PROPOSAL PREPARATION

One set of volumes of a typical giant proposal (November 1968). Left to right: Michael Pelehach, Project Director for the VFX (F-14); Dr. Tom Cheatham, Vice-President and Director of Grumman Aircraft Engineering Corporation; John Michael, Proposal Manager. (Courtesy of Grumman Aerospace Corporation, Bethpage, New York 11714.)

PROPOSAL PREPARATION

RODNEY D. STEWART

ANN L. STEWART

A Wiley-Interscience Publication
JOHN WILEY & SONS

New York   •   Chichester   •   Brisbane   •   Toronto   •   Singapore

Library of Congress Cataloging in Publication Data:

Stewart, Rodney D.
  Proposal preparation.

  "A Wiley-Interscience publication."
  Bibliography: p.
  Includes index.
  1. Proposal writing in business.   I. Stewart, Ann L.
II. Title.

HF5718.5.S85   1984   808'.066658   83-19827
ISBN 0-471-87288-1

Printed in the United States of America

10 9 8 7 6 5

To Bob and Carol

PREFACE

Early in this century the United States Army ran a newspaper advertisement broadcasting a request for proposed bids on the production of a military aircraft having the following specifications: "Ability to travel in air for one hour, travel forty miles per hour, carry one passenger, and land undamaged. Bidders are required to put up a bond to certify financial responsibility."

Although the procurement process has increased in complexity substantially since this early example of a solicitation, the basic tenets of proposal development have not altered significantly. This book will show the proposer how to convey the basic information required to demonstrate capability, competence, compliance, comprehension, and credibility in the proposal. It also describes the proposal *evaluation* process in a way that will give the vital clues needed to prepare a winning proposal, and suggests a standardized methodology.

The importance of excellence in proposal preparation is underscored by the unique position of the proposal developer in the competitive market. Companies operating in consumer markets spend vast amounts of money to cause the customer to come to them so that they may have the opportunity to make a sale. In contrast, *the proposal goes to the customer* and must induce, mostly by itself, a sufficient desire in the recipient to complete the buying action.

In the proposal document, the proposer must persuade the customer that: (1) the proposed solution is the best one available for his or her problem; (2) adequate personnel, facilities, and equipment have been estimated and allocated to perform the job to the required schedule; (3) the price proposed is fair in relation to the value received; and most importantly, (4) the proposer is the most qualified and best equipped to do the job. This information is conveyed in three sections or volumes of the proposal: the technical volume, the organization and management volume, and the cost volume. This book is organized to permit in-depth study of each of these major parts of a proposal (Chapter 6, 7, and 8), and it provides vital information on preproposal marketing and planning steps that must be taken prior to the start of the proposal development process.

Appendix 1 is an outline for a company proposal manual, and Appendix 2 will be useful as a final proposal review checklist.

Comprehensive information is also provided on the mechanical aspects of writing and publishing the proposal.

The book you are about to read is designed to serve as a handy reference for the professional developer of proposals; as a guide to management in establishing proposal teams, methods, and techniques; as a textbook for students or new entrants into the field of proposal preparation; or for the interested and curious reader who merely wants to expand his or her knowledge of this most interesting and challenging aspect of the modern business world.

Each chapter should be studied carefully to determine techniques that have proven successful, to apply these techniques to the proposal at hand, and to establish a track record of excellence that will assure a high capture rate for continuing and new business.

May all your proposals be winners!!

RODNEY D. STEWART
ANN L. STEWART

Huntsville, Alabama
January, 1984

IN APPRECIATION

We wish to express our appreciation to all those who graciously provided information, advice, and assistance in the preparation of this book. Particularly appreciated were comments and suggestions made by our dear friend and business associate, Mr. Harry D. Cleaver, and information provided by Ms. Bobbie Graham. We appreciate the use of the COSTFORM™ prototype computer software provided to us by Mr. Eddie Roberts, president of Diversified Data Systems, Incorporated, of Hunstville, Alabama, in preparing the cost estimate for the case study in Chapter 12.

R.D.S.
A.L.S.

CONTENTS

Chapter 1

WHY "PROPOSAL PREPARATION"? 1

The Age of High Technology   1
Sophistication in Source Evaluation   2
The Effect of Government Laws and Regulations   2
The Proposal: Training Ground for Performance   3
Commonality of Approach   3

    Fixed-Price "Advertised" Bids, 3
    Negotiated Procurements, 4
    In-Company Proposals, 4

Six Basic Steps in Proposal Preparation   6

    Marketing, 7
    Analyzing, 7
    Planning, 7
    Designing, 8
    Estimating, 8
    Publishing, 9

Urgency: A Common Trait of Proposals   9

Chapter 2

PREPROPOSAL MARKETING: AND THE DECISION TO BID, 11

The Market Survey: Identifying the Customer   11
Planting and Cultivating the Seed   13

The "AIDA" Approach, 13
Build in "Acceptance Time," 15
Activate Latent Needs, 15
Help the Customer Decide, 16

Evaluating the Need   16

Keeping Company Objectives in Focus, 16
Matching Company-Unique Capabilities to the Need, 17
Watch for Opportunities for "Synergism," 17
Beware of the "Cuspetitor," 17

Determining Long-Term Effects   18
Profitability Optimization, 18
Profitability Factor, 20
Growth Rate Assessment and Goals, 21

The Decision to Bid   24

Determining Competitive Advantage, 25
Determining Technological Advantage, 26
Determining Geographical Advantage, 27
Determining Political Advantages, 28
Determining Price Advantage, 28

When the "Winner" is Really the Loser   28

Chapter 3

PLANNING THE PROPOSAL ACTIVITIES, 31

Predevelopment, Design, Breadboard, and Prototype Testing   32
Preliminary Unsolicited Proposals   34
Written Questions to the Customer   36
Proposal Clarification Conferences   36
The Proposal Preparation Activities   37

Time Required for Proposal Preparation, 37
Facilities Required for Proposal Preparation, 40
The Proposal Team, 40
Resources Required to Propose, 40

Follow-Up Activities to Proposal Preparation   41

The "Best and Final" Offer, 41
Contract Negotiations, 42

Establishing an Overall Proposal Preparation Schedule   43

   The "Kickoff" Meeting, 43
   The "Review of Ground Rules" Meeting, 44
   The Technical and Resources Input and Review Meeting, 44
   Summary Meetings and Presentations, 44

Establishing a Detailed Proposal Preparation Schedule   45

   Review of Request for Proposal (RFP) Requirements, 45
   Define the Proposal Effort, 45
   Preproposal Functions, 45
   Plan of Action or "Kickoff" Meeting, 46
   Preparation of Rough Draft of Proposal Volumes, 46
   Detailed Review of Technical and Cost Volumes, 47
   Proposal Writing and Publication, 47
   Packaging the Proposal, 47
   Proposal Delivery, 47

Proposal Supplements   47

   Scale Models and Mockups, 48
   Motion Pictures and Video Tapes, 48
   Computer Software Demonstration Programs, 48

Typical Proposal Flow   51

Chapter 4

ORGANIZING THE PROPOSAL TEAM, 52

Skills Required for Proposal Preparation   54
   Business and Finance Skills, 54
   Engineering and Technical Skills, and Functional Managers, 54
   Manufacturing and Assembly Skills, 55
   Management Skills, 55
   Mathematical and Statistical Skills, 55
   Production Planning and Industrial Engineering Skills, 55
   Writing and Publishing Skills, 56

Proposal Team Composition   56

   Proposal Manager, 58
   Proposal Administrator, 62
   Sales Engineer, 63
   Technical Volume Manager, 64

Organization and Management Volume Manager, 65
Cost Volume Manager, 65
Publications Manager, 66

Summary   66

Chapter 5

THE REQUEST FOR PROPOSAL—WHAT TO EXPECT, 69

Opportunities to Influence the Request for Proposal   69

Opportunity 1: Influencing Initial Requirement, 71
Opportunity 2: The Draft RFP, 71
Opportunity 3: The Pre-Bid Meeting, 71
Opportunity 4: The Proposal, 72
Opportunity 5: Proposal Clarifications, 72
Opportunity 6: The Best and Final Offer, 72
Opportunity 7: The Final Negotiations, 72

The Content of a Request for Proposal   72

General Instructions to Bidders, 73
The Contract Document or "Schedule," 84
General Provisions, 92

Other Technical and Programmatic Data Included in the RFP   92
Other Types and Sizes of Requests for Proposals   92

Standard Products or Supplies, 93
General Support Service Contracts, 93

A Final Comment on Request for Proposal Quality   95
Government RFP's: Evolving Requirements   95

Chapter 6

THE TECHNICAL PROPOSAL, 98

The Work Statement: Basis for the Technical Proposal   100
Three Basic Functions of the Technical Proposal   100

Description of the Work, 100
The Means of Accomplishing the Work, 106

Demonstrating an Understanding of the Requirements   121
Description of Customer Involvement   121

Discussion of Problem Areas   122
Typical Technical Proposal Outlines   122

Chapter 7

THE ORGANIZATION AND MANAGEMENT PROPOSAL, 125

The Work Element Structure (Work Breakdown Structure)   126

Hierarchical Relationship of a Work Element Structure, 126
Functional Elements Described, 128
Physical Elements Described, 128
Treatment of Recurring and Nonrecurring Activities, 128
Work Element Structure Interrelationships, 129
Treatment of Work Elements, 130

The Project Plan   131

Visibility, 133

The Company's Organization   134

Relationship to Corporate Headquarters and Resources, 134
Interdivisional Relationships, 134
Other Internal Company or Division Support, 135
Relationship with Associates and Subcontractor(s), 135
Indirect, General and Administrative, and Fee Rates, 135

The Project Organization   138

Project Direction, 139
Project and Cost Control Management, 140
Information Management (Documents and Data), 141
Procurement Management, 141
Logistics Management, 141
Safety Management, 142
Other Management Areas, 142

Project Labor Rates and Factors   142
The Make or Buy Plan   143
Key Personnel and Résumés   144

Education, 144
Experience Categories, 144
Awards, Honors, and Other Outside Activities, 145

Skill Mix Among Key Personnel, 145
Staffing, 145

Plant Facilities and Equipment   146

Specialized Equipment and Facilities, 146
General Purpose Equipment and Facilities, 146
Compatibility of Equipment with Personnel Skills, 147
High Technology, Advanced Equipment, 147

Company Past Experience and Successes   147
Methods of Achieving Efficiency, Economy, and Effectiveness,   148

Attracting and/or Retaining High Quality Personnel, 150
Combining Skills in the Right Mixture to Achieve Optimum
    Skill Utilization, 150
Motivating Employees to Produce High Quality Work, 150
Adjustment of Skill Levels as the Work Progresses, 151
Evaluating Progress and Making Corrections, 151
Adoption of New Procedures, Methods, and Equipment, 151
    Employee Training, 151
Control of Indirect (Overhead and Burden) Costs, 152

Organization and Management Proposal Flow   154

Chapter 8

THE COST PROPOSAL, 155

Credibility: A Key Objective   155

Credibility Area 1: Matching the Work Content to the
    Resources Available, 156
Credibility Area 2: Appropriate Time-Allocation
    of Resources, 156
Credibility Area 3: Labor-Hour Estimates, 157
Credibility Area 4: Traceability of Resource Estimates, 157
Credibility Area 5: Supporting Data and Backup Material, 157

The Cost Proposal Content   159
The Proposal Estimating Process   159

Estimating Based on the Work Element Structure, 161

The Proposal Cost Elements   162

Labor Costs, 162
Materials and Subcontract Costs, 164

Treatment of Other Necessary Ground Rules   165

Spares and Spare Parts, 165
Maintenance and Repair Manuals, 165
Optional Equipment and Services, 166

Estimating Material Costs   166

Drawing Takeoff (If Detailed Drawings Already Exist), 166
Material Handbooks and Supplier Catalogs, 167
Quantity Buy and Inventory Considerations, 167
Scrap and Waste Considerations, 168
Bills of Material, 168
Subcontracts, 169

Treatment of Documentation   169
The Process Plan   170
Manufacturing Activities   170
Construction Activities   172
In-Process Inspection   172
Testing   173
Special Tooling and Test Equipment   173
Computer Software Proposal Cost Estimating   174
Labor Allowances   174
Cost Growth Allowances   175
Estimating Supervision, Direct Management, and Other
Direct Charges   176
Costing in the Proposal Flow   176

Chapter 9

PROPOSAL WRITING AND PUBLICATION, 190

The Proposal Quality As a Reflection of Work Quality   191
The Writer's Role in Proposal Preparation   191

Synergism in Proposal Writing, 191
Words Stimulate, 192
Documenting and Explaining a Record of Success, 193
The Proposal Writer as a Storyteller, 193

Publication of the Proposal   193

Word Processing: A Boon to Proposal Publishers   194
The Publication Department's Role in Proposal Preparation   194

   Tables and Illustrations, 200
   Integrating Tables and Illustrations into text, 201
   Proposal Covers and Bindings, 201

The Proposal Format   202

   The Letter of Transmittal, 203
   Front Matter, 203
   The Proposal Executive Summary, 204
   Technical, Organization and Management, and Cost,
      Volumes, 205
   Appendices, 206
   Tables of Contents, Indices, Lists of Terms and
      Abbreviations, 206
   Index Tabs and Figure Positioning, 206

Publishing the Giant Proposal   207

   Developing Content, 208
   Processing the Giant Proposal, 211
   Production Operations, 212
   Distribution and Delivery, 214

The Customer Should "Experience" the Proposal   214
Proposal Publication Closes the Loop   214

Chapter 10

HOW IS THE PROPOSAL EVALUATED? 215

Source Evaluation Versus Source Selection   215
Source Evaluation Boards: How They Work   216

   The Proposal, 216
   Plant or On-Site Visits, 217
   References and Experience Verification, 217
   Oral Presentations, 217
   Written Questions and Answers, 217
   Best and Final Offers, 218

Organization of a Source Evaluation Activity   218

   Source Evaluation Ground Rules, 218

Source Evaluation Personnel, 218
Functions of the Source Evaluation Board, 219
Physical Location for the Evaluation Process, 221
Source Evaluation Schedule, 221

Evaluation Factors and Criteria   223

Performance Suitability Factors, 224
Cost Factors, 227
Experience and Past Performance, 227
Other Factors, 227

Weighting and Scoring Procedures   228
Cost Proposal Adjustment and "Most Probable Cost"   229
Detailed Evaluation Procedures   231

Management Plan, 232
Excellence of Proposed Design, 232
Key Personnel, 233
Corporate or Company Resources, 233
Experience and Past Performance, 233
Other Factors, 234

Learning from Past Mistakes   235
The Purchasing Agent's Motives   236
Continuing Evolution in Source Evaluation   238

Chapter 11

A FEW KEY ELEMENTS REQUIRED FOR SUCCESS, 239

Technical Excellence: A Must   239

Meeting the Specifications, 240
Providing On-Schedule Performance, 240
Providing Consistency in Quality, 240

Innovation and Creativity   241

Use of High Technology Methods and Materials, 241
Efficient Design and Manufacturing Techniques, 241
The "People-Oriented" Approach, 242

Stability or Flexibility of Labor Base?   243

Stable Base of Skilled Personnel, 243

Hiring at the Low End, 244
The Use of Consultants and Subcontractors, 244
Part-Time and Temporary Employees, 244
Cross-Training of Work Force, 245

Competency in Scheduling   246
Proposal Review by Management and Others   247
Honesty and Integrity   247
Final Guidance   248

Be Complete!, 248
Be Organized!, 248
Be Objective!, 248
Be Informed!, 248
Be Innovative!, 249
Be Factual!, 249
Be Professional!, 249
Follow Up!, 249

Chapter 12

A CASE STUDY: PROPOSAL FOR "COSTREND™," 250

Marketing   250
Analysis   251
Planning   251
Design   252
Estimating   252
Publication   252
Letter of Transmittal   252
Technical Proposal   253

Introduction, 253
Basic System Description, 254
Background and History, 256
System Specifications, 256
Growth Potential, 257
Development Schedule, 258

Organization and Management Proposal   261

Company Background and Experience, 261
Project Organization, 261
Company Financial Capability 261
Key Project Personnel, 262

Cost Proposal   264

   Introduction, 264
   Costing Rationale, 266
   Material Costs, 267
   Other Direct Charges, 267
   Overhead Costs, 267
   Detailed Cost Breakout, 267
   Cost Summary, 267

Appendix 1. Sample Proposal Preparation Manual   279
Appendix 2. Checklist for Proposal Review   310

Bibliography   314

Index   315

1

WHY "PROPOSAL PREPARATION"?

Do you not know that those who run in a race will run, but only one
receives the prize? Run in a way that you may win!
I Cor. 9:24

This book is about proposals and their preparation. What is a proposal? A proposal is a plan of action for fullfilling a need. It is a sales document that is honest, factual, and responsive to the needs of others. It is a written description of work to be performed that provides enough information for a customer to make a purchase decision.

There are three principal reasons why proposal preparation is becoming an important skill in the 1980s and beyond:

1. Greater complexity and technical content of work activities and work outputs, both in the public and private sectors.
2. Increasing sophistication of source evaluation and selection techniques.
3. Growth of the number and complexity of requirements imposed by customers or clients in the procurement and purchasing processes.

This chapter discusses these influences on the business and technical community and describes the benefits of developing proposal preparation skills and the basic steps and flow processes required to meet the proposal preparation needs brought about by their impact.

THE AGE OF HIGH TECHNOLOGY

As John Naisbitt points out in his book, *Megatrends* (Warner, 1982), higher technology products and services are abounding in the commercial

1

marketplace as well as in business and industry. The purchaser of work outputs and work activities is more frequently encountering multiple options rather than either/or decisions. The number of variables to be considered in making a purchase decision is increasing because of the growing number and complexity of products and services offered. These trends have resulted in the need for greater reliance on more objective and analytical approaches to expenditure decision making; and the use of analytical approaches to source selection requires that the suppliers of goods, services, or projects provide formal, organized, and detailed information on the characteristics and price of the proposed product or service. Consumers—individuals, businesses, industries, and government agencies—are demanding good value for what they can afford to pay. Documented evidence must be provided along with sales information to assure these consumers that they are getting the highest quality available for their money. The written proposal is the document that is designed to perform this function.

SOPHISTICATION IN SOURCE EVALUATION

Today, even the more unsophisticated customer is likely to have some rather sophisticated analytical tools and methods at his or her disposal. Personal, professional, engineering, and business computers and their related computer software permit a rapid and economical comparison and analysis of multiple options with multiple features. The growing availability and capability of the computer, greater knowledge about its use for analytical comparisons, and the seemingly constant decrease in cost per computing power have resulted in increased automation, speed, and accuracy in making the economic and technical decisions required to identify the most attractive choice among the many available alternatives. Using the computer and other high technology tools and methods of management, structured analysis and organized procedures are evolving source evaluation into an increasingly systematic and objective process. Further, some evaluation teams have access to large numbers of skilled technical and management personnel and occasionally have more time and resources allocated for their evaluation than the bidder had to prepare the proposal. Availability of advanced tools and techniques for the buyer requires the seller to use equally advanced tools, techniques, and methods in generating the sales approach. The written proposal presents the resulting sales information in a way that will favor the offered work activity over that of competitors when subjected to a searching comparative analysis.

THE EFFECT OF GOVERNMENT LAWS AND REGULATIONS

Government procurement regulations, laws, and socioeconomic objectives have far-reaching effects on the conduct of business in the United

States. Growth in the number of these regulations, laws, and policies in the past several decades has had a pronounced effect on the amount of information that must be accumulated (and usually reported) prior to entering into a new venture. In a 1972 study group report published by the Commission on Government Procurement, one hundred and one laws were cited as affecting the procurement process for major systems alone. Eighty of these were associated with purely socioeconomic objectives. Recently the Department of Defense issued an instruction referencing thirty-five directives covering thirty-nine acquisition management and system design principles required in developing and producing major systems (DOD Instruction 5000.2 "Major System Acquisition Procedures;" March 8, 1983). These laws and regulations impact the procurement process—and they have increased the amount of detailed information required to submit responsive proposals both in the private and public sectors.

THE PROPOSAL: TRAINING GROUND FOR PERFORMANCE

Another factor that has a bearing on the importance of the proposal preparation process is the fact that the proposal preparation activity itself is an excellent training ground for actual performance of the work. The proposal preparation activity organizes the team, establishes conceptual design, initiates planning, identifies needed equipment or facilities, formulates needed work methods and procedures, creates employee interest and involvement, and "debugs" the work activity or work output. The proposal preparation activity not only serves to fully inform the customer of what he or she can expect in the way of job performance, but, equally as important, it familiarizes the proposer with the scope, intent, and content of the work. A flaw in design, planning, or estimating found during proposal preparation creates less impact than if found during work progress when it is too late to make a change in the contract.

COMMONALITY OF APPROACH

Experience has shown that there is a common thread of methodology that exists in virtually all proposal preparation situations. There are certain principles, practices, and procedures that hold true among the various categories of proposals whether it is an industrial process, a manufactured product, a multimillion dollar construction project, or a business service that is being proposed.

The several categories of proposals are described below:

Fixed-Price "Advertised" Bids

Fixed-price bids and quotes in response to "advertised" procurements are common methods of providing information to potential customers for work activities and work outputs that are relatively straightforward in content. The bid may be in the form of a sealed bid referencing a specification or scope of work, or it may be accompanied by some form of proposal. In either case, it is to the advantage of the bidder to have completed the steps outlined in this book, even though all of the information produced is not supplied to the potential customer. The internal marketing analysis, planning, preliminary design, estimating, and publication steps will result in a more realistic bid and one which will more nearly represent a task that can actually be accomplished with the projected resources.

Negotiated Procurements

It is in preparation for solicited or unsolicited bidding on fixed price or cost-reimbursable negotiated procurements that improved skills in proposal preparation will enjoy the greatest rewards. Proposals for large procurements, particularly in the field of federal, state, and local government projects, involve extensive substantiation and supporting data. The larger the procurement, the more likely the procuring organization is to establish formal evaluation and competitive negotiation procedures. When the proposal is being reviewed by a team of experts rather than a single purchasing agent, the full spectrum of proposal preparation skills must come into play. Figure 1.1, a typical proposal flow chart for a negotiated procurement, will be used throughout this book to describe the proposal preparation process.

In-Company Proposals

In-company proposals (those that are not submitted to a potential customer or buyer) are solicited or unsolicited proposals that are prepared *within* a company to convince management, the stockholders, or a department head that the company should proceed with a work activity or work output that will improve the company's efficiency, economy, or effectiveness or enhance the potential of capturing future work. Typical of in-company proposals are: (1) the acquisition of new equipment, facilities, methods, or techniques that will improve company profitability; and (2) independent research and development that the company sponsors with its own funds. A proposal for the location of a new plant or office facility is a typical type of in-company proposal that frequently employs all of the skills, methods, and techniques of proposal preparation.

Figure 1.2 shows some typical internal and external proposal types that are commonly encountered in the business and industrial community.

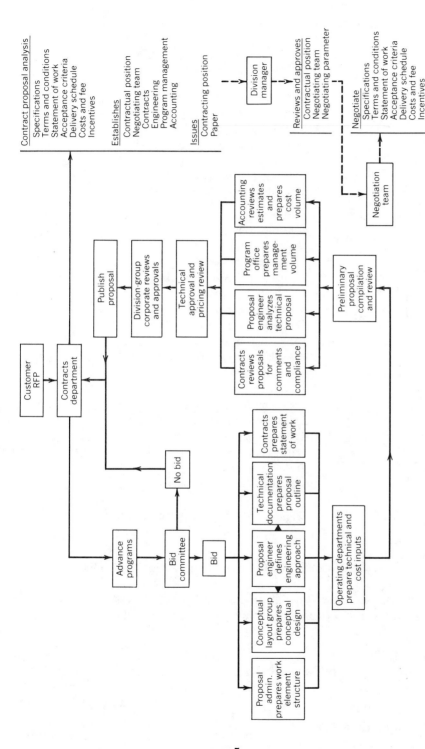

Figure 1.1. Proposal flow chart.

5

Internal Proposals

Independent research proposals
New product line proposals
Operational procedures proposals
Plant relocation proposals
Process engineering proposals
Product improvement proposals

External Proposals

Architect-engineer proposals
Book proposals
Construction proposals
Design proposals
Development proposals
Engineering change proposals
Maintenence proposals
Manufacturing proposals
Materials supply proposals
Parts supply proposals
Research grants proposals
Services proposals
Subsystems proposals
System production proposals
Systems development proposals
Testing proposals
"Time and materials" proposals
Tooling proposals
Training and education proposals

Figure 1.2. Types of proposal.

SIX BASIC STEPS IN PROPOSAL PREPARATION

There are six basic steps in proposal preparation that are taken (not necessarily in the order listed) to prepare a proposal. They are:

1. Marketing
2. Analyzing (and bid decision)
3. Planning
4. Designing
5. Estimating
6. Publishing

Although these steps are taken generally in the order listed, the marketing, analysis, and planning steps continue throughout the process.

Marketing

The principal step required to start out in a business venture is to find or identify a need and fill it. As a subset to this step, one can identify or generate new needs that are waiting to be filled by making available a work activity or work output for which the need is dependent on its availability. Fashion designers, for example, know that they can generate a need for a new style of clothing by widely advertising and publicizing the new style as "the latest and most chic." Successful businessmen realize that the idea of a need must be planted in the minds of their customers long before the proposal cycle is initiated. Throughout the proposal preparation process the marketing function plays an important role in shaping and directing the policies, ground rules, and procedures used in preparation of the proposal. As will be mentioned later, care must be taken to counterbalance the marketing department's optimism and desire to win new work for the company with realistic independent planning, scheduling, and estimating of the project by the performing elements of the organization.

Analyzing

It is through an analysis of the customer's needs and the proposing company's capabilities of performing useful work that identifiable needs and potential proposals are generated. This analysis will take many factors into account, but the criteria for selection of an identified need for further pursuit in the form of a specific proposal will most frequently be the *profitability* of the venture.

Planning

Experience in our country as well as in other countries has shown that meticulous planning and testing prior to work initiation or product introduction helps assure that the work activity or work output will be profitable and beneficial to producer and consumer alike. Good planning and definition will help avoid "dead end" projects, partially completed projects, and unnecessary duplication or overlap of work activities. A better job of proposal preparation, backed by conceptual or preliminary design and testing effort, means less wasted effort, more projects completed on time and within cost, and fewer "dead end" projects. Businesses are developing an awareness of the need for more systematic planning and financial analysis before initiating a venture. Recognition of the significant effect of economic factors and the need for good planning has expanded the scope and content of the proposal from a simple document into a comprehensive technical, organizational business plan for accomplishing a work activity or producing a work output.

Planning, an essential step in proposal preparation, coupled with its close cousin, *scheduling*, is required to provide the realism and credibility needed in the proposal. In planning a work activity or work output, it is necessary to concentrate on as few alternatives as possible. One must beware of the professional planner who wants to be in a continuous planning mode with two or more alternatives being simultaneously analyzed in depth. Comparison of alternatives early in the need-identification phase is always helpful; but an early choice of a single alternative is usually very beneficial. The choice of a single alternative forces the resolution of key questions and assumes that the work can and will be performed in a selected manner. Planning includes all of the technical, organization, and management aspects of the project and considers all marketing inputs such as projected quantities, cost targets, and capture potential for the work.

Designing

Design work that is done as part of proposal preparation is usually conceptual design or preliminary design, although a final design of the work activity or work output will occasionally be required. When a proposal is to be submitted for performing final design work, conceptual or preliminary designs are all that is needed. Design work for proposal preparation includes preliminary sketches, plant layouts, flow diagrams, scale models, mockups, and prototypes. The degree of completion of design work as evidenced by the number and types of drawings, models, mockups, components, or prototypes is often a source evaluation factor. The design step of the proposal preparation process usually culminates in the preparation of the technical volume or technical section of the proposal.

Estimating

Estimating is one of the most important steps in the proposal preparation process. Estimating includes predicting or forecasting the amounts of materials, numbers of labor hours, and costs required to accomplish the job. Credible estimating cannot be done without adequate planning and preliminary design of the work activity or work output being proposed. Estimating requires unique skills, usually multidisciplinary in nature, that must either be acquired by experience or by training in a special mixture of technical and business disciplines. This unique mix is most nearly approached by the industrial engineering profession but includes business skills that analyze and optimize profitability that have not traditionally been a part of the industrial engineering discipline. The estimating step of the proposal preparation process culminates in the cost volume or cost section of a proposal.

Publishing

The publication step of proposal preparation includes the organization, writing, editing, art work, printing, and binding of the proposal document or proposal documents. The publication capability and publication team should be an integral, responsive part of the proposing company's organization. Opportunities for using high technology in the proposal publication process must be taken if one is to submit a competitive proposal. The appearance and accuracy of a proposal, although not usually numerically scored by the evaluator or by the evaluation team, are important factors in the general impression of the proposal. They can engender confidence and could be a basis for initial acceptance or rejection. Fancy or elaborate formats or displays are unnecessary and in many instances are even undesirable as they give an impression of lack of cost consciousness. A neat, accurate, easily read, easily referenced proposal is an aid to evaluators and is an indication to the customer of the type of work that he can expect to receive in reporting and documentation during the performance of the work.

URGENCY: A COMMON TRAIT OF PROPOSALS

Because there is usually a limited time available to respond to Requests for Proposals or Requests for Quotations, urgency of publication is a common characteristic of proposals. The proposal preparation process involves the marshalling, managing, and utilizing of a broad range of disciplines, skills, and specialists in a very short time period and often under conditions of great stress: to (1) present the solution to the problem; and (2) compel action or adoption by the customer. This urgency of action and the stressful environment that exists in the days or weeks immediately preceding the proposal submission is the reason for in-depth preproposal marketing and planning of the proposal activities themselves as explained in Chapters 2 and 3. If preplanning is done properly, the urgency will not be a source of confusion or frustration to the proposal team, the proposal managers, or the company.

We would like to close this first chapter on "Why 'Proposal Preparation'?" with what one might call "basic truths" about proposal preparation and its treatment in this book:

There are basic work elements and work activities that are common to all proposals. We emphasize the commonality rather than the differences because we would like to share this information with the widest possible audience and have it applied to the greatest variety of proposal situations.

There are some sure-fire instructions that will help produce a more credible, accurate, and attractive proposal.

The first step in the proposal preparation process is introspection by the proposer to determine if he or she truly feels able to do the job better (by better we mean more advantageously to the customer) than anyone else.

A really good proposal is often like a breath of fresh air and many a completely unknown bidder has confounded the big name competition and won against a company that thought they had the bid "all sewed up."

In an almost-even contest, the scales might be tipped toward a favored bidder, but a poor proposal cannot win against a really good proposal, no matter who wrote it.

A good proposal leaves nothing to chance. "Straight-line-control" is employed to cover all bases.

One cannot win a contract just because one *believes* he or she can win—although that must come first. A person must put this belief into words and actions. This is the proposal—the document that puts a belief into words and actions. These actions involve launching out in faith to actually perform some of the preliminary laboratory work, design, and development steps.

There is no need if the customer does not know there is a work activity or work output to fullfill it. A proposal is the means of letting a customer know.

The successful proposer is the one who can identify relevant information, process it, and present it more efficiently and effectively than his or her competitors.

Survival in a tough competitive environment is often thought to be possible only at the expense of someone else. This is true only in the sense of the losing proposers. A successful proposal is a win-win situation for the winning supplier and the customer because they both gain. The successful proposer looks for and finds the synergistic effect between himself and his customer.

The plain fact is that it is all but impossible to win with a poor proposal, no matter how effectively other marketing activities have been carried out, especially if there are better proposals submitted. On the other hand, many contracts are won by those submitting superior proposals with *no other marketing activity whatsoever!*

2

PREPROPOSAL MARKETING: AND THE DECISION TO BID

And your ear will hear a word behind you, this is the way, walk in it, whenever you turn to the right or to the left.
Isa. 30:21

The success of the entire proposal preparation activity depends to a large degree on steps that are taken far in advance of actual proposal submission. These steps are associated with the marketing of the work output or work activity to one or more customers. Marketing involves identifying a potential customer, letting the potential customer know that a work activity or work output exists to fill his or her needs, and getting the customer to commit to pay a stated price for performance of the work.

THE MARKET SURVEY: IDENTIFYING THE CUSTOMER

In identifying a potential customer and a specific need for work activities or work outputs, one has access to a wealth of readily available, sometimes free information. A principal source of information—often overlooked by marketing personnel—is the information published by state, federal, and local governments. It is available at little or no cost. Government data is full of useful socioeconomic, geographical, and demographic data that reveals the buying habits of individuals, companies, and government agencies themselves. Labor markets where skilled personnel are available along with complete wage histories and projections can be obtained from the Bureau of Labor Statistics, one of the largest statistics-gathering, analysis and reporting organizations in the free world. Literally thousands of other special reports ranging from agricultural to industrial and business subjects can be obtained at nominal costs from federal, state, and local agencies. These special reports and studies cover an almost unimaginable variety of subjects useful to the marketer. They cover expansion and growth trends, economic trends, and taxation and tariff effects on business, industry, and the economy.

Professional and industrial associations, trade shows, trade magazines, and business magazines and newspapers also contain sizeable amounts of useful marketing information. If used selectively and wisely, this information can result in the identification of market needs and even specific potential customers. The *Commerce Business Daily* alone lists hundreds of procurement opportunites every day. Publications of professional and technical societies such as the American Marketing Association have much useful information on techniques and methods as well as clues to potential open markets.

Wholesalers, retailers, and distributors of products possess real life statistics on how various products stack up in the marketplace. They know which products are selling the fastest and know when needs or demands are building up in the marketplace. These organizations predict how products or services rate in comparison to competitors.

Market research organizations which specialize in gathering specific data for the introduction of a new product or line of products are becoming more sophisticated in their information gathering, analysis, and reporting techniques. These organizations can be hired at a nominal fee to do the "pick-and-shovel" work to provide needed market data for entering into a new venture.

Stockbrokers and banks have, and are willing to disburse, a wealth of information about the volume of business, net worth, profit history, growth, and overall financial health of companies. Not only do they have financial data from other companies but they are also quite willing to analyze and predict future growth, acquisition, and merger trends.

In-depth knowledge of the customer—a vital requirement during the preproposal marketing period—can be obtained by the open literature, company-supplied information, and above all by personal contacts with management as well as workers within the customer's organization. It is important to obtain as much information as possible about the customer's procurement or purchasing methods, techniques, organization, and personnel. If one "knows his way around" in the purchasing and procurement circles, work statements, contract provisions, and contract boiler plate can be prepared easily.

Marketing policies and overall company policies as far as practicable should also be known. It should be remembered that the customer is supplying products or services to an end-customer. This end-customer is the final recipient of the results of the bidder's work, and satisfaction of the end recipient is important to assure continued need for the marketer's input to the final work output.

It is important to know the customer's other product lines to permit as much "synergism" as possible in the final work content. If the customer has a product or service similar to the proposer's, a mutually beneficial interdependence or combination of the product lines may be beneficial. The customer may also supply services or products needed or desired by the proposer. A willingness to use the customer's products will enhance the marketer's knowledge of the customer's company and could have a potential impact on decisions regarding the proposed work activity or output.

A friendly, cooperative relationship with the customer, rather than an adversative one, will open up the opportunities for greater synergism and for a greater two-way flow of information. Not only will the marketing representative learn more about the customer's organization but the customer will learn more about the proposer's capabilities, aspirations, and competence. Knowing the key personnel of the customer opens up the flow of information that is necessary for the proposing team to evaluate the requirements fully and responsively.The marketeer should make it a point to personally contact and become acquainted with those who originate the need, those who implement the procurement, and those who make the final procurement selection decision. This personal contact and acquaintance period must come in the early preproposal phases because communication is often severely limited or cut off entirely when the competitive process heightens in intensity.

With these sources of information available, the marketing representative is well equipped to identify a market area, select one or more specific potential customers, plant the seed of the idea to identify or generate the need, and embark upon the preproposal marketing activities which will lead to a decision to bid or not to bid on the proposed work.

PLANTING AND CULTIVATING THE SEED

The secret of success is finding a need and filling it; and as mentioned in Chapter 1, a proposal is a plan of action to fulfill a need. Needs can either be existing, latent, or generated. Regardless of the source of the need, the potential customer must be made aware of an available work activity or work output and this awareness must be cultivated and nurtured until it becomes an interest, a desire, and an action on the part of a customer.

The "AIDA" Approach

Marketing professionals use what is known as the "AIDA" approach in making a sale. The same steps are generally those required in preproposal marketing. The "AIDA" approach involves gaining the customer's *A*ttention, creating *I*nterest, nurturing a *D*esire for the service or product, and stimulating *A*ction to request or purchase the work. The proposer should be prepared to establish relationships with potential customers *while the* *customer is formulating his or her needs*, and the proposer should be prepared to actually plant the notion in the customer's mind for the specific work *or* the specific work requirements.

Gaining the Customer's Attention.   Gaining the customer's attention involves the transmission of information to the customer regarding a process, product, project, or service that is available to fulfill an actual, latent, or previously undeveloped need. The business customer's attention can best be gained by emphasizing that the work to be performed will improve overall profitability by increasing efficiency, economy, effectiveness, or overall growth of the company.

Many ways are available for gaining the customer's attention—advertising, direct mail, telephone, and so on—but by far the most effective, particularly for large procurements, is personal contact. Personal contact provides a two-way communication that is more effective than any other means in bringing together a need with a way to fulfill that need. Personal contact permits an early exploration by both parties into the potentials of any work activity or work output, and allows the supplier and customer to communicate in real time in an atmosphere of personal empathy and in a way that enhances the germination and evolution of fruitful work. A personal visit is by far more persuasive than a bill-board, magazine advertisement, television commercial, or direct-mail brochure when it comes to interacting with a customer to develop or identify a means of fullfilling a need.

The personal contact technique should be used extensively by the proposer in the early phases of any new work activity to develop a close and preferably indistinguishable interrelationship between the required task or project and the supplied task or project. To do this effectively, the seller must have considerable freedom and flexibility. He must be bound only by overall business principles rather than detailed procedural constraints in order to retain negotiation and discussion flexibility. As the work activity is defined and scoped through the interactive customer-supplier interrelationship, then fixed parameters, rules, and business arrangements can evolve.

Creating Customer Interest.   Once the customer's attention is gained, the seller must create interest and enthusiasm for the service or product being offered. This is accomplished by fostering a familiarity with the potential work to be performed, the organization that will perform it, and the overall benefits of the completed work. Continued communication, including but not limited to additional personal contacts, will create a more than passive interest in the customer and will serve to further define the work to be performed.

Nurturing Customer Desire.   As preproposal marketing proceeds, the customer's desire should be nurtured, maintained, and increased through the supply of additional information that will reinforce the realism and urgency of the need. This is done by personal, telephone, and written contact to convey information that will accentuate the positive aspects of the project and diminish any negative aspects or objections that are surfaced during the discussion and evolution of the work's characteristics. The purpose of this step is to bring the customer's desire to a point where he or she is not only willing but is actively seeking an opportunity to take the action required to engage the services of the seller.

Stimulating Customer Action. In the proposal preparation process, the final customer action that must be taken is the signing of a contract with the proposer's firm to perform the work. There are often interim customer actions that must be stimulated, however, one of which is the issuance of a request for proposal (RFP) or a request for quotation (RFQ). It may be either verbal or written. The purpose of this step is to assure that the customer has everything required to *act* on the desire that has been developed. Customer action can be best stimulated by requiring a definite response within a given time period or by making the customer aware that there are other organizations competing for the proposer's services that may take action sooner. In addition to stimulating customer action, these activities improve the proposer's competitive position because of the proposer's intimate knowledge of the request for proposal or request for quotation.

Build in "Acceptance Time"

The acquisition process for any new work activity or work output must include sufficient "acceptance time." Acceptance time is the time required for an organization and its key individuals to absorb, understand, adjust to, and become advocates of the proposed work. Acceptance time is usually proportional to the amount or degree of deviation of the work content from existing practice. Very large multiple-year projects may take months or even years to initiate simply because of their size and complexity and the resources required. Overall marketing strategy should build in enough acceptance time, and through patience, perseverance, and hard work, the project will materialize into a fruitful venture.

Activate Latent Needs

A latent need is one in which the customer has a vague idea of a need but can't fully describe it because the work activities or work outputs available to satisfy the needs are not known. The key to the identification of a latent need is to make the customer aware of what is available. This step usually does not require a full-blown proposal but can be accomplished by simply informing the customer that there is something that will (or might) fill the not yet fully defined need.

Help the Customer Decide

Not only can one plant the seed of desire in the mind of a potential customer but one can develop more specific details about the characteristics of the item or service to be provided. This facet of proposal marketing requires that the salesperson be intimately familiar with the technical characteristics of the product or service being marketed. It is in this area of marketing that great care must be taken not to mislead the customer into believing that performance will be above that which can actually be provided. The most recent example of shortcomings in this area is in the computer hardware and software industries. A number of computer-users have been misled concerning the present or future capabilities of their computer equipment. A dissatisfied customer, who is disgruntled about the actual versus advertised performance of his or her recent acquisition can do more harm than many satisfied customers can do good to credibility and future sales. Helping the customer decide can begin at the inception of the need and continue throughout the preproposal, negotiation, and contract performance periods. One must realize that in defining a need for a customer, it is necessary that the selling company must be capable of fulfilling that need in order to have a successful business relationship. The person or company who can identify relevant marketing information and process it more efficiently and effectively than his or her counterpart in competing firms will be successful at this first but essential phase of marketing.

EVALUATING THE NEED

Since the establishment of the need *includes* the continued assumption that the proposer's company can fulfill that need (if at any time, it is determined that the customer's need cannot be fulfilled, preproposal discussions should be terminated), the next step is to determine that the proposing company can do the job *better* than anyone else. By doing the job better, we mean doing it in a way and at a cost that is most advantageous to the *customer*. The reason the customer's advantage is paramount is that the customer is the one who is doing the evaluating. The selection decision will not be based on the greatest (or least) advantages to the supplier. On the other hand, the proposer must keep in mind his company's overall goals and select only pursuits that will ultimately accomplish these goals.

Keeping Company Objectives in Focus

In the preproposal time frame, it is essential, as a proposer, to keep the overall company objectives in mind as well as those objectives that have been established for this particular procurement. Is the objective to make a short-term profit to improve cash flow or cash on hand? Or is it the primary objective of the company to improve its net worth and/or long term business potential over a number of years? It is a proven fact that in business the second objective is the one having the greater potential of creating sizeable wealth in the long run. But if the company's cash flow is in trouble, a decision to market a "dead-end" job may be necessary to solve the short-term cash flow problem. In general, it is best to search for work that will accomplish the long term objectives and goals of the company. If this can be done while at the same time improving short term cash flow, then the best of two worlds has been attained.

Matching Company-Unique Capabilities to the Need

In matching the company capability to the need (or in matching need to company capability), consideration should be given to specialized team skills, equipment, facilities, personnel, and experience, as well as the unique ideas available to perform the proposed work. Specialization is important when looking for a specific job acquisition. Competitive advantage over other firms bidding for the same work will lie principally in one or more of the six areas listed above. Even though the project may be open for competition, if a particular company has on its payroll a qualified expert in a skill required to do the job and the competitor does not, that particular company has the greatest potential of winning. The company's pattern of acquisition of new equipment, skills, and capabilities can thus influence the type and magnitude of its new work.

Watch for Opportunities for "Synergism"

Often new work acquisitions can have a synergistic effect with current or other new company products or services. When a college professor combines teaching with writing, when a homemaker combines homemaking with a catering service, or when a physician combines research with medical practice, they are engaged in synergistic activities which are mutually supportive and mutually beneficial. Synergistic activities are those that can use the outputs, resources, facilities, or knowledge acquired to help each other. Some companies have found that a by-product from one product line can give rise to a whole new product line based on the by-product of the first. Other companies have found that services related to a product are often more profitable than sales of the original product itself. Synergism has a way of giving more to the customer for his or her dollar while at the same time providing a more profitable venture for the performer.

Beware of the "CUSPETITOR"

The "cuspetitor" is the company which is potentially both a customer and a competitor. The importance of knowing the organization one is dealing with is emphasized when working with this type of company. Many companies have worked long and hard on detailed proposals only to have the "customer" absorb, modify, and sell the proposal ideas and approaches as his or her own. Then there is also the customer who lets the contractor do the more difficult design and development work and then takes over in the more profitable production phase. It is best to establish at the outset in dealing with potential customers that certain product lines or service areas are within the customer's purview or area of competence and that others are within the proposer's area of expertise. This early informed but important agreement will provide smoother sailing during negotiations with a new customer and will eliminate possible areas of suspicion or distrust relative to overlapping target markets or possibilities of competition *between* customer and supplier.

DETERMINING LONG-TERM EFFECTS

In marketing a new work activity or work output it is essential to be certain that this new activity will be profitable in the long run to the company. It is also desirable to know that the work will be more profitable than other projects or activities that could be pursued with the same investment of resources. For these reasons, it is not only desirable but essential that some form of long range analysis be performed. This should determine the profitability of the venture in relation to other alternatives and whether the new activity will result in a net worth growth equal to or better than that experienced in the past or desired by the company. It will also identify and evaluate any other long-term benefits to the company in acquiring the new work. Since companies are in business to be profitable, a profitability analysis and profitability optimization study should be conducted before investing in the efforts required to submit a formal proposal for the work and to implement the subsequent expenditures that must be undertaken to successfully compete in the chosen marketplace with the chosen customer.

Profitability Optimization

A profitability optimization study includes consideration of past and desired company profitability; the profitability of the new acquisition and its alternatives; the company's past and desired growth rate; the increase or decrease in growth rate brought about by the new work; and other factors such as changes in company capacity or capability, diversification, or follow-on work brought about by the new work acquisition. The ten steps required to do a profitability optimization study are shown on Figure 2.1. The profitability of a venture is the return on the investment for that venture. It is the quality of possessing an operating profit while contribut-

Step 1

Establish long term company growth goals, profitability goals, and goals for increasing capability and capacity. Establish excellent cost estimating systems and methods.

Step 2

Determine *present* and *past* company profit category, profitability index, and net worth growth from past financial reports. If divisional financial reports are available, do this on a divisional or departmental basis.

Step 3

Determine cash flows of expenditures and incomes for the project, product, acquisition, or service under study. Determine which are nonrecurring investments and which are recurring incomes and costs.

a. Establish one or more assumed payment modes for expenditures (cash payment, lease, or mortgage loan).
b. Determine all federal and state tax benefits based on the *latest* tax laws.
c. Determine depreciation allowances for equipment and salvage values.
d. Determine increase in company capability and capacity in workforce, equipment, and market potential due to the new activity (nonmonetary value but very important).

Step 4

Bring *all* expenditures and incomes back to present value using a *discount rate* computed based on the most recently available economic projections of *interest rates* and *inflation rates*.

Step 5

Determine profitability index using the *present value* of incomes, expenditures, and non-recurring investments.

Step 6

Determine net worth growth effects of the new project on overall company net worth growth.

Step 7

Compare the profitability of the new work activity or acquisition with past history by comparing its:

a. Profitability index with overall past company profitability index.
b. Net worth growth effects with overall past company net worth growth.
c. Increase in capacity and capability compared with past company capacity and capability.

Step 8

Compare the effect of profitability index, net worth, and capability/capacity increases for each alternative new project or method of acquisition of a new project.

(Continued)

Step 9

Select for implementation, propose, negotiate, and carry out the alternate that best fits company growth and profitability goals.

Step 10

Keep excellent financial records on progress of implementation of the new work activity or acquisition to see—*on a real time basis*—if it is living up to its expectations. If it is not, be prepared to cancel the project provided you have thoroughly evaluated the consequences of cancellation.

Figure 2.1.   Steps in Optimizing Profitability.

ing to the growth of the company. If growth is measured by an increase in net worth, then a positive growth can be achieved when the net worth increases.

Businesses should acquire new work with a high "profitability factor" rather than merely a high profit percentage. This is emphasized by the fact that *growth* is necessary (1) in order to attract capital to provide continued merit advancement of a work force and (2) to provide continued modernization of plant equipment and facilities. Questions that will have an effect on the profitability of a venture are:

1.   Does the work include the expenditure of some nonrecurring resources that will result in work usable in the performance of the *next* job?
2.   Does the work *improve* the overall competitive position in the industry?
3.   Is the new work challenging, and does it represent a significant advance above the current work activities to permit acquisition of new capabilities?
4.   Is the work synergistic (interrelated or mutually supporting) to other activities the company is engaged in?
5.   Does the work improve the *future* growth potential, sales potential, profit potential, and diversification potential?
6.   Will the work improve the company's net worth?

Profitability Factor

The profitability factor is a means of testing a work activity or work output to determine if its profitability is greater or less than past work or other work that is currently under consideration for acquisition. The following is the equation for the profitability factor:

$$\text{Profitability Factor} = \frac{\text{Volume (Units)} \times (\text{Unit Price} - \text{Unit Cost})}{\text{Investment (\$)} \times \text{Time}}$$

For example, if a company had a present net worth of $1.5 million and a past overall profitability (or return on the investment) of two percent per year and had a prospect for selling one thousand transformers per year for three years at $25.00 each, the profitability factor (PF) for a cost of $17.00 each and an investment of $100,000 per year would be:

$$PF = \frac{3,000 \times (25 - 17)}{100,000 \times 3} = .08 \text{ or } 8\%$$

The company would accept the job because the profitability factor of eight percent is four times the past profitability of two percent.

If the actual unit cost turns out to be $24.00 per unit and the equipment budget is overrun by $25,000, the profitability equation is changed as follows:

$$PF = \frac{3,000 \times (25 - 24)}{375,000} = .008 \text{ or } .8\%$$

The profit of $3,000 is offset by the two percent normally expected gain on $125,000 which would have been $2,500 per year or $7,500 for three years. Subtracting the $3,000 profit from the normally expected growth ($7,500 − $3,000) results in a $4,500 net loss for the venture. This example illustrates the importance of good forecasting and estimating of manufacturing costs and production equipment costs and shows how profitability can be decreased drastically if faulty estimating is encountered.

Part of the information provided to the bid committee to assist in making a decision to bid on a particular work activity or work output should be an assessment of the profitability factor of the proposed work in comparison with past and desired company profitability. This profitability factor should be compared with that of alternate new acquisitions to determine which venture will best meet the future profitability needs and desires of the company.

Growth Rate Assessment and Goals

The growth rate of the company can be measured best by examining the balance sheets of the company. Balance sheets tabulate both the assets and liabilities. Since they are "balance" sheets, liabilities are made equal to the assets exactly by including shareholders' equity as part of the liabilities. To determine growth rate, net worth must be computed by subtracting liabilities (not including shareholders equities) from assets. Let us use as an example, Scientific Software Services (SSS), a hypothetical professional service specializing in providing computer programs—software—for a wide range of computer based technical and business monitoring and estimating systems. The SSS annual financial report for 1983 contained balance sheets for assets and liabilities, and an income statement as shown on Figures 2.2, 2.3, and 2.4 respectively. Since financial reports usually show the previous year's financial figures, growth in net worth can be calculated as well as the increase or decrease in the company's profit percentage. In this example, the liabilities (exclusive of stockholders' equity) are subtracted from the company's assets at the end of each of the two years to find the company's net worth at the end of 1982 and 1983. The net worth *increase* for 1983 was found by subtracting the net worth at the end of 1982 from the net worth at the end of 1983. This net worth *increase* was divided by the 1983 net worth to provide an indication of growth during the past year. The phenomenal growth of forty percent occurred, as shown on the bottom of Figure 2.2. Obviously, SSS is a highly successful, growing, profitable company.

The profit percentage rate for Scientific Software Services can be computed for the two years by analysis of the statements of income shown on Figure 2.4. The profit percentage rate is found by dividing the net income by the total expenses and multiplying by one hundred to convert to a

BALANCE SHEETS

	December 31	
ASSETS	1983	1982
CURRENT ASSETS		
Cash....................................	$ 13,840	$ 25,303
Time deposits and certificates of deposit ...	245,001	25,001
Short-term investments	15,061	
Accounts receivable	358,329	245,570
Inventory................................		650
Prepaid expenses and other	4,030	3,711
Total current assets	636,261	300,235
PROPERTY		
Laboratory equipment.....................	107,724	74,975
Furniture and fixtures	92,533	38,794
Leasehold improvements..................	11,003	3,050
Equipment held under capitalized lease	30,862	30,862
Vehicles.................................		26,004
Total.............................	242,122	173,685
Less accumulated depreciation	65,687	42,354
Property—net........................	176,435	131,331
OTHER ASSETS		
Notes receivable—net of discount..........	8,669	
Other	9,668	
Total other assets	18,337	
TOTAL	$831,033	$431,566
Liabilities	431,814	191,653
(Capital) net worth	399,219	239,913
	239,913	
Increase	$159,306	

Growth $= \dfrac{159,306}{399,219} = 39.9\%$

Figure 2.2.   Assets, Scientific Software Services, Inc.

| | December 31 | |
LIABILITIES AND STOCKHOLDERS' EQUITY	1983	1982
CURRENT LIABILITIES		
Accounts payable	$ 35,087	$ 33,944
Accrued interest	5,598	2,566
Accrued payroll and related taxes	5,467	1,323
Accrued employee stock grants		26,400
Accrued profit-sharing contribution	74,124	20,620
Income taxes payable	110,294	12,284
Notes payable (current portion)	42,827	34,483
Accrued vacation benefits	26,536	
Other	3,475	
Total current liabilities	303,408	131,620
LONG-TERM LIABILITIES		
Notes payable (amounts due after one year, net of discount)	128,406	57,618
Accrued interest		2,415
Total long-term liabilities	128,406	60,033
COMMITMENTS		
STOCKHOLDERS' EQUITY		
Common stock—$.20 par value; authorized, 500,000 shares, issued, 409,380 shares in 1983 and 249,940 shares in 1982, outstanding, 409,180 shares in 1983 and 198,400 shares in 1982	81,876	49,988
Paid-in capital		110,273
Retained earnings (profit)	317,743	82,229
Total	399,619	242,490
Treasury stock—at cost; 200 shares in 1983 and 51,540 shares in 1982	(400)	(2,577)
Stockholders' equity—net	399,219	239,913
TOTAL	$831,033	$431,566
Shareholder equity	− 399,219	− 239,913
Liabilities (not including shareholder's equity)	$431,814	$191,653

Figure 2.3. Liabilities and stockholders' equity, Scientific Software Services, Inc.

percentage figure. Note that SSS not only experienced a forty percent growth, but its profit percentage rate increased from 5.89 percent in 1982 to 12.03 percent in 1983.

If it is the goal of Scientific Software Services to continue with a high profitability factor as a result of continued growth, the company must assure itself that the new work it acquires has a profitability potential equal to or greater than its past performance. Since Scientific Software Services is in the enviable position of being in a fast growing field that has a continued high demand for services, its bid committee may elect to reject many high profit ventures in favor of those with a high profitability factor. Note that the profitability factor increased from .30 in 1982 to .68 in 1983.

The important message of the profitability analysis is this: a company cannot expect to have continued high or growing profitability if new projects are accepted that have a lower profitability than those projects carried out in the past. Further, the growth rate of a company cannot be

FOR THE YEARS ENDED DECEMBER 31	1983	1982
REVENUES		
Sales	$2,632,586	$1,297,319
Other	4,648	1,350
Total	2,637,234	1,298,669
EXPENSES		
Cost of sales............................	1,004,194	569,098
Selling, general and administrative		
[Over 50% of revenues: should be about 10%]............................	1,237,086	651,388
Interest	11,986	6,746
Other	1,042	—
Total	2,254,308	1,227,232
INCOME BEFORE PROVISION FOR TAXES ON INCOME	382,926	71,437
PROVISION FOR TAXES ON INCOME		
Current	110,405	400
Deferred	1,300	(1,300)
Total	111,705	(900)
NET INCOME	$ 271,221	$ 72,337
Overall probability factor = $\frac{\text{net income}}{\text{net worth}}$	.68	.30
Company profit rate, net/expenses = ...	12.03%	5.89%
EARNINGS PER COMMON SHARE...........	$.66	$.18

Figure 2.4. Statement of income, Scientific Software Services, Inc.

expected to continue if its new work activities do not contribute to growth rate as much as those projects completed in the past.

In addition to a numerical financial analysis such as that mentioned above, it is also necessary for the marketing function to make other information available to company management and to the bid committee before an intelligent bid/no bid decision can be made. This information includes answers to questions like: "Is it likely that other new work will grow out of this new work acquisition?" Often a company acquires a sizeable competitive advantage for the *next* job if it performs the current job in an outstanding manner. The proposed work may offer the company the opportunity to make new friends and new contacts that will result in expanding its product line and customer base. Further, performance of the proposed work may just give the company the edge in experience needed to rout potential customers.

THE DECISION TO BID

In addressing the decision to bid, one must first determine the goals of bidding and performing the work. There are "no-win" bids and "win" bids. Why would a company want to bid on a job knowing or believing that it was not going to win the contract? There are several reasons. One is that the company may have just entered the field and may need experience in putting together and submitting a proposal. The proposal activity itself usually provides a good experience base for going after new work. Another reason is that the company may want to gain recognition or publicity as a potential supplier. It may merely want to let the customer know that it is "in-the-running" for a particular service or product line. Pricing policies for proposals which are submitted on a "no-win" basis are flexible because the price can be made high enough to cover personnel, facilities, or equipment acquisition to do the job as well as a sizeable profit.

For this discussion, however, we are assuming that the bid committee will be basing its bid decision on the criteria that the company should have a high potential if not a certainty of winning the resulting contract.

Not only is it necessary to decide on a winning strategy (rather than a no-win strategy), but it is necessary to determine the *reasons* for wanting to win. Because the proposal style and content will depend upon them, it is necessary to convey these reasons to the proposal team. Reasons for wanting to win the contract fall into three categories: (1) immediate cash flow improvement, (2) keep the team going, and (3) long term growth and prosperity. In category 1 proposals, the purpose is to make an immediate gain, profit, or increase in cash flow to save the company from impending financial difficulties or to raise cash for an important new project or capital acquisition. Little thought is given to follow-on effort, continued business with the same customer, or long-term profitability. Category 2 proposals are submitted for work that will keep the team employed, active, and available until more attractive or applicable work can be found. Even less consideration to long term growth potential, profitability, and expansion is given in these cases. Category 3 proposals—needless to say the most desirable—are to assure that the company is acquiring work that will bring long term and continually increasing growth and prosperity. These proposals can include those that will capture a portion of the *future* market as well as the existing market.

The bid committee must consider the company's competitive advantage, technological advantage, geographical advantage, political advantage, and price advantage.

Determining Competitive Advantage

It is very difficult to precisely assess the potential of capturing any specific new work activity or work output, but one can conceive of and describe variables that have an effect on capture potential and organize these into a systematic method of comparison. This numerical or quantifiable method of comparison can then be used in combination with the expert judgment of the bid committee to arrive at a bid decision. Two quantifiable factors that can usually be assessed or estimated fairly accurately before a competition are (1) the number of probable bidders and (2) the experience of the company and key personnel in the proposed work. A "competitive ratio," R, can be envisioned which is an indicator of capture potential based on numbers of bidders and the company's experience base. The equation for competitive ratio is shown on Figure 2.5. The company should strive toward high competitive ratios by entering markets where there are not too many competitors and by entering markets where their experience is directly applicable to the proposed work.

The potential of capturing one of a number of jobs on which proposals have been submitted can be computed by adding the competitive ratios of the several proposals as shown on Figure 2.6. If a desired "capture ratio" has been established for a company's proposals, the composite competitive ratio can be used to compare the projected capture potential with desired capture potential.

Determining Technological Advantage

Of the five factors that the bid committee must evaluate in making a decision (competitive, technological, geographical, political, and price advantages), the technological factor is the one that can, in itself, cause a unanimous "no" vote. Therefore, it is considered first in the bid committee's deliberations. The technological advantage will depend principally on whether the firm has a superior product when measured from a standpoint of performance, capacity, quality, speed, accuracy, or any of many other specified characteristics. A unique design or configuration of a product, or uniquely useful features of a service can give a company an immediate technological advantage over its competitors. The bid committee's assessment in this area should also evaluate the technology that is being used to produce the product or deliver the service. Use of modern, advanced

1. Competitive ratio is for comparative analysis only.
2. It is a function of experience level and number of bidders.
3. It does not take into account geographical, technological, and political advantages.
4. Inputs and computation:
   N = number of bidders
   $E1$ = percent of project team that has the exact amount of *generalized* experience required
   $E2$ = percent of project team that has the exact amount of *specialized* experience required
   $E3$ = percent of the job that represents *company* experience
   $$R = \frac{E1 \cdot E2 \cdot E3}{10,000\,N}$$
5. If R = 100%: "We're going to get the job."
   If R = 0%: "We're *not* going to get the job."
6. Competitive ratio is an indicator of capture potential based on number of bidders and experience.

Figure 2.5.   Determining the Proposal's Competitive Ratio, R.

1. Sum the competitive ratios (R) for proposals 1, 2, 3 ----N to determine the *potential**
    of receiving work in any given calendar period covered by these proposals.

    W = *Potential** of receiving work

    $$W = \frac{R1}{100} + \frac{R2}{100} + \frac{R3}{100} + \frac{RN}{100} \times 100$$

    (If W is 100%, *potential* of receiving more than one job is W − 100.)

2. Compare W/R with desired (or required) capture ratio**

Potential is not to be confused with *probability*, a statistically derived factor.
**Capture ratio is the percent of proposals that must be successful.

Figure 2.6. Composite Competitive Ratio.

equipment and facilities designed for speed of delivery and responsiveness
to customer requirements will rate high when assessing technological
advantage. Questions such as: "Is the company employing the latest com-
puter-based technologies for design, manufacturing, testing, materials
handling, logistics, and management reporting?" should be answered and
assessed. Like the other areas of assessment described below, these will
necessarily be subjective in nature. But some recognition of the state-of-
the-art in performing the work relative to that of competitors will be
needed to fully assess technological advantage.

Determining Geographical Advantage

The physical plant or activity location may be of significant value in any
given new acquisition proposal activity. Location in an area where skilled
personnel are plentiful is an important factor in being able to attract the
quality of worker required to do the job. Proximity to the customer may be
an advantage but not necessarily an overriding one. Geographical advantage may also give a price advantage because of lower labor rates, lower
transportation and travel costs, lower energy costs (due to climate), or
lower communications costs. A geographical advantage may also turn into
a political advantage, particularly in underdeveloped, distressed areas
with high unemployment and in desperate need of jobs, new industry, and
new work.

In determining the geographical advantage, certain quantifiable factors can be developed that will give an objective view of the advantage over
competitors. Communications costs to one location versus another location
can be computed in dollars and cents as can travel costs and transportation
costs. Labor costs in various geographical areas, obtained from the Bureau
of Labor Statistics, can provide quantitative information, verifiable by a
government source that labor rates will be lower (or higher) than any other
geographical location. The company in a mild climate area or one which
has inexpensive energy sources has an advantage because of these factors.

Proximity to major suppliers may offer an advantageous cost and schedule as well as geographical advantage.

Determining Political Advantages

The bid committee should also assess the political overtones, if any, of the proposed procurement. Does the new procurement fall into a depressed industry or is it one in which skills of the now unemployed can be effectively used? Does the work offer an opportunity for minorities, veterans, or the handicapped to participate? Are there political factors such as congressional support, public support, media support, or special interest group support that would lean toward one company performing the work as opposed to those other companies that are engaged in the competition? Likewise, through market research information, it can be determined if the company is in any way favored by the customer—or even *his or her* customer. All of these factors are "politically oriented" inputs to the bid/no bid decision.

Determining Price Advantage

Even though a detailed cost estimate has not been developed at the time the bid/no bid decision has to be made, there are factors other than those already mentioned above that enter into the potential price advantage in the competition. Significant of these factors is overhead rate. If overhead is traditionally low, this one factor (all other factors being equal) could be a price advantage. Other factors, mentioned earlier, are low labor rates, availability of inexpensive energy sources, and proximity to raw material sources.

Estimation of a rough order-of-magnitude price prior to the bid/no bid decision will allow evaluation of:

1. Cost in relation to price.
2. Price in relation to known budgets.
3. Price in relation to supply and demand.
4. Price in relation to the competitor's most probable prices.

A cursory evaluation of these four areas will provide the bid committee with quantitative financial data on which to determine overall most probable pricing advantage.

WHEN THE "WINNER" IS REALLY THE LOSER

Armed with excellent marketing information, the bid committee can make a knowledgeable decision whether to bid or to forego the opportunity

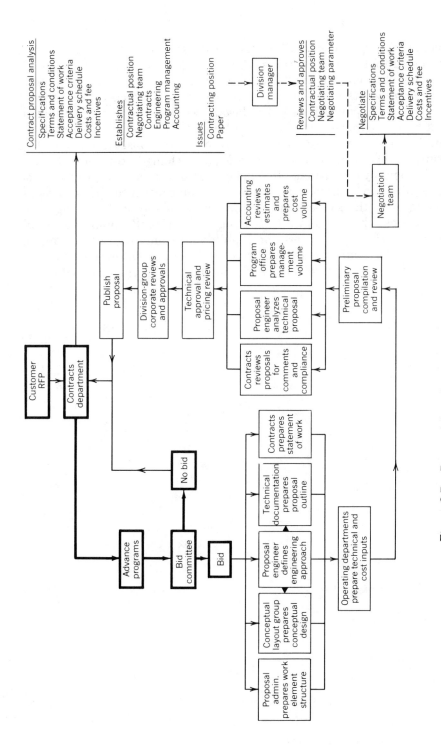

Figure 2.7. Proposal flow chart showing bid/no bid decision.

29

to bid in favor of the pursuit of other business opportunities. It has often been said that there is nothing more courageous than a knowledgeable "no-bid" decision. We might add also, that there is sometimes nothing more *profitable* than an informed, courageous no-bid decision. (See Figure 2.7.) Many companies have bid and won coveted contracts only to find out that their preproposal marketing techniques were so lacking that major pitfalls in the proposed contract were obscured. Obscure contract fine print, a propensity to include unanticipated changes, contractually covered actions by the customer that delay the work, or untimely cancellation or termination of parts or all of the work can cause a company to regret having "won" the competition. A company should rely on the courage of its convictions when it comes to bidding on marginally profitable or ill-defined work, and long-term profitability will improve rather than decrease. If the required marketing homework is done, however, certainty of winning will justify the very best in the proposal preparation effort.

3

PLANNING THE PROPOSAL ACTIVITIES

*Be strong and courageous, and get to work, do not be frightened by
the size of the task.*
I Chron. 28:20

Some who prepare proposals have the misconception that proposal preparation starts with receipt of a request for proposal and is completed when the proposal is submitted to the customer. Nothing could be further from the truth! The proposal activities of any company are inextricably enmeshed in its overall business acquisition activities and business acquisition plans. A company's overall marketing strategy, its research and development program for new products and services, and its capital acquisition and expansion plans all form a part of the business acquisition process, of which proposal preparation is only a part. Because of this integral relationship of the proposal with other business related activities, it is often difficult to identify exactly where proposal preparation begins.

When an entrepreneur conceives an idea, he or she must then start taking actions that will ultimately result in the manifestation of a final work activity or work output. The steps taken to bring the idea from the conceptual stage to a place where it will fulfill a real need and produce real prosperity can be thought of as part of the proposal preparation process. Although the entrepreneur, scientist, engineer, or businessperson may have no thought (at the time he or she conceives and starts developing the idea) of submitting a formal written proposal document, he or she invariably will have to do so in some form sooner or later if the idea is to be put into practice. Hence, any description or treatment of the overall proposal preparation process must include a "cradle-to-the-grave" analysis of the overall business acquisition process from the viewpoint of how the activities preceding and following actual proposal submittal affect the proposal

31

itself, and how these activities influence the potential of receiving an authorization, funds, or contract to proceed with the work. This chapter will describe some of the often neglected and always important steps in the process and will point out ways that a company can enhance, even assure, a winning record. When it is decided which of these methods or techniques will be used, they must be scheduled, staffed, and funded to compliment the proposal effort.

PREDEVELOPMENT, DESIGN, BREADBOARD, AND PROTOTYPE TESTING

The credibility of a proposal for any new work activity or work output is affected significantly by the amount of forethought that has been put into the design of the product or service through in-depth design, analyses, operations research studies, literature reviews, market surveys, and customer attitude polls. All of these activities represent important but "soft" work definition activities. That is, these preproposal activities do not usually include sufficient hard evidence that the product will work properly in its intended environment or that the service can be performed in the time period and with the quality desired by the customer.

To provide convincing evidence of the viability of a new work activity or work output there is no substitute for preliminary activation of the work process to produce a "straw-man," "prototype," "breadboard," or "dry run" of the proposed work output or work activity. This convincing evidence, once planned and completed, must then be skillfully documented in anticipation that this evidence may be the deciding factor in the selection of the proposing organization to do the work. If the proposal is based strictly on theory, or what is theoretically possible, it will have little opportunity for success. If it is based on actual demonstrated results, there is a far better chance of success. All other factors being equal, the more thoroughly tested and demonstrated work output or work activity will be the one that has the best opportunity of fulfilling the stated need, provided that the demonstrations are adequately and skillfully documented in the proposal.

If the proposed work output is a product or project, it is desirable to demonstrate in the proposal that a prototype has been designed, built, tested, and operated under conditions similar to or more stringent than those that would be expected to be encountered in actual use. If it has not been feasible or practical to build a complete prototype, it is often beneficial to show that working models or operating models of the components or subsystems of the final product have been successfully tested in the environment in which they are expected to operate when combined with the total system. This type of testing is often accomplished by what is commonly known as a "breadboard" or "brassboard."

A breadboard or brassboard is a laboratory or shop working model of the total system that may or may not look like the final product or system but that will operate in the same way as the final system. An example of a breadboard would be an electronic circuit in which all components and interconnecting wires are placed in their proper electronic position relative to each other but are not packaged in the same way that they will be packaged in the final product. A breadboard usually pays no attention to size or convenience to the customer or consumer in arrangement of components but emphasizes convenience of visibility, component removal and replacement, and operational testing to the laboratory technician or test engineer. A brassboard is a similar arrangement for hydraulic, pneumatic, or mechanically interconnected components. A breadboard or brassboard design may be layed out flat on a test bench, while the final product that consists of the same components may be packaged in a small, three-dimensional "black" box. The breadboard or brassboard can be used for a wide range of operational testing to evaluate the effect of performance changes and component interactions without immediately affecting the overall final packaging of the completed design. The value of the breadboard or brassboard to the proposal activity, then, is to provide tangible evidence (test data) that proves that the product or system works, albeit in a physical form other than the final configuration.

To supplement the breadboard or brassboard tests, and to show that planning and forethought have gone into the final configuration, the design, construction, and documentation of a "soft" or "hard" mockup is a good investment. A soft mockup is one built of wood, soft metals, plastic, foam, or even cardboard or paper. A skillful maker of soft mockups can develop a three-dimensional model of "string and glue" that, when painted and photographed, looks like the actual completed product. Soft mockups can be built in full scale size or in reduced scale size, depending on the pre-proposal time and funds available. Reduced scale soft mockups or models are economical and, when photographed with suitable scale model size references such as a scale model man, car, or house, will look like the real thing. Hard mockups are usually constructed of the same or similar materials to those to be used in the final product but the model may or may not be a working or operational model. Both types of mockups have the advantage of allowing the customer to visualize through a reproduced photograph in the proposal what the completed product will actually look like, and lend credibility, realism, and visual reinforcement to the confidence of the proposal reader or evaluator because the work output can be realistically depicted in physical form.

Processes and services (work activities) are more difficult to verify during the preproposal process through physical evidence of workability; however, there are ways that tangible evidence can be generated and documented for the edification of the potential buyer. One way to demonstrate a work activity, of course, is to have actually carried out the activity on a small scale prior to proposal submittal. This is similar to "reducing-to-practice" a patented process prior to putting it into full scale production. Laboratory results, time and motion studies of a dry run of the process, motion pictures of work activity being accomplished, and live demonstrations of the work activity can all be ways of supplementing the proposal material with physical evidence of the speed, quality, or results.

PRELIMINARY UNSOLICITED PROPOSALS

One way to establish relationships with potential customers is through preliminary unsolicited proposals. Since these proposals can go directly to the people in an organization who will make the decisions rather than through the normal contracting or procurement organization, they can be very useful in providing a direct input to the customer's technical decision makers during the time of formulation of requirements. Through the use of preliminary unsolicited proposals, information can be informally provided to the customer that he will find useful in preparing the request for proposal. When a company has provided input that has been used in developing the request for proposal, it is aware of the approach and perhaps even the content before the request for proposal is formally issued on the open market. Preliminary unsolicited proposals also have the advantage of making the decision makers in the customer's organization aware at an early date in the procurement process of the capabilities, interest, and the quality of work a firm can provide. Such a revelation to the customer could result in a sole-source procurement provided that the customer is convinced that the company is the only one that is truly qualified to do the task on the schedule and within the costs allocated. It is necessary to preplan the submittal of any preliminary unsolicited proposals. These proposals should be integrated into the overall new business acquisition strategy; their value considered, and their use adopted if it is believed that they will enhance a competitive position. (One note of caution in submitting preliminary unsolicited proposals: an unethical potential customer might find it to his advantage to leak data or information from the proposal to competitors. The proposer should beware of this possibility and determine the risk of this occurrence before submitting the preliminary unsolicited proposal).

Since it is often difficult to discern where preproposal marketing leaves off and proposal preparation begins, it is necessary to schedule and plan preproposal conferences with the customer as a continuation of the marketing process and to provide continuity of communication with the customer in this manner. Once the customer has been led through the four steps of the marketing process (attention gained, interest created, desire stimulated, and action taken), continued contact and communication with the customer will be required until the sale has been consummated through the signing of the contract. Since the marketing or sales department's job is essentially completed when the customer has been stimulated to take the action of sending a request for proposal or a request for quotation, the proposal team must take over the baton of customer contact and communication and continue this intercourse into the more detailed technical, organizational, and cost aspects of the project.

This is when the marketing department phases in the operational team that will be defining the more subtle and detailed aspects of the work activity or work output. The proposal manager and the sales engineer (see Chapter 4) will be key individuals in this process and should coordinate the continuity of customer contacts early in the overall proposal preparation process. Detailed communication with the customer should proceed as far as possible into the proposal submittal process. If the proposal is competitive with other proposals, sometimes the customer will institute a "blackout" period during which further communications with the potential suppliers are prohibited. If communications with the customer are continuous and effective, the maximum amount of benefit can be gleaned from customer contact prior to the blackout period.

Once the blackout period is instituted, it should not be violated or circumvented. The customer will not appreciate those who try to extract information concerning the status of the procurement while the evaluation activity is in process. By the time the blackout period is started, all of the information needed to prepare an effective and winning proposal should have been collected from the customer. Once the blackout period has begun, information is passed on equally to all bidders through formal communications procedures instituted by the customer. These formal procedures usually serve to provide the customer with supplemental information about the capabilities or the work to be performed, and are carried out during the evaluation process after the proposal has already been submitted.

Prior to proposal submittal, and subsequent to issuance of the request for proposal, the customer will often arrange a formal preproposal conference to which all bidders are invited and allowed to ask questions to clarify the intent and content of the request for proposal. Attendance at these conferences by marketing personnel and key proposal team members is usually desirable because these conferences offer the opportunity to hear the types of questions that are being asked by the competitors. These meetings or conferences frequently do not yield substantive information because competitors will not want to reveal their key concerns or lack of knowledge. But some questions, usually procedural, will be asked, and each potential bidder will be allowed to submit written as well as oral questions about the procurement at this time. The written questions, as well as some of the oral questions may not be answered by the customer at the time of the bidders' conference but will be answered in writing later with answers to all questions going to all bidders. The cardinal rule of a bidders conference at which competitors are present is to ask only those questions that are necessary and to ask intelligent questions rather than ones that may unknowingly reveal potential weaknesses in the competition. The one-on-one meetings already held with the customers prior to the formal phase of the competition will be far more valuable in gaining significant information that will be useful in preparing the proposal.

The key point in all communications with the customer is to *listen carefully*! The customer knows what he or she wants, and it is the purpose of a proposed work activity or work output to fulfill that need. Key information will be missed if a company is more concerned with what it would rather supply than what the customer actually wants and will result in failure to get the job. The fact having been established in the marketing phase that the job has a high enough potential profitability to cause one to want it, it is essential to *listen carefully* to the customer's requirements and react responsively and sensitively to them.

WRITTEN QUESTIONS TO THE CUSTOMER

In planning the overall steps of the proposal preparation process, it is necessary to devote specific time and resources to the function of providing written questions to the customer about the procurement if provision has been made in the request for proposal for a formal question submittal. Thoughtful and careful preparation of these questions is necessary because these questions actually serve two functions. The more obvious of these functions is to get answers or clarifications about the request for proposal content. The other function of carefully prepared written questions is to indicate intelligence, competence, insight, and interest in prospective work. Although competitors may also formally receive the same answers, the customer usually does not indicate which bidder has asked the question. Therefore, much less is revealed to a competitor than in the oral preproposal question and answer period. Oddly enough, an absence of questions from the bidder may (erroneously) indicate a lack of interest, competence, or understanding of the project requirements rather than a complete understanding. The strategy of formal written communication with the customer, then, should be a subject of preproposal discussion and policy within a company.

PROPOSAL CLARIFICATION CONFERENCES

For large procurements, particularly those that are of the "negotiated procurement" category, the customer may call in one bidder at a time to obtain additional information about his proposal *after* it has been submitted. In this type of conference, the best people should be there and they should be well briefed on the answers to provide and the supplemental information to present. Preceding these conferences the customer has usually formulated written questions about the proposal and submitted them several weeks prior to the proposal conference to allow time to prepare suitable oral answers as well as written replies or proposal addenda. Since this meeting will be "one-on-one" with the customer without competitors present, there is an opportunity to reveal much more valuable information to the customer and probably even glean some overall information from the customer as to his major concerns, doubts, leanings, and trends in the selection. There may or may not be an opportunity to add further supplemental written information to the customer after this conference. If an erroneous statement has been made or an incomplete answer to a question has been given in this conference, a follow-up letter to clarify the answer, whether solicited or not, will be appreciated by the customer.

THE PROPOSAL PREPARATION ACTIVITIES

Planning the proposal preparation activities involves laying out and dedicating the *time* required for proposal preparation, allocating and identifying of the *facilities* required, appointing or designating the *team* and team members, and estimating and authorizing the *resources* required to do the job. A well-planned proposal preparation activity is essential for the development of a high quality proposal. The proposal preparation activity, particularly for larger proposals, must be meticulously planned, and estimated just as the activity being proposed must be meticulously planned and estimated. In estimating the time, facilities, team, and resources required to complete the proposal preparation process, it is handy to use a checklist like that shown on Figure 3.1.

Time Required for Proposal Preparation

The competitive nature of the procurement process makes the factor of *time* the most important factor in planning the proposal preparation process. A fast-response unsolicited or solicited proposal may result in one firm being the only bidder for a job, and may result in a sole-source procurement. In most solicited competitive procurements, the time allocated for proposal preparation is only a small fraction of that required for actual performance of the job itself, yet some of the aspects of job performance must be at least addressed if not initiated during the proposal preparation process. The construction of models, mockups, breadboards, and prototypes and their testing and documentation usually take more time than that usually allowed for proposal preparation. Therefore this work must be initiated and even completed *prior to* receipt of the request for proposal. The short time allocated for proposal preparation precludes last minute decisions and haphazard planning. Many companies, through

I   Review RFP Requirements

1. Identify each item called for by the RFP through use of a checklist.
2. Identify company approach and develop marketing strategy.
3. Provide inputs or feedback to the customer if appropriate.

II   Define Proposal Effort

1. Identify tasks required for proposal preparation.
2. Estimate number of personnel and time required for each task.
3. Establish a proposal schedule.
4. Determine security classification and information protection and handling techniques.

III   Perform Preproposal Functions

1. Establish specific approach.
2. Determine extent of proposal (austere, standard, or elaborate).
3. Define work activity or work output to be proposed.
4. Develop a proposal outline and an estimate of the number of pages.
5. Establish proposal preparation man-hours by task.
6. Identify team members and work area location.
7. Initiate proposal funding request and obtain management approval.
8. Select critique committee (red team).
9. Establish a target price for the work to be proposed.

IV   Hold Plan-of-Action or Kickoff Meeting

1. Present program to be proposed to proposal team.
2. Distribute work package.
   a. Proposal preparation schedule.
   b. Proposal outline.
   c. Program outline (preliminary work statement if developed to this extent at this time.)
   d. Assumptions and ground rules.
   e. Preliminary designs and specifications.
   f. Work element structure and dictionary.
3. Assign individual responsibilities and allocate labor-hours.
4. Marketing manager or manager briefs team on customer, program history, and competitive situations.

V   Prepare Rough Draft

1. Expand proposal outline.
2. Develop and refine preliminary work statement.

3. Prepare materials and drawing lists.
4. Prepare labor-hours estimates for the proposed work.
5. Develop new facilities requirements
6. Monitor facility requirements for RFP compliance.
7. Review program schedule for compliance with work statement and RFP.
8. Develop introduction, summary, and a draft letter of transmittal.
9. Maintain proposal funds budget surveillance to control labor-hour expenditures.
10. Obtain line management ideas early.
11. Review labor-hour estimates and materials costs to be sure they are consistent with the RFP and expected customer funding.

VI   Detailed Review of Technical and Cost Volumes

1. Study preliminary cost breakdown.
2. Eliminate any unnecessary or excess tasks and/or labor-hours.
3. Assure a competitive price and technology that is consistent with RFP and customer funding.

VII   Critique Committee Review all Volumes

1. Obtain critique committee or red team comments and extent of rewrite required.
2. Rework proposal in accordance with critique committee or red team comments.
3. Submit for final type by sections.
4. Review final corrected copy.
5. Check figure sequence and page sequence.

VIII   Produce the Proposal

1. Finalize letter of transmittal and obtain signature.
2. Complete final artwork.
3. Complete final copy editing.
4. Print the proposal.
5. Collate, assemble, and bind volumes.
6. Check over all bound volumes and all copies for completeness.

IX   Package the Proposal

1. Assemble volumes into complete sets.
2. Provide the required number of copies.
3. Package into convenient size envelopes or boxes.

X   Mail or Hand Carry the Proposal to the Customer

Figure 3.1.   Proposal Preparation Checklist.

inadequate proposal planning, have entered the competition too late and have had to play a game of "catch-up" throughout the proposal competition. Because marketing is feeding information to the proposal team continuously even *during* the proposal preparation process, there is usually a scarcity of time during the proposal preparation process. Hence, it is vital that detailed time-planning be done for the proposal preparation process. Deadlines must be established for each phase of the proposal preparation process and these deadlines must be met. There can be no room for slippage or delays because the submittal date is usually fixed. Time delays must be made up *within* the schedule (rather than by extending the schedules) by the use of overtime, additional personnel, or multishift operation. Since the proposal team is an integral unit (see Chapter 4), the last two of these alternatives are less attractive and oftentime become the only way to make up for proposal preparation schedule slips. A courageous no-bid decision is much better than accepting a proposal preparation job with insufficient proposal preparation time.

Facilities Required for Proposal Preparation

The principal facilities required for the actual proposal preparation process are (1) an isolated office space or area for the proposal preparation team and (2) a publication production facility. These facilities must be supplemented in the preproposal phase by any shops, test laboratories, and test facilities required to develop tangible evidence of work quality and credibility through physical demonstrations of prototypes and dry runs. Action must be taken to assure that these facilities are made available to the team on a dedicated basis during and throughout the proposal preparation period.

The Proposal Team

Preplanning of proposed activities is an essential element in indentifying the personnel required for the proposal team and determining the skill categories and skill levels required for these personnel. A look forward to Chapter 4 will show that some very specialized and competent people are required for proposal preparation. Planning by company management to identify, allocate, and assign these personnel to the team during the proposal preparation process is necessary to assure that other ongoing work being performed by the company is not adversely affected by the reassignment of these highly qualified team members to the urgent job of proposal preparation during the new work acquisition process.

Resources Required to Propose

Proposal preparation requires money and manpower. In the preproposal marketing and planning process, a detailed cost estimate should be made of the costs of preparing the proposal and this estimate should be used to develop a budget which is then placed under the control of the proposal manager. Proposal preparation costs can vary as an order of magnitude of the percentage of the costs of the proposed work (from one to ten percent of the costs of the proposed work). Therefore, a rough estimate of proposal preparation costs is usually not acceptable to company management. The same principles spelled out in Chapter 8, "The Cost Proposal," can be used in estimating the cost of the proposal itself. This is a vital part of the proposal planning activity and will help to identify all of the activities and actions that must be accomplished to do the total proposal preparation job.

FOLLOW-UP ACTIVITIES TO PROPOSAL PREPARATION

Because members of the proposal preparation team may become negotiators and/or performers of the work itself, the job is not finished when the proposal is submitted to the customer. The proposal activities include other follow-up activities that must be planned and carried out before a contract is signed. These activities, although not a part of the physical preparation of the proposal document, must be included in planning the proposal activities because they require the continued allocation of time, facilities, the proposal preparation team members, and monetary and manpower resources. The two principal postproposal activities are preparation of the best and final offer (if one is allowed for in the procurement process) and negotiation of contract provisions, scope of work, contract price, and fee.

The "Best and Final" Offer

In many negotiated procurements a provision is made for the offer or to submit a "best and final" offer prior to completion of the evaluation process and the selection of the winning firm. A deadline date is usually provided in the request for proposal beyond which best and final offers will not be accepted. Although best and final offers vary in content and depth, the principal constituent of a best and final offer is always a final quoted price for accomplishment of the work. Often the procuring company or agency requires little backup material for this revised bid price, and it is usually not necessary to resubmit the entire cost proposal. Even though backup material is often not required, it is wise and prudent for the proposing firm to do a detailed revision of its cost estimate and its proposed pricing adjustments to this revised cost estimate. The reason for this is that the work activity or work output must be adjusted to match the newly proposed price by modifying the work content, skill categories or levels, timing of schedule elements, or specifications. Time and effort must be allocated in the overall proposal activity schedule to accomplish modification of company work plans to meet the new quoted price.

Contract Negotiations

It is the practice of some procuring organizations to conduct parallel negotiations with several bidders before making a final source selection decision. This "reverse auctioning" process is often time and manpower consuming because company funds must be expended on a job before the assurance is available that the job is won. Proposal preplanning should recognize this fact in these instances, and careful planning should be done to assure the availability of team members and resources to carry out the various phases of the negotiation process.

Planning for the Negotiation of the Work Statement.   Whether source selection is completed before or after negotiations, both technical and management proposal team members may be involved in negotiation of the contract work statement and specifications. The key to negotiating the contract work statement and specifications will be to go over all words and numbers in the contract *very carefully* to ensure that the work contracted for can be accomplished with the resources available to do the work. Many losses have been incurred and companies ruined because they failed to evaluate fully subtle wording or numerical requirements during contract negotiations. It is essential for the proposer to understand what is being sold and for the customer to know what he or she is buying. Sufficient manpower and resources should be allocated to the new work acquisition effort to assure a thorough and systematic approach to work scope and specification negotiations.

Planning for the Negotiation of Contract Price.   Negotiation of contract price (or cost if a cost-reimburseable contract is contemplated) should involve individuals from the technical, cost, and management proposal teams who can support company negotiators in dealing with the customer. Principally, it is the cost proposal team members who will be the most useful in this negotiation because they have access to and can explain detailed labor-hour and material estimates from a high-granularity cost proposal. The cost proposal team members are also most likely to know if and how much contingency or allowance for cost growth has been included in each cost element within each work element within each calendar time period. Although these contingencies and allowances for cost growth may or may not be revealed to the customer, it is vital that the negotiator have this information at his or her fingertips. The most common ploy of customers who are negotiating on a limited budget is to try to eliminate or at least to reduce the contingency costs and allowances for cost growth. Unless a work output or work activity is thoroughly defined in painstaking detail, elimination of cost growth allowances could be a precursor to an eventual overrun in cost resulting in a loss in profit (fee) or even in reimbursement for materials and direct labor. Very few jobs are so well defined that it is possible to eliminate all contingencies and allowances for cost growth. Sufficient manpower and resources must be planned as early as the preproposal phase to assure that the proper individuals will be available for this aspect of the negotiation process.

Planning for the Negotiation of Fee. Early in the proposal preparation process it is necessary to establish a policy on what profit or fee will be required to make the whole venture worthwhile. As pointed out in Chapter 2, the quality of "profitability" is one that has to be considered and evaluated early in the process and used as a basis for a bid decision. If the venture has an extremely high profitability (long term or life-cycle profit and growth advantage), then a lower immediate profit or fee can be accepted. On the other hand, if profitability as related to growth and long term benefits are limited or nil, a high front-end fee or profit should be demanded. Because the fee or profit negotiation is usually performed by corporate or company negotiators or company management, little support of the proposal preparation team except perhaps the proposal manager and cost manager will be required. But time must be allocated in the overall business acquisition cycle to negotiate profit or fee. If the fee structure is to be based on an award fee or incentive fee arrangement, fee negotiation time must be increased in proportion to the fee structure complexity.

ESTABLISHING AN OVERALL PROPOSAL PREPARATION SCHEDULE

Where the proposal cycle is expected to take several weeks or months, and where inputs will be required from various organizations and/or disciplines, an essential tool is a detailed proposal schedule. The minimum key milestones in a proposal preparation schedule are (1) a "kickoff" meeting; (2) a "review of ground rules" meeting; (3) "technical and resources input and review" meeting; and (4) summary meetings and presentations. Descriptions of these meetings and their approximate places in the proposal preparation cycle follow.

The "Kickoff" Meeting

The very first formal milestone in a proposal preparation schedule is the kickoff meeting. This is a meeting of all the individuals who are expected to have an input to the proposal. It usually includes individuals who are proficient in technical disciplines involved in the work to be performed; business-oriented individuals who are aware of the financial factors to be considered in developing the proposal; project-oriented individuals who are familiar with the project ground rules and constraints; and, finally, the proposal manager and the proposal preparation team.

Sufficient time should be allowed in the kickoff meeting to describe all project ground rules, constraints, and assumptions; to hand out copies of selected portions of the request for proposal, technical specifications, drawings, schedules, and work element descriptions and resource estimating forms; and to discuss these items and answer any questions that might arise. It is also an appropriate time to clarify proposal preparation assignments among the various disciplines represented in the event that organizational charters are not clear as to who should support which part of the proposal.

The "Review of Ground Rules" Meeting

Several days after the kickoff meeting, when the participants have had the opportunity to study the material, a review of ground rules meeting should be conducted. In this meeting the proposal manager answers questions regarding the proposal preparation, assumptions, ground rules, and assignments. If the members of the proposal preparation team are experienced in developing technical descriptions and resource estimates for their respective disciplines, very little discussion may be needed. However, if this is the first proposal preparation cycle for one or more of the team members, it may be necessary to provide these team members with additional information, guidance, and instruction.

The Technical and Resources Input and Review Meeting

Sometime after the kickoff and review of ground rules meetings, each team member that has a technical and resources (labor-hour and/or materials) input is asked to present his input before the entire proposal team. Hence starts one of the most important parts of the proposal preparation process: the interaction of team members to reduce duplications, overlaps, and omissions in technical descriptions and resource data.

The proposal manager should, in this meeting, make maximum use of the synergistic effect of team interaction. In any multidisciplinary activity, it is the synthesis of information and actions that produces wise decisions rather than the mere volume of data. In this review meeting the presentor responsible for each discipline area has the opportunity to justify and explain the rationale for technical descriptions and estimates in view of his peers—an activity that tends to iron out inconsistencies, overstatements, and incompatibilities. Occasionally, inconsistencies, overlaps, duplications, and omissions will be so significant that a second input and review meeting will be required in order to collect and synthesize all proposal inputs.

Summary Meetings and Presentations

Once the proposal inputs have been collected, adjusted, and "priced" or "costed," the proposal is presented in a package as a dry run to the proposal team. This dry run can produce visibility into further inconsistencies or errors that have crept into the proposal during the process of consolidation and reconciliation. A final review with the company management could also bring about some changes in the proposal because of last minute changes in ground rules.

As shown on Figure 3.1, there are other steps leading up to and surrounding these key meetings. These other steps are developed and explained more thoroughly throughout this book but are summarized briefly here in a form that will allow the proposal activity planner and estimator to plan and estimate the resources required to carry out a total proposal preparation activity.

ESTABLISHING A DETAILED PROPOSAL PREPARATION SCHEDULE

Review of Request for Proposal (RFP) Requirements

The review of RFP requirements (or company requirements if the proposal is to be unsolicited) is the first step in the detailed process leading to the publication and delivery of a completed proposal document. The first step in this RFP review is to develop a summary or checklist of the RFP. Since many RFPs are long and complex, this step eliminates much confusion and provides in-depth visibility as well as an overview of RFP requirements. Concurrent with this step, assuming that a decision to bid has already been made, is the development or formulation of an overall company approach and marketing strategy that will be used in developing the proposal. Then the results of the RFP review should be evaluated for places where supplemental information is needed either from marketing or from the customer. If the customer has made provision for written or oral questions from potential bidders, a formal list of questions is prepared and submitted to the customer (the results or answers to these questions will be returned in the form of a letter or an addendum to the RFP). Keep in mind that competitors will also be afforded an opportunity to receive the answers to any questions.

Define the Proposal Effort

This and the following step include the activities that are spelled out in this chapter. It includes identification of all the tasks required for proposal preparation; estimation of the number and types of personnel, equipment, facilities, and time required to prepare the proposal; establishment of a proposal preparation schedule; and determination of security classifications, logistics, and handling techniques.

Preproposal Functions

Preproposal functions commence with the establishment of a specific proposal approach that fits within the request for proposal requirements and the overall company marketing approach. A determination is made of the extent of the proposal; that is, will it be an austere, standard, or elaborate proposal? This decision will be guided by the assessment of marketing and company management concerning the worth to the company of winning the contract as well as the resources available to submit the proposal. The work activity or work output to be proposed must then be defined in detail. This is done by preparing a work element structure and work element structure dictionary. A detailed outline of the proposal is developed along with an estimate of the number of pages, figures, tables, and appendices that will be included. Proposal preparation labor-hours are estimated and budgeted by task, work team members and the work area location is identified, and a funding request or proposal task authorization is initiated to obtain management approval to proceed with the proposal preparation activity. A "critique committee," "red team," or "murder board" is selected to review the final proposal draft before it is sent to production, and a target price is established for the work to be performed.

Plan of Action or "Kickoff" Meeting

As mentioned earlier, all key proposal team members are invited to a "plan-of-action" or "kickoff" meeting. In this meeting the proposal manager, company marketing or sales manager, or other knowledgeable company officer describes the work activity or work output to be proposed. A work package is distributed which includes a proposal preparation schedule; a detailed proposal outline; a preliminary work statement (if available); and a list of proposal team assignments, responsibilities, and labor-hour allocations. Also distributed are proposal assumptions and ground rules, preliminary designs and specifications, the work element structure and dictionary, and blank forms for submittal of technical and resource data. The marketing manager or sales manager also briefs the proposal preparation team on the customer's characteristics and desires, program history, and competitive situations.

Preparation of Rough Draft of Proposal Volumes

When the proposal team has been thoroughly briefed, work commences on expansion and deepening of the proposal outline, and development and refinement of the preliminary work statement. Materials and drawing lists are prepared, and labor-hour estimates are prepared for the proposed work. Concurrently, facilities and equipment lists and descriptions are developed. Both the facility requirements and the program schedule are monitored for request for proposal compliance. The introduction, summary, and draft letter of transmittal is prepared.

Throughout the time period of rough draft preparation, surveillance of the proposal funds budget is maintained to control labor-hour expenditures, line management ideas are interjected into the draft, and estimated labor-hour estimates and material cost estimates are reviewed to be sure they are consistent with the RFP and the expected customer funding.

Detailed Review of Technical and Cost Volumes

Once the preliminary or rough draft of the proposal is completed, a detailed, in-depth review is made of the technical and cost volumes by studying the preliminary cost breakdown and eliminating any unnecessary or excess tasks and/or labor-hours, thereby assuring a competitive price and technology that is consistent with the request for proposal and the available funding.

Proposal Writing and Publication

Finalizing proposal writing and production starts with a polishing of the letter of transmittal and approval and signature of the letter of transmittal by company management. Final artwork and copy editing are completed, and the proposal is "sent to press." When printing is completed; collation, assembly, binding, and checking of all copies are performed by the production staff.

Packaging the Proposal

Proposal volumes are assembled into complete sets, copy counts are verified, and the proposals are packaged into convenient size envelopes or boxes.

Proposal Delivery

Often one or more copies of the proposal are handcarried to the customer to personally assure that the deadline date is met. The remaining copies are mailed or shipped by a reliable and fast mail or parcel carrier.

PROPOSAL SUPPLEMENTS

For very large or complex proposals it is sometimes both necessary and desirable to supply other material than the actual written proposal volumes. Scale models, mockups, briefings, brochures, motion pictures, video tapes, computer software demonstration disks or tapes, and other tangible material may have to be developed, produced, and delivered to the customer at appropriate points in the new work acquisition cycle. Planning for the production and delivery of these items must be done at the outset of the proposal cycle to permit effort to proceed parallel to the written material.

Scale Models and Mockups

Earlier it was mentioned that photographs of models and mockups may be desirable to display realism and credibility in the proposal document. The bidder should also consider the possibility of providing an actual scale model, working model, or mockup to the customer as part of the proposal. A three-dimensional representation of a completed product or project helps the customer visualize what the final configuration will look like better than detailed engineering drawings and specifications. Also, the customer may need to use such a scale model or mockup to illustrate to his or her customer; management; or even to the public through the media the principles, advantages, or operation of the item.

Scale models are particularly appropriate in large architect-engineer tasks, construction tasks, public works projects, and high technology hardware such as aerospace and defense systems. Also to be considered is the value of a scale or working model, a cutaway model showing operation, or an operational breadboard or brassboard to supplement a proposal of any size. The production of the model itself must be well planned, organized, and carried out with forethought and prudence in order to make it a truly useful item in the marketing of a proposal.

Motion Pictures and Video Tapes

When a process or a work activity is the subject of the proposal, a motion picture, video tape, slides, or audio tapes may also supplement a proposal. The expense of these media should be weighed against potential benefits. Technology improvements in these areas of presentation are reducing costs significantly, and a well-produced video tape, graphic presentation, or slide show might be the additional icing on the cake that will assure palatability of the entire proposal. Audio-visual production should be planned and carried out parallel to the preparation of written material to assure consistency and compatability of the written and audio visual presentations.

Computer Software Demonstration Programs

When computer software is all or part of the work activity or work output being marketed, an essential element to provide with the proposal is a hands-on computer demonstration. Because computers are still relatively new to many industries, businesses, and government agencies, it is often necessary to educate the customer on computer software capabilities. When the potential customer is unfamiliar with computers, there is no substitute for a real-time, live demonstration of a preliminary version, or even a similar version of the software that is being marketed. Since portability and communications links for computers have been improved immeasurably in the past few years, on-site demonstrations of software

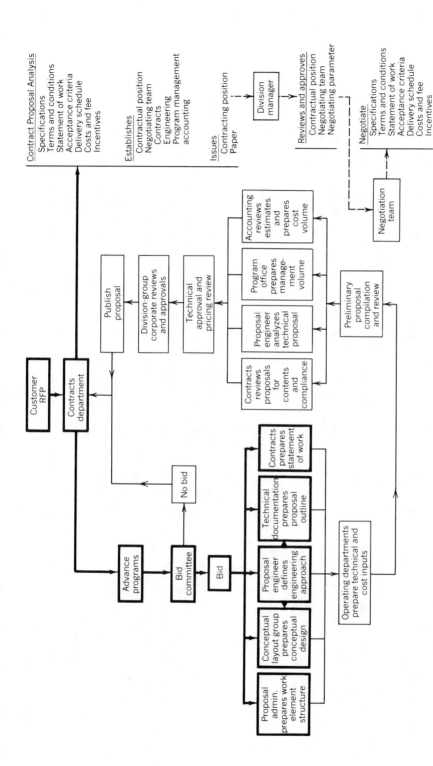

Figure 3.2. Proposal flow chart showing typical organization and responsibilities.

PROPOSAL CHECKLIST   CONTRACT EFFORT   PROPOSAL VOLUMES   DATE

TYPE OF PROPOSAL

— COST TYPE
— FIXED PRICE
— ROM

— ENG STUDY
— BREADBOARD
— PROTOTYPE

— PRODUCTION — FIELD SUPPORT
— SPARES
— DATA

— LETTER
— TECHNICAL
— MANAGEMENT
— COST

PROPOSAL TITLE: _____
PROPOSAL MANAGER: _____
PROPOSAL ADMINISTRATOR: _____

NOTES: _____

ATTACHMENTS: YES   NO
W.E.S.   —   —
PROGRAM SCHEDULE   —   —
PROPOSAL SCHEDULE   —   —

   YES   NO
TECHNICAL SUMMARY   —   —
ESTIMATING INSTRUCTIONS   —   —
TASK DESCRIPTIONS   —   —

EFFORT REQUIRED	ADMIN.	PROG. STAFF	IMAGE INFO.	SECURITY DOC.	ADV. TECH LAB	REL. ENG.	MECH	ELEC. ENG.	SYSTEMS ENG.	DESIGN & DRAFT.	MFG. ENG.	TEST	PRODUCT ASSUR.	DATA MGMT.	CONTRACTS	ACCTG.
ATTEND KICK-OFF MEETING																
PREPARE TECHNICAL WRITE-UP																
PREPARE COST ESTIMATE																
PREPARE BILL OF MATERIALS																
PREPARE SPARES LIST																
ITEMIZE CAPITAL EQUIPMENT																

Figure 3.3. Checklist for responsibility assignments.

programs on microcomputers and phone-connected data terminals are not only feasible but relatively economical. Cost and time required to develop a demonstration software package consisting of a tape, disk, or diskette, and to arrange to demonstrate its operation to the customer should be considered. This resource expenditure and development effort may well be the *coup-de-grâce* that convinces the customer to select a particular firm for the job.

TYPICAL PROPOSAL FLOW

On Figure 3.2, each organization involved in the proposal preparation process is represented, and the activities of each of these organizations is briefly depicted. The flow chart lets each organization know where it fits into the overall proposal preparation picture and indicates to these organizations where they will be receiving their inputs from and to whom they will be providing inputs. The configuration of this chart will vary with organizational structure and with the type of proposal being submitted. The proposal flow chart will also identify all major elements of the proposal preparation process and will be an effective aid to the identification and planning of resources required to effectively carry out the total proposal process.

To be sure all involved segments of the organization are aware of the effort required, a proposal checklist similar to that shown on Figure 3.3 is prepared and submitted to each organization expected to contribute to the proposal effort.

4

ORGANIZING THE PROPOSAL TEAM

Do you see a man skilled in his work? He will stand before kings.
Prov. 22:29

Since proposals are prepared by people, a large amount of attention must be given to the types, numbers, and skill levels of people assembled to do the proposal preparation job. Proposal preparation teams can range in size from one or two persons to fifty or one hundred, depending on the size of the work activity or work output being proposed. Each member of the team must be selected based on his or her qualifications to provide the specific information needed in the proposal and must be given an accurate and complete description of the work to be performed. We will initiate our description of the proposal preparation process in this chapter by referring to a medium sized proposal and one which requires multiple proposal volumes. (See Chapter 5.)

Once the Bid Committee has made an affirmative decision to bid, the decision is documented with a signed proposal task authorization (a typical example proposal task authorization is shown on Figure 4.1), the proposal manager is selected, and a proposal schedule is prepared. If the proposal manager is selected beforehand, he attends the Bid Committee meeting and takes part in the above actions; otherwise, the data package including the request for proposal and all rationale used to support the bid decision is forwarded to the selected proposal manager for immediate action.

It is the responsibility of the proposal manager to put together a cohesive team which includes all the skills required to produce the proposal. The team must be functionally oriented and designed to create the specific proposal.

Proposal Task Authorization	Work order	Task	Rev. No.

Title	Prime division

Log No.	Customer	Business area

Rep. No. or cust. msg. No.	Security classification	Department having prime responsibility

Proposal work statement

Business potential (estimated contract price)—is requirement budgeted?

Yes ☐ No ☐ Unknown ☐

Marketing Strategy
  Contract possibility
  Past relationship with customer
  Prime competitors
  Conversion date
  Contract type
  ☐ CPFF ☐ CPIF ☐ FFP ☐ T&M ☐ FPI ☐ Other

Proposal task budget

Previous auth. _____

This auth. _____

Total auth. _____
(Incl. this PTA)

End Item User	DOD	NASA	Other gov't	Comm'l	Comm'l purchaser supplying gov't

Proposal budget

Department		Jan	Feb	Mar	Apr	May	Jun	Jul	Aug	Sep	Oct	Nov	Dec	Total MM	$
	Lab $														
	N/L $													✕	
	Lab $														
	N/L $													✕	
	Lab $														
	N/L $													✕	
	Lab $														
	N/L $													✕	
	Lab $														
	N/L $													✕	
Total Lab $															
Total N/L $													✕	
*Totals $														This auth.	

Does this contract require significant additional capital equipment or facilities (describe)	$ Amount cap. eq.

Identify key contributors required for this proposal	Proposal manager	Submission date

Marketing (1)	Date	Dir. adv. plan (2)	Date	Dir. adv. prog. (3)	Date
Director (1)	Date	Gen. mgr. (2)	Date	Controller (4)	Date
Div. controller (1)	Date	Asst. controller (3)	Date	Sr. V. Pres. (4)	Date

*If in excess of $1,000 requires bid comm. approvals—
total authorization determines approval level:
(1) $1,000 or less ☐ (2) over $1,000 ☐ (3) over $10,000 ☐ (4) over $25,000 ☐

Figure 4.1. Proposal task authorization.

SKILLS REQUIRED FOR PROPOSAL PREPARATION

A number of different skills are needed in the preparation of the proposal. Whether these skills are possessed by one person or by an organization, it is necessary to arrange for their availability and application to the proposal preparation process during the appropriate time phase of the proposal activity. The quality of the mix of skill types and the skill levels used to develop proposals has a great bearing on the overall credibility, accuracy, and completeness of the resulting proposal. A few of the generic skills used in proposal preparation follow, along with a description of the functions performed by these skill types and an indication of the skill levels required for credibility and quality in proposal preparation.

Business and Finance Skills

Business and finance skills are an essential part of the proposal preparation process, particularly in the preparation of the cost volume. A knowledge of accounting procedures and techniques and an awareness of changing economics and business policies are needed. For example, a person with this knowledge will have a full appreciation of many of the "hidden costs" that must be covered by the cost proposal such as: (1) direct charges that are added to basic direct costs by "factoring;" (2) overhead costs; (3) general and administrative costs; and (4) profit or fee. Assuming that the purpose of bidding on a proposal is to make a profit, the cost volume must be constructed in a way that it will do more than merely recover the costs of labor and materials. Business and finance skills are mandatory to understand this fact so that all costs of the work output will be included in the cost volume with sufficient allowance for profit.

Engineering and Technical Skills, and Functional Managers

Engineering and technical skills, as reflected in actual on-the-job experience, are the basis for a sound, competitive, and realistic proposal. A completed proposal must be based on a practical knowledge of the work activity as well as the theory of design of the work activity or work output. Although educational background and knowledge of theory are important, this "book knowledge" must be supplemented by actual hands-on experience in producing a similar or identical work output. Therefore, experts in the technical field required by the request for proposal must be available to the proposal team. In addition to the technical experts, functional line managers should be made available to the proposal team at least on a part-time basis. These are the people who will be supervising the technical aspects of the work and who will be able to contribute realism and credibility to the technical approach as well as to the estimates of resources required to do the job.

Manufacturing and Assembly Skills

For work activities or work outputs that involve manufacturing and assembly operations, detailed knowledge of each manufacturing, assembly, test, and/or inspection function is essential. This detailed knowledge requires people who have had experience in manufacturing and assembly operations. The most valuable attribute of these individuals is their ability to originate and organize the manufacturing and assembly plan for the proposed work output and to plan the effort to eliminate gaps, overlaps, and duplications. Should the proposal involve production line operations, these skills are even more important. The most common fault in manufacturing plans is the omission of essential steps in the process. Simple steps such as receiving and unpacking raw materials or parts, inspection of incoming parts, in-process inspection, attaching labels and markings, and packaging and shipping of the final product are often inadvertently omitted. Team members skilled in manufacturing and assembly will assure proposal accuracy and credibility in these areas.

Management Skills

Part of any proposal team's expertise must consist of abilities in the area of project management. A skilled and experienced project manager will be able to best correlate the need for workers, material, equipment, and systems with the proposed work output or work activity. He will be able to envision and plan the management tools, resources, and expertise required to effectively carry out the proposed job; and he will be able to effectively communicate the management control, schedule control, and cost control aspects of the job to the customer.

Mathematical and Statistical Skills

Higher mathematics and the application of statistics are not always required in the development of credible and supportable proposals, but in high technology and multidisciplinary work activities and work outputs, these skills are becoming more and more critical. Often, a design will not be fully developed and various mathematical or statistical techniques will be necessary to develop data for the technical and cost volumes. When new products are designed and new services are envisioned, it is always best to verify the performance and cost projections by use of mathematical and statistical techniques.

Production Planning and Industrial Engineering Skills

Production planning and industrial engineering skills are closely related to the manufacturing and assembly skills mentioned earlier, but these skills are usually learned and applied at a higher organizational level. Where the manufacturing and assembly skills used in proposal preparation are derived from hands-on experience by workers or their immediate supervisors, production planning and industrial engineering skills are acquired from an overall knowledge of the workload and work flow in an office, factory, or processing plant. Production planning and industrial engineering skills are particularly important for work activities or work outputs that involve higher rates or larger quantities of production. Knowledge of automation and labor saving techniques in the shop, factory, or office become important in these applications.

Writing and Publishing Skills

Since the proposal is primarily a sales document, it must present the best possible picture of the proposing company. Writing style, contents, quality of reproduction and paper, even the choice of cover or binding may have an effect on the evaluating team. Individuals capable of writing and editing material while working under pressure are essential. It is necessary for the proposal team to have available a knowledge of the mechanics of the publishing process, including expertise in types of printing; reproduction; typesetting; word processing; uses of various inks and papers; and all types of oral, written, and graphic media.

In soliciting the skilled personnel required to work on proposals, the recruiter should remind the participants that the proposal preparation process is often regarded as an essential step in developing the careers of future project managers, business managers, and corporate management. Because an in-depth knowledge of the company and one or more of its products or services is developed during preparation of a proposal, proposal team participation has historically been a vital asset in the career paths of future managers. Management usually puts its best people on proposals, and, therefore, expects these best people to develop into positions of higher responsibility and authority.

PROPOSAL TEAM COMPOSITION

The proposal team usually consists of (1) a proposal manager, (2) a proposal administrator, (3) a sales engineer, (4) a technical volume manager, (5) an organization and management manager, (6) a cost volume manager, and (7) a publications manager. Positions 4, 5, and 6 are often called "Book Bosses." In addition, the proposal team often includes representatives of performing organizations, such as: engineering, manufacturing, purchasing, property, and contracts. (See Figure 4.2 for a typical organization chart for a proposal team for a large proposal.) The activities of the team will be performed far more effectively if all members are

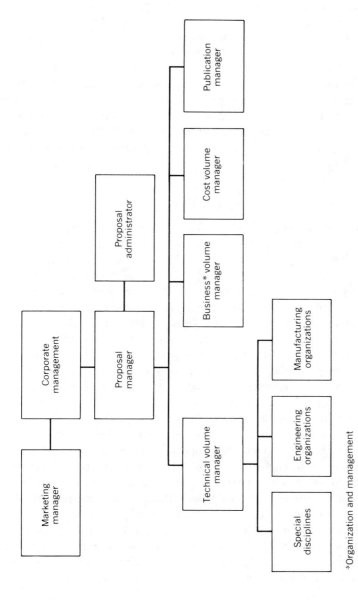

Figure 4.2. Proposal team organization.

*Organization and management

57

located in the same area. Since the proposal administrator is charged with day-to-day control of the team, coordination will be more efficient if the team location is adjacent to his regular work area.

An effective proposal team is the result of bringing together individuals from a wide variety of unrelated organizations. Their action can be performed most effectively in accordance with a well thought out and documented plan or schedule. An overall proposal schedule is usually developed by the proposal manager prior to the formation of the team. Within this overall schedule, each team member should be informed in writing of the task or tasks assigned and the expected schedule of performance. This internal control within the team not only provides the team members with a clear definition of what is expected of them but also forces the proposal manager and proposal administrator to define clearly the results expected.

Proposal Manager

The proposal manager is responsible for the planning, organization, direction, and control of the entire proposal project. Good, competent, aggressive leadership is crucial to the preparation of winning proposals. Proposal managers are often selected before the decision to bid is made so that some preliminary work can be done: (1) members of the team can be selected; (2) routine proposal sections can be prepared in advance thus reducing the hectic and sometimes frantic demands of the preparation period; (3) résumés of possible key personnel can be collected; (4) a synopsis of contracts and jobs performed that are similar to the requirements in the request for proposal can be prepared; and (5) a concise history of the company can be specifically tailored to the needs of the request for proposal.

The first task of the proposal manager is to define the theme or the proposal approach by preparing a proposal outline. This outline should be compatible with the request for proposal outline and will help ensure responsiveness to the request for proposal. It will also aid in collecting and measuring the output and performance of the members of the team. It should include a table of contents, as well as short descriptions of each section of the proposal, along with number of pages, due date, person responsible, and authorized hours. (See Figure 4.3 for a sample outline of a single-volume proposal.) It will indicate how much emphasis is placed on each particular topic, thereby further defining the theme for this particular proposal. *Above all, it should reflect responsiveness to the request for proposal!*

Once the outline is established (and time is of the essence), the proposal manager convenes the kickoff meeting, sometimes called the plan of action meeting. The first meeting of the proposal team quite often occurs within the twenty-four hour period following the authorization to propose.

Proposal Outline

1. Expand or simplify outline to meet specific proposal requirements.
2. Cross-check to assure that all RFP requirements are covered.

Headings—Outline	**Contents**
Title page	Title, classification, and preparing organization
Foreward	Authority for submittal of this proposal.
Table of contents	List of sections, headings, figures, tables, and appendices.
Introduction and summary	Summarize the proposal in 3 to 5 percent of total pages in the proposal. This should contain the justification for award of contract to the company.

Section I

Work statement	The Work Statement is the contractual commitment. (Do not explain here how work will be performed.)
Scope Objective List by task of work to be performed Delivery commitments	

Section II

Technical approach	Prepare detailed outline required to be responsive to RFP. Introductory statement presenting requirements to be met and problems associated therewith. (Drawings and sketches are helpful.)
Schedule	Time-phased milestones are related to work statement and logic network.
Engineering plan	Analysis and design. (Many subparagraphs may be added in this area.)
Material section	Types of material and reasons for selecting.
Tooling plan	Design and fabrication.
Manufacturing plan	Fabrication (Production flow diagrams may be useful.) Assembly Shipping
Quality Assurance plan	Relate to customer's objectives.
Logistics plan Spares Support	Show how this benefits the customer.

(Continued)

Headings—Outline	Contents
Section III	
Management	Define: scope of management required; the program management group; where group fits; program control, cost control, and personnel qualifications.
Section IV	
Related experience	Pertinent, applicable, and true.
Section V	
Capabilities and facilities	Those needed and available, and source for those not presently available.
Section VI	
Costs	Detailed cost estimate with rationale.
Section VII	
Appendices	Derivations, statistics, and technical detail.

Figure 4.3. Format for a Single-Volume Proposal.

Attendees include the proposal administrator, the sales engineer, technical volume manager, organization and management volume manager, cost volume manager, publications manager and representatives from all contributing, operating, and support departments as determined by the proposal manager. At this meeting all pertinent information is distributed and discussed. The following are examples of the type of materials supplied to each attendee:

1. Proposal Control Form (Figure 4.4).
2. Copy of request for proposal or request for quotation.
3. Overall proposal preparation schedule and budgets.
4. Marketing intelligence and proposal strategy.
5. Basic proposal theme and technical/costing guidelines.
6. Detailed proposal preparation schedules for all proposal contributors.
7. Assignment of tasks, as appropriate.
8. Coverage of any other proposal effort items as applicable.

At this time, the proposal manager may appoint a technical team to study the technical aspects of the proposal and determine conceptual analysis and design including risk areas and program scope.

Proposal Title: _____

RFP title and number: _____

Customer name and address: _____

Proposal charge number: _____

Proposal manager: _____

Proposal administrator: _____

Contract administrator: _____

Financial representative: _____

Technical writer: _____

Courier expediter: _____

Critical dates: _____

    Technical section to tech writing: _____

    Cost section to accounting: _____

    Sign-off meeting: _____

    Delivery to publication activity: _____

    Mailing date: _____

Figure 4.4. Proposal control form.

It is also the responsibility of the proposal manager to conduct other general team meetings. These meetings occur periodically during proposal preparation to assure adherence to the proposal outline and proposal schedule and to review material in progress. Contradictions, overlaps, and items of questionable value come to light before the final proposal is printed. These other meetings include an evaluation meeting (technical/ cost evaluation), a review meeting (critics' review), and a management approval meeting. While these meetings are general in nature and involve the whole team, other meetings are also conducted that bring together the smallest possible group of team members needed to solve the problem.

The primary concern of the proposal manager is quality. It is the proposal manager's responsibility to integrate all outputs of the team into a high quality, persuasive, flowing, sales document. Technical quality is measured by the responsiveness of the proposal to the request for proposal. The proposal manager must be prepared to answer a number of questions: Does the proposal describe the desirable results the customer will receive by purchasing the proposed solution to the problem? Do these results reflect performance equal to or better than the requirements described in the request for proposal, and are they favorable when compared to competitors? Are the key technical results outlined in the proposal those most wanted by the customer? Does the management volume clearly describe the personnel responsible for each particular task, and how and when they will know when they have accomplished each task? Does the cost volume indicate a cost that is fair and reasonable? Is supporting cost data sufficiently detailed and presented in a readable format? Is the cost volume consistent with the technical and management solutions proposed? These questions, and many more of the same type have been developed in tabular form and are shown in Appendix 2. It is up to the proposal manager to evaluate and shape the document to meet all these criteria.

Duties of the proposal manager or the selected project manager include responsibility for formulating the proposed project organization, describing how this project organization will work within the overall company framework, and selecting key personnel who are qualified to fill the proposed positions.

In addition, the proposal manager's expertise includes a knowledge of the customer's organization and procurement procedures. Perhaps the most important qualification, however, is the ability to direct and control the activities of others. Since proposal teams often work long hours for extended periods of time, morale and team spirit play an active part in the success or failure of the organization. Therefore, it is essential that the proposal manager have their full confidence in directing their day-to-day activities.

Perhaps one of the most important tasks of the proposal manager is the preparation of an interesting, well thought out letter of transmittal that will motivate the reader to adequately and thoroughly review and study the proposal. Supervision of the activities required to produce, package, and transmit the proposal is the final task of the proposal manager, as assisted by the proposal administrator.

The proposal team is created to respond to a particular proposal request; it is shaped by the characteristics of the request for proposal or request for quotation and by the characteristics of the company itself. Since it must draw on a wide variety of diverse skills and resources throughout the company, it is all the more important that a "team spirit" prevail. The creation, motivation, and control of the team demands dynamic leadership. Winning proposals are the result of team effort, and it is up to the proposal manager to inspire the team to do the best job possible in an incredibly short time. There is no room for petty arguments or disagreements. First and foremost is the objective to win the contract award, to translate the data accumulated into a sale for the company.

Proposal Administrator

The proposal administrator is selected from a permanent proposal preparation group trained in proposal preparation procedures. Business oriented and familiar with company objectives from a broad standpoint, this person has a thorough knowledge of the company plans, accounting system and possible constraints, and availability of company resources. He or she is fully informed on the status of all current and proposed programs. Functions involving day-to-day administration of the proposal team are delegated to the proposal administrator by the proposal manager. Such items as cost control, schedule preparation and monitoring, and technical details of graphic and reproduction support are usually delegated to the proposal administrator. He or she is thoroughly knowledgeable in communication skills, particularly in oral, written, and graphic media. Not only is the proposal administrator able to instruct the team, but he or she is also familiar with the mechanics involved in the proposal preparation process. As stated earlier, locating the proposal team close to the office of the proposal administrator (or locating the proposal administrator in or near to the proposal work area) will improve communications between the team members and the proposal administrator and make his or her job of controlling the output of the team much easier. The proposal work area should be isolated from day-to-day operational activities of the plant to prevent distractions and to give the proposal administrator full control of the team.

Among the specific duties that may be included in the proposal administrator's job are the management and tracking of labor-hours and dollars spent during preparation of the proposal, the monitoring of team performance in adherence to schedules, and the control and integration of all text, tables, and illustrations used in the proposal. The proposal administrator also ensures the security of proprietary and classified material. Should the proposal require supplements such as brochures, briefings, or models, they are prepared under the direction of the proposal administrator in conjunction with the sales engineer.

Sales Engineer

Describing what the customer wants is the primary task of the sales engineer. A close personal working relationship with the customer during the preproposal period gives this person an opportunity to find out exactly what the customer is looking for in relation to the contents of the technical, organization and management, and cost volumes. He or she may have an opportunity to influence the contents of the request for proposal, thus giving the company an "edge" on the competition. Once the request for proposal is issued, the sales engineer is able to expedite delivery and arrange for attendance and favorable consideration of proposal team members at the bidder's conference. Because of a unique position as a contact with the customer, the sales engineer may be useful in oral briefings or presentations, should they be needed, or in personally hand-carrying the finished proposal to the customer. Such activities give the sales engineer an opportunity to further the relationship with the customer thus making this person even more valuable to his or her company later on in the negotiation and contract award phases of procurement.

Early in the proposal process the sales engineer prepares an information package that provides significant information and data about the customer. It contains a detailed analysis of the organization of the customer as well as specific details about the background, education, and personal biases of those who will evaluate the proposal.

Another contribution of the sales engineer is the preparation of a program history package. He or she provides the proposal team with information of the history and background of the program, both within the customer's organization and his or her own company. It includes the business plan and estimates on future development plans thus enabling the proposal manager to determine growth potential of the work activity or work output. The proposal manager is then able to make educated decisions based on these facts and give the team an overview of the entire project at the kick-off meeting so that each member will be "up to speed" and better able to perform the tasks assigned.

One area the sales engineer is particularly useful in is market intelligence. Who is the competition? What are the strengths and weaknesses of the competitors, and just how hard are they competing for the job? Have any of the competitors worked for the customer before and if so, what kind of relationship did they have? What is the relationship of the competitor with the customer now? By keeping his or her eyes and ears open in the marketplace, the sales engineer can usually find the answers to these and other questions the proposal manager may have. It behooves the proposal manager to make the best use possible of his or her sales engineer in gathering any information that will make a proposal a winning one.

Technical Volume Manager

The prime responsibility of the technical volume manager is the preparation of the technical volume in accordance with the outline prepared by the proposal manager. Duties are to carry out all of the functions and meet all of the ground rules spelled out in Chapter 6. Technical specialists are available in engineering, design, manufacturing, or any other organizations of the company that have the expertise required by the request for proposal. The technical volume manager integrates and coordinates the inputs of these specialists to ensure that they meet the specifications of the outline.

Labor-hour estimates, materials lists, and skill mixes are developed which are sent to the cost volume manager to develop the cost estimate for the proposal. The technical volume manager is uniquely qualified to develop the test plan and schedule in which the type, scope, and rationale of all tests recommended in the work activity or work output are defined. Spare parts and logistics support recommendations and the program schedules, flow diagrams, technical change procedures, and facilities requirements are prepared by the technical volume manager.

The technical volume manager uses all of the specialists within the organization to accomplish the job. Each individual is required to describe the contribution of a unique specialty to the total project in writing and show the relationship to the solution of the customer's problem. With so many diverse specialties, the technical volume manager must integrate the material carefully; this can best be done by following the proposal manager's outline consistently. Any deviations or adjustments should only be made with the concurrence of the proposal manager and, frequently, key members of the team.

Organization and Management Volume Manager

The organization and management volume manager has the responsibility for carrying out all of the activities and adhering to all of the guidelines spelled out in the request for proposal and described in detail in Chapter 7. Intimately familiar with the company organization, this individual must know how work activities or work outputs are initiated, proposed, negotiated, and carried out by the company. He or she must be (1) generally familiar with plant facilities and equipment and the method that the company uses to capitalize these assets; (2) familiar with past company experience and capabilities and be able to bring together a convincing argument that this company can do a better job of successfully completing the proposed work than any of the competitors; and (3) familiar with methods of achieving efficiency, economy, and effectiveness in an organization and credibly apply these methods to perform the proposed work on a timely basis.

Cost Volume Manager

The cost volume manager should be familiar with estimating techniques, methods, and procedures in general as well as the specific pricing and estimating principals, policies, and procedures of the company. He or she is responsible for establishing and acquiring the physical tools required to do the complete cost estimating and pricing job. This includes the development or acquisition of cost estimating computer programs and the rental, purchase, or use of computers to do the mathematics and printing of cost information, particularly if the cost volume is a large one. The cost volume manager must assure that all rationale is credible, up-to-date, consistent with the resource estimates, and included in the cost proposal volume or either of the other two proposal volumes if appropriate. Although the cost proposal volume manager's job comes next to last in the proposal cycle, this job is vital and crucial to the success of the overall bid. Mathematical errors should be relatively easy to avoid with the use of modern computers, but a subtle mathematical error in the rationale or backup material can destroy the credibility of the entire proposal. A person who has a background in business matters, publication techniques, and technical operations of the company, the cost volume manager must be ready and willing to spend the dedicated hours required to complete a cost volume that is consistent within itself as well as with the other proposal volumes.

Publications Manager

The real hero in proposal preparation is the publications manager. For large proposals this person must accomplish in six to nine weeks, sometimes even less, all of the activities that a publisher of textbooks or handbooks performs in six to nine months. The publications manager is responsible for the editing, typing or typesetting, artwork, tables and figures, review, printing, assembly, binding and shipping of a multi-volume document with multiple copies. This is done under enormous pressure because a missed deadline could mean a missed contract. With the financial health of tens, hundreds, or even thousands of workers at stake, to say nothing of the financial health of the company itself, the publications manager is looked to as the person who will produce an attractive, professional, error-free document. This must be done with the added burdens of deadlines missed by individuals or organizations who precede this final step in the proposal cycle, the constant overview and critique by management, and the steady harassment by several "bosses:" the three proposal volume managers or book bosses. This hectic life is abundantly supplied with the multiple gremlins of missed meals, lost sleep, and the all-important "last-minute-change." Needless to say the proposal publications manager must have a thick skin, an even-tempered disposition, and a stick-to-itiveness exceeded only by knowledge of the multiple facets of the publication production process.

Many large companies divide the responsibilities described here for the proposal manager, proposal administrator, and publications manager (three people) differently and give them to two people, the proposal manager and the proposal operations manager. Other companies with smaller staffs and budgets fold all of the duties into one person. The important point here is that all of the described functions must be done by a designated capable and responsible team member.

SUMMARY

It cannot be overemphasized that the most important feature of the proposal team is team spirit. If the proposal manager has the leadership qualities needed, he or she will be able to motivate the members of the team and keep them on schedule. Preparing a "winning proposal" should be the objective of the entire team. Sufficient time should be taken at the beginning of the process to ensure that each member knows exactly what is expected and when it is expected to be done. Once a schedule is established and each task defined and assigned, it is up to the proposal manager and proposal administrator to follow the process through to its conclusion. (A typical proposal schedule is shown in Figure 4.5).

	Days after RFP
Market research and preliminary bid decision	0–45 days prior
Organize proposal team	0–45 days prior
Preliminary review of RFP or requirement	1
Kickoff meeting and issue proposal task authorization	1
Preliminary feedback and discussion of ground rules	2
Initial input response from team and first cut pricing	45
Team input review meeting	49
Instructions developed for revisions	51
Final input from team members	53
Analysis, pricing, rework, and management reviews	53–56
Publication	56–59
Submittal	59
Follow-up	60 until contract award

Figure 4.5.   Proposal Schedule (based on a 60-day response time).

The underlying theme of the proposal team is "go to the experts." Whatever section is to be prepared, the best person possible should do it: the one who knows how to do the job, when it should be accomplished in the course of the work activity or work output, where the most suitable location is to do it, and why it should be done a certain way. It will be very helpful to the team if the proposal manager institutes quality control milestones providing the members targets and clear rationale upon which to pace their efforts.

Once the proposal has been published and sent to the customer, a good proposal manager will keep the team members informed of progress as it is being evaluated. All pertinent facts, whether the proposal wins or loses, will be given to the team by a good proposal manager. This personal touch not only indicates that the proposal manager is aware of their contribution to the project, but also shows the team members what they did right or wrong in that proposal so that they can correct the situation the next time.

In summary, the following rules of thumb can be applied to the proposal team:

1. Use proposal specialists for those proposal tasks that are similar from one request for proposal to the next.
2. Use those who will actually perform the proposed work to do technical volumes and provide cost estimating inputs.

3. On major proposals, the proposal team should be dedicated to the effort for one hundred percent of the working hours in each work-day. Overtime must also be provided if required.

4. The dedicated team should be in a single location.

5. Anyone that will be involved in subsequent negotiations should be involved in the proposal effort from the start.

6. Corporate management should ensure team availability as required after initial proposal submittal.

5

THE REQUEST FOR PROPOSAL—WHAT TO EXPECT

Give to him who asks of you, and do not turn away from him.
Matt. 5:42

Unless the proposal is to be an unsolicited proposal, it most likely will be prepared in response to a request for proposal or request for quotation. A request for proposal or request for quotation can consist of anything from a telephone call or a letter to a large, multipage multivolume document. The requestor will always ask for a price and may also ask for some backup material for price, terms, and conditions of any resulting contract and detailed specifications of the work activity or work output that is proposed. The cardinal rule to follow in the treatment of a request for proposal or request for quotation is to give the customer what is asked—but skillful treatment of "unreasonable" requests may be the key that spells success. The customer must fully understand the cost, schedule, and performance impacts of each request for proposal requirement.

Before discussing request for proposal requirements in detail, it is important to note that there are key points in the procurement process where one can influence these requirements.

OPPORTUNITIES TO INFLUENCE THE REQUEST FOR PROPOSAL

For proposals resulting from a request for proposal or request for quotation, the proposer may interact with the procuring agency or company in a more complex manner than merely receiving a request for proposal and submitting a proposal. Figure 5.1 shows, in flow diagram format, twenty

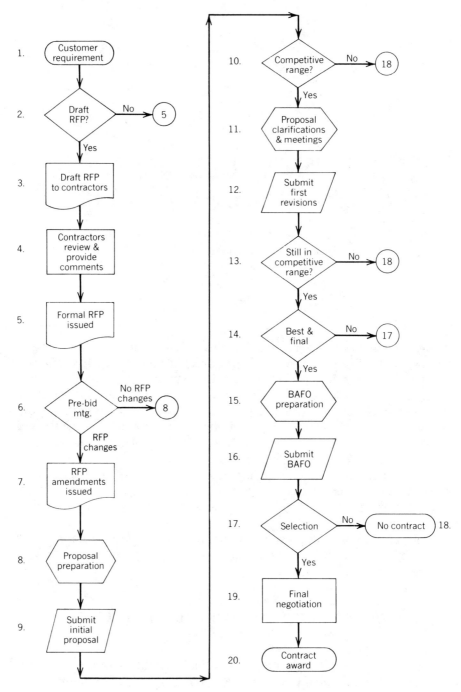

Figure 5.1. RFP procurement flow chart.

steps that may occur in the customer/supplier interaction process from the time the customer formulates the project requirements until the time the contract is awarded. If all of these steps are employed in a procurement cycle, there will be no less than *seven* opportunities to provide additional information to the customer that may enhance competitive position.

Opportunity 1: Influencing Initial Requirement

Remember that step "zero" in the overall process is to plant the seed for the idea in the customer's mind. Presuming this has been done, and that the "customer requirement" is a result of an initial sales effort, there has already been an opportunity to provide a significant input to the customer before the process even starts.

Opportunity 2: The Draft Request for Proposal

Some customers informally solicit comments on their requests for proposal from prospective bidders prior to formal issuance of the request for proposal (steps 3 and 4 of Figure 5.1). This is an ideal time to provide significant inputs relative to work scope, work timing, and work performance standards; and an active participation in providing inputs at this stage in request for proposal preparation will enhance one's knowledge of what to expect and may even result in the interjection of specifications that will favor one's product or service, or one's firm.

Opportunity 3: The Prebid Meeting

When a prebid meeting is held, the questions that are posed by potential bidders *can* influence the issuance as well as content of any amendments or revisions to the request for proposal. It is recognized that any questions from potential bidders provide clues to competitors of technical or management approaches since all bidders are usually represented in a bidder's conference held for clarification of request for proposal requirements. But the value of the information transmitted to the customer and the value of the customer's responses may far outweigh the advantages of "tipping one's hand" relative to the proposal approach. Intelligent questions about the request for proposal requirements convey information to the customer about (1) interest in providing a responsive proposal (indicated by well thought out questions; (2) knowledgeability of the project or subject; and (3) desire to fulfill all project requirements. The answers to these three points will help *formulate* a more responsive proposal.

Opportunity 4: The Proposal

Step 9 on Figure 5.1, submittal of the initial proposal, is the *principal* opportunity to provide comprehensive information on why a particular firm should be chosen to perform the work. This step is the culmination of the preparation activity for the initial formal proposal.

Opportunity 5: Proposal Clarifications

Proposal clarifications requested by the customer, or special meetings established to allow a proposer to clarify the content of the proposal (step 11 on Figure 5.1), are opportunities to provide still more information to the customer about competence and responsiveness. By analyzing the phrasing and content of the customer's questions, one can also gain valuable information on evolving customer requirements that, when combined with the original request for proposal and amendments, will give a company an edge on the competition.

Opportunity 6: The Best and Final Offer

The "Best and Final Offer," step 16 on Figure 5.1, is the final place where an input can be made to the customer prior to source selection. This best and final offer can include not only a final "price" but also supplemental technical, schedule, management, or organizational data based on information gained from the previous contacts with the customer.

Opportunity 7: The Final Negotiations

After a company is selected to perform the work, of course, there will once again be an opportunity to provide information to the customer as part of the final contract negotiation process (step 19 on Figure 5.1).

The above listing of "opportunities" illustrates that there are various channels of communication during the request for proposal and selection process that will enable the customer to spell out his requirements and the supplier to present his capabilities. To know in advance of request for proposal submittal that these channels exist will help in understanding the degree and method of responsiveness required to respond to the request for proposal itself.

THE CONTENT OF A REQUEST FOR PROPOSAL

It is necessary for proposers to gain, in advance of proposal preparation, an insight into the many facets and elements of a request for proposal.

Whether the request is from a government agency, a private concern, a university, or a nonprofit corporation, many of the same elements will be included in proposal or quotation requests. The following information can be used as a checklist for the *types of information* that may be required in a proposal for either government or industry. It will also demonstrate some methods and techniques of dealing with proposal requests, even if they are of the more detailed type normally encountered when state, local, and federal government agencies are requesting products, projects, or services.

A detailed request for proposal will normally be sent to bidders as an enclosure to a letter of transmittal that invites a bid and describes the procurement in general terms. The letter of transmittal may also contain instructions as to how many copies of the proposal should be submitted, the deadline date for proposal submittal, the address to which the proposal is to be sent, and any special proposal packaging and handling provisions. This letter will also ask for an acknowledgement of receipt of the request for proposal within a given time period if there is an intention to bid.

A large request for proposal normally includes five basic parts: (1) general instructions to bidders; (2) a proposed contract draft or "schedule;" (3) general contract provisions; (4) the statement of work; and (5) appendices. Smaller requests for proposal or requests for quotation may contain only part of this information. The authors are in possession of four recent United States government requests for proposal, three for services and one for a high technology development project. They represent small, medium, large, and very large documents consisting of 75 pages (small), 166 pages (medium), 506 pages (large), and 760 pages (very large) respectively. (Any request for proposal consisting of 1,000 pages or more can only be termed enormous, mammoth, voluminous, or huge!) For the purpose of this discussion, we will describe the content and approach to the "very large" request for proposal. This discussion will provide information on the major aspects of a request for proposal or request for quotation that one is likely to encounter in doing business with industry *or* government in either large *or* small procurements.

General Instructions to Bidders

The first part of a very large request for proposal is the section that includes general instructions to the bidder. This part of the request for proposal contains instructions, conditions, and notices to the bidder; certifications, representations, and other statements that must be made and/or agreed to by the bidder when he submits his proposal; and a description of proposal evaluation factors and methods that will be used in grading the proposal. In the typical "very large" request for proposal that was evaluated, this first part of the request for proposal occupied 105 pages, or about fourteen percent of the total number of pages in the request for proposal.

Instructions, Conditions, and Notices. The "Instructions, Conditions, and Notices" section (or other suitable or appropriate title) of the request for proposal contains general information about the project and the proposed contract, site visits by the proposer to the place of work performance, preaward on-site reviews by the potential customer, desired proposal validity times, and other general clauses and conditions required by law or by the customer's procurement policy. Some typical parts of this section are described below.

Contract planning. The contract planning section describes the program, the program phases, the type(s) of contract, funds available (if appropriate), and specific procurement provisions. The following is an excerpt from a recent Request for Proposal issued by the National Aeronautics and Space Administration for a "Tethered Satellite" project (a satellite designed to be tethered to the space shuttle and towed through the upper atmosphere to obtain scientific readings concerning upper atmosphere composition, pollution content, ozone layer concentration, and other upper atmosphere data):

It is planned that the Tethered Satellite Project will be implemented in two phases: an Advanced Development Phase to be followed by a Design and Development (Phase C/D). This RFP solicits proposals for both phases. A firm contract is planned for the Advanced Development Phase, with a firm option for the Design and Development Phase.

The Advanced Development Phase will be a pre-development type contract with a period of performance of sixteen (16) months. Approximately $1,100,000 has been projected to be available for the Advanced Development Phase.

The Design and Development Phase will be a mission type contract with a period of performance of approximately forty (40) months. If the option for this phase is exercised, the contract will be initiated immediately following the Advanced Development Phase. The contractor is advised that initiation of the Design and Development Phase is contingent upon congressional approval for a new start.

The Advanced Development procurement will be awarded utilizing a cost plus fixed fee (CPFF) contract. The Design and Development (C/D) procurement will be negotiated as a firm option, utilizing a Cost Plus Award Fee (CPAF) contract. Any resulting contracts will contain all provisions required by law and regulations and such other provisions as may be required to adequately protect the interests of the Government. The clauses and the provisions applicable are set forth in the sample contract contained herein.

Competition has been limited to the two (2) Phase B study contractors, one of which will be selected as a result of this RFP to perform both the Advanced Development Phase and, if contracted, the Design and Development (C/D) Phase of the TSS Project.

However, if NASA determines the proposed concepts inadequately fulfill mission need objectives, all design concepts together with the result of agency in-house study effort may be made available to industry to propose on any concept design or development solicitation.[1]

[1] Request for Proposal for Tethered Satellite. NASA Marshall Space Flight Center, 1982.

The contract planning section will also include a description of the overall, long term schedule for the project and will include a bar chart schedule similar to that shown on Figure 5.2 to illustrate the time relationship between major program elements.

Estimating and pricing. General instructions to the bidder relative to submittal of estimating and pricing information are included in this section. The forms to be used are referenced and a requirement is included that pricing and estimating techniques will be described in the proposal. One recent request for proposal states that "All pricing or estimating techniques should be clearly explained in detail (projections, rates, ratios) and should support the proposed cost in such a manner that audit, computation, and verification can be accomplished. Price visibility and traceability to the *lowest practical cost level* is essential [emphasis provided]."[2] The meaning of *lowest practical cost level* is understood better when the *cost proposal instructions*, contained in another section of the request for proposal, are taken into consideration.

Proposal instructions. Specific proposal instructions provided in the request for proposal include a number of areas of policy that the customer wishes to convey to the bidder. One such clause cautions against the use of unnecessarily elaborate proposals.

> Unnecessarily elaborate brochures or other presentations beyond those sufficient to present a complete and effective proposal are not desired and may be construed as an indication of the offeror's lack of cost consciousness. Elaborate art work, expensive paper and bindings, and expensive visual or other presentation aids are neither necessary nor desired.[3]

The policy on whether or not proposal preparation costs can be covered in the proposed contract estimate is also included in this part of the request for proposal. Government requests are usually strong in pointing out that sending a request for proposal to a prospective bidder does not commit the government to pay any costs incurred in submission of the proposal or in "making necessary studies or designs for the preparation thereof." They further state that no costs may be incurred in anticipation of the contract with the exception that "any such costs incurred at the proposer's risk may later be charged to any resulting contract to the extent that they would have been allowable if incurred after the date of the contract and to the extent authorized by the contracting officer."[4] This appears to be a loophole that will allow *some* proposal preparation costs to be charged to the resulting contract under certain specific conditions.

[2] Ibid.
[3] Ibid.
[4] Ibid.

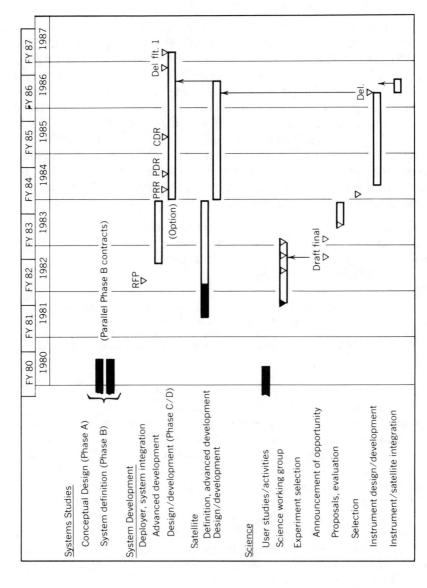

Figure 5.2. Long-term project schedule.

Treatment of "proposal data" by the customer is covered in most requests for proposal to assure the bidder that the information presented in a proposal, particularly if it is proprietary in nature, will be protected from transmission to the proposer's competitors or to any company or organization outside that of the customer's. Generally, the customer will and should use a bidder's technical, organizational, and cost data for evaluation purposes only. Stating this in the request for proposal assures the customer of maximum disclosure of a company's plans, ideas, and capabilities.

A "proposal validity period," usually ninety days after proposal submission, is specified in most requests for proposal. The bidder can easily change this period but would be wise not to shorten it unduly because evaluation procedures frequently extend beyond their prescheduled dates, forcing a delay in selection and contract negotiations. Requests for proposal also state that the issuance of the request for proposal does not obligate the customer to sign a contract with *any* of the bidders. In the event that the customer is not satisfied that any of the bids will meet the stated requirements, the procurement can be cancelled completely. Each request for proposal also contains a policy on late proposals and withdrawal of proposals. (Customers usually reserve the right to accept late proposals.)

Miscellaneous clauses. Miscellaneous clauses are also included in this section even though some of them are amplified, clarified, or repeated for emphasis in other sections of the request for proposal. Typically, these clauses pertain to the following subjects:

1. Security classification of the work
2. Technical direction of the work
3. Contracting officer's responsibility
4. New technology policy
5. Inventions and patents policy
6. Equal opportunity provisions
7. Small and disadvantaged business use
8. Visits by bidders to the work performance site
9. On-site visits by the proposal evaluation team
10. Customer furnished equipment assumptions
11. Information required on proposed consultants:
    a. Résumés—including education, experience and technical publications.
    b. Unique capability possessed by the individual(s) making his/her/their use on this program necessary and advantageous (basis for selection).

     c. Estimated hours and rate(s).

     d. Estimated cost and supporting data.

     e. Estimated contract duration.

12. Safety and health policies.

Representations, Certifications, and Other Statements of the Offeror. In most government requests for proposal, and in some industrial and commercial requests for proposal, the bidder is required to make certain certifications concerning adherence to specific laws, policies, and directives that have been enacted and are in force in state, federal, or local governments. Most of these laws, policies, and directives have resulted in the provision of "socioeconomic" objectives. The "representations and certifications" are merely forms to be filled out and returned to the government prior to or along with the proposal to help assure that all state, federal, and local laws will be complied with in the performance of the work. Typical "representations and certifications" are listed below along with a brief description of what each is designed to accomplish.

Buy-American Trade Agreements Certificate. The proposer lists, in this certification, all end products that are not American made. (The certificate implies that preference will be given to a supplier who is providing the most American made products.) In a related certification the proposer must estimate what percentage of the proposed contract price represents foreign effort.

Certificate of Contingent Fee. The proposer states, in this certification, whether or not any company or person, other than a full-time bona fide employee working for the proposer has been employed to solicit or to secure the contract. The proposer also states whether or not he has paid or agreed to pay any company or person (other than an employee) any fee, commission, percentage, or brokerage fee contingent upon or resulting from the award of the contract. A positive response to either of these questions will more than likely bring further questions from the procurement officer of the company or person accepting the fee to the proposing company and/or to the customer. The purpose of this certification is to help assure that there is no conflict of interest situation in the possible award of a contract.

Equal opportunity. In this certification, the proposer states whether or not all equal opportunity compliance reports required by Executive Order Number 10925 "Equal Opportunity Program" have been filed.

Affirmative action program. The proposer states in this certification whether or not the proposing company has developed and maintained an equal opportunity affirmative action plan at each geographical plant location.

Small business, small disadvantaged business, and nonsegregated facilities. In these certifications, the proposer certifies whether or not he or she is a small business concern, a regular dealer-manufacturer, an individual, partnership, or corporation; and whether or not the proposing company is a small business concern owned and controlled by socially and economically disadvantaged individuals. Definitions of a small business and a disadvantaged small business are included in Section 8(a) of the Small Business Act. Some government and industrial requests for proposal are directed specifically to small businesses. In others, small businesses are favored. In still others there is no preference one way or the other but the customer must merely know whether or not the bidder is a small business to complete its reports to the government on the percentage of small businesses in the overall contract or subcontract structure.

In a related certification, the proposer certifies that the proposing company does not have or condone facilities such as waiting rooms, work areas, restrooms and washrooms, restaurants and other eating areas, transportation facilities, or housing facilities that are segregated on the basis of race, color, religion, or national origin. This certification draws attention to and helps the enforcement of equal opportunity laws or clauses in the proposed contract.

Clean air and water certification. This certification is used to assure the customer that the proposer is using facilities that conform to the Clean Air Act and the Federal Water Pollution Control Act.

Certification of current cost and pricing data. This certification is used by the proposer to authenticate the fact that cost and pricing data used in the proposal are accurate, complete, and current as of the date of contract negotiation. Therefore, this certification is not submitted until contract award and negotiation is complete.

Cost accounting standards and practices. Bidders who are proposing to the government as prime contractors or major subcontractors are required to execute a series of forms which certify that their cost accounting systems meet certain standards; that they will disclose the principles, practices, and procedures used in cost accounting; and that they will inform the customer if any changes are made in their cost accounting practices. Whether these certifications must be filed or not depends on the total amount of business a firm does with the government (over 10 million dollars per year) and the size of the procurement (over 100,000 dollars).

Government facilities. Contractors or subcontractors to the federal government must certify if they are using government facilities, if any of those facilities are to be used in the proposed contract, or if additional government facilities are required. If the proposer is a government contractor the proposer must certify as to whether property control and accounting procedures have been approved by the government.

Keep in mind one thing about representations and certifications: a large part of them will go away completely for most commercial and industrial procurements. In the private sector, most of these practices are maintained merely as a matter or preserving company dignity and prudence and are an integral part of good business sense. Public sector contracts have fallen under legislative controls and guidelines that require special documentation of these certifications because of the failure of a few to hold to continued good business practices or because of pressures to correct past political and social inadequacies.

Evaluation Methods and Procedures.   Requests for proposal will normally give the proposer a clue as to how his proposal will be evaluated. In some instances a complete section of the request for proposal will be devoted to methods, procedures, factors, criteria, and cost evaluation. If the customer plans to use a source evaluation board, which is usually the case for large, multimillion dollar government procurements, he will preestablish mission suitability factors which are weighted based on a total score of, say, 1,000 points. Within each "factor" are criteria to which a further breakout and apportionment of the weight of each mission suitability factor is applied. Misson suitability factors are normally scored, while cost factors and certain other factors such as experience and past performance are generally not scored by the source evaluation board while they are taken into account in the overall evaluation process. (See Chapter 10, "How the Proposal Is Evaluated.")

Although weightings assigned to mission suitability factors and criteria are not listed in the request for proposal, a very interesting paragraph is usually contained in the request for proposal which will give a series of clues that can be used to derive an approximate breakout of the weighting. The reader must patiently study this paragraph, noting the interrelationships of the various factors and criteria, to guess what specific numerical weighting has been applied to each factor and criterion. Through a process of iteration, one can come reasonably close to the most probable breakout or weighting of the total allocated points.

For example, a typical request for proposal contains a listing and description of the following mission suitability evaluation factors and criteria:

   A. Excellence of Proposed Design
      Criteria
      1. Syst. Eng. & Analysis
      2. Design & Development
      3. Mfg. Test & Opns.
   B. Organization & Management
      Criteria
      1. Team Auth. & Control
      2. Team Org. & Structure

C. Key Personnel
    Criteria
    1. Proj. Mgr. & Commitment
    2. Key Personnel Exper.,
        Capabilities & Commit.

A typical paragraph in the request for proposal reads as follows:

> For evaluation purposes, *Excellence of Proposed Design* is the MOST IMPORTANT factor and is of substantially higher value than the sum of the other factors. *Organization and Management* is equal to *Key Personnel.* In the evaluation criteria, *Systems Engineering* is MOST IMPORTANT and significantly higher in value than *Design and Development*, which is VERY IMPORTANT and moderately higher in value than *Manufacturing, Test, and Operations. Manufacturing, Test, and Operations* is IMPORTANT and moderately higher in value than either *Team Authority and Control* or *Project Manager Experience and Commitment*, which are also important and equal in value. *Key Personnel Experience, Capabilities, and Commitment* is LESS IMPORTANT than either *Team Authority and Control* or *Project Manager Experience and Commitment*, by a moderate value, and is equal in value to *Team Organization and Structure.*

Through an iterative process, by arbitrarily assigning various weights to each factor and criterion within a framework of 1,000 points, the authors developed the following as a plausible and probable weighting:

A. Excellence of Proposed Design   650
    Criteria
    1. Syst. Eng. & Analysis   Most Important   375
    2. Design & Development   Very Important   150
    3. Mfg. Test & Opns.   Important   125
B. Organization & Management   175
    Criteria
    1. Team Auth. & Control   Important   100
    2. Team Org. & Structure   75
C. Key Personnel   175
    Criteria
    1. Proj. Mgr. & Commitment   Important   100
    2. Key Personnel Exper.,
        Capabilities & Commit.   Important   75   ____

                                                 Total   1,000

Although the above point distribution may not be exactly what was assigned by the source evaluation board, the interrelationships stated in the request for proposal hold; therefore, the actual assigned weights cannot be too far off from the above. Assuming that a proposal will be scored against factors and criteria, a proposer can develop a weighting distribution. He will then gain a valuable insight into the emphasis to be placed on these criteria and will be able to structure a proposal with emphasis in the corresponding subject areas.

Technical, Management, and Cost Proposal Format and Contents. The RFP section on "General Instructions to Bidders" also includes a description of the expected contents of the technical proposal, organization and management proposal, and cost proposal. This section may go so far as to specify the number of volumes in a proposal, the maximum number of pages in each volume, the number of copies of each volume required, the type of line spacing required (double, single, or space-and-a-half), a page numbering system, a policy on the use of foldouts and double-sided printing, and even how many proposal copies should be included in each shipping carton. The main information derived from this part of the request for proposal, however, is the desired *content* of the technical, management, and cost volumes.

Technical proposal volume(s). Instructions as to the content of technical proposal volumes will include a requirement for (1) a description of the work activity or work output being proposed and (2) implementation plans and schedules that describe how and when the work is to be performed.

A large part of the technical work to be performed manifests itself in a "Data Procurement Document," "Data Requirements List," or "Technical Reports Listing" that usually appears as an appendix to the request for proposal. In this data procurement document, the customer lists and describes the various drawings, specifications, progress reports, manuals, training documents, operating plans, and maintenance procedures that will be required under the proposed contract. Content, format, frequency of distribution, and number of copies required are included in this document for each report that is to be required under the contract. Since documentation is a large cost in itself, and since the documentation of work must reflect work content, a thorough analysis of the documentation requirements in the request for proposal is a must. A data procurement document for a recent very large government request for proposal consisted, in itself, of three hundred pages.

Organization and management proposal volume(s). The request for proposal specifies what type of information should be provided to explain and substantiate a company's experience, past performance, and corporate interest and investment; the company and project organization that will be assigned to do the work; the qualifications, experience, and training of key project personnel; and how the work will be managed.

Other information that is often required (or desirable) to include in the organization and management volume or volumes consists of: (1) personnel practices and labor relations experience; (2) procurement policies, practices, and procedures; (3) "make-or-buy" policies; (4) configuration management; (5) quality, reliability, and safety management; (6) cost and schedule reporting; (7) logistics; (8) design reviews; and (9) documentation to be submitted during performance of the resulting contract. The request for proposal will usually require some discussion of: (1) how the work of the organizations and personnel who will be participating in the project will be integrated; (2) the method of general planning and master scheduling to be used; (3) how task assignments will be made and followed up; (4) the method to be used for internal review, job tracking, and setting priorities; and (5) how you will detect problems, determine the appropriate corrective action, and assign it to a responsible individual or organization.

Cost proposal volume. A cost volume must contain resources estimates, costing methodology, and rationale sufficient to allow the customer to establish the fact that the work will be cost-effective and that cost estimates are realistic.

The request for proposal will usually specify the exact format required in the cost proposal. To date, there has been very little uniformity and consistency in the format and content of cost proposal requests among various government and industrial agencies and organizations. There is no reason for this to continue, since the basic resource information required to do a complex task or series of tasks can be presented in a relatively uniform or consistent format. Some government agencies have become aware of the need for greater standardization, consistency, and condensation of cost data in proposals to the government, but, at this writing, there is still much to be done in both government and industry, to simplify and reduce cost data requirements in requests for proposals. Increased simplification and uniformity in cost estimating and cost reporting systems would reduce the bidder's man-hours required to *prepare* proposals, the customer's man-hours required to *evaluate* proposals, and would enhance the collection of actual cost data, comparison of actual costs between projects, and comparison of actual costs with estimated costs.

Greater standardization in cost proposals has been difficult in the past because each company has its own unique accounting system that has more than likely grown with the company for a number of years and has become relatively fixed and inflexible. With the advent of computerized financial management and cost estimation, and cost reporting systems, it has become feasible to convert cost data from a company's traditional accounting system into almost any format required in a very short period of time. The modern computer, then, has paved the way toward greater possibility of standardization and comparison of cost data. Until a relatively standard approach is developed for cost accounting, estimating, and reporting, however, the potential bidder for both governmental and industrial contracts may expect to see a wide variation in cost proposal requirements in requests for proposal. A flexible and adaptive computer system that will format output cost information in a large variety of ways is a must for any organization that expects to bid to different agencies or companies.

The cost proposal requirements in requests for proposal include ground rules for cost estimating, suggested or required cost estimating methodology, formats for proposal of resources, and descriptions of the bidder's estimating methods and rationale. The request for proposal provides definitions of various categories and elements of cost to permit a close correlation of the cost proposal presentation with customer understanding. The request for proposal will also specify different levels of depth of cost proposal data for different phases of the project.

The Contract Document or "Schedule"

The contract document or contract "schedule" (as it is often called in government circles) is the legal document that is negotiated and mutually agreed to by buyer and seller prior to commencement of the work. The contract document is inserted in the request for proposal to assure the proposer that he understands the legal terms and conditions of the contract and to provide a basis for specific comments, exceptions, deviations, or additions that may surface during the proposal preparation process. The contract schedule contains the following "Articles" which describe the legal agreements made between the seller and the buyer:

Statement of Work.   The statement of work, which is usually referred to or included in Article I of the contract schedule, includes an introduction and scope, mission objectives, roles and responsibilities, and specific contractor tasks. Included in the statement of work or as references or appendices are work activity or work output specifications, the data procurement document, the work breakdown structure or work element structure dictionary, product assurance and safety requirements, and other technical and/or programmatic data.

The statement of work, if prepared in a detailed manner by the customer and included in the request for proposal, can and should form the basis for the technical proposal volume, as it covers generally as well as specifically all of the work to be performed as the principal "deliverable" under the proposed contract. If it is not prepared and included in the request for proposal, the bidder will have to prepare a detailed statement of work as part of the proposal. The statement of work defines all work contained in the work element structure. Ideally, there is a close if not identical correlation between the statement of work and the work element structure dictionary, with even an identical numbering system if feasible. The statement of work not only provides all deliverable hardware, software, and services, but also spells out all the work that will be required to deliver these items and to prepare and deliver all required documentation. Hence, the statement of work is a document that will eventually serve as a legally binding contract document that integrates and interrelates the work elements with deliverable and nondeliverable hardware, software, documentation, and services. Prepared with great care, it is the basis for the entire cost and resources estimates and is integrally tied to the time schedules for the conduct of work. It is recognized that the development plan portion of the technical proposal volume as well as the organization and management proposal will bear heavily on the content of the statement of work, which is the detailed word description of what is going to be accomplished under the proposed contract. Thus, it is an essential part of a proposal.

Statement of work introduction and scope. The contract schedule or document, as amplified by the statement of work introduction, states that the selected contractor "shall" furnish the management, labor, facilities, and materials required to design, develop, procure, manufacture, assemble, test, deliver, and/or operate (as applicable) the item described in the design and performance specification. The design and performance specification is usually included as a reference or appendix at this point in the statement of work. The scope of work also identifies specific deliverable items and states when they are to be delivered.

Mission objectives. If the work output or work activity being proposed is a part of a larger work activity or work output, the overall mission objectives of the larger work activity or work output are described here in the statement of work. This information is provided not only to give a clear understanding to both parties as to the relationship of the work to an overall plan of action but to assure that the resulting contract starts and stays in tune with an overall mission objective, which may consist of parts other than that being proposed.

Roles and responsibilities. A clear and concise description is included in the statement of work to define specific roles and responsibilities of the proposed supplier and the customer. If there are to be any customer-supplied direction, approvals, parts, labor, or facilities, they are physically described or referenced along with the dates or times the customer commits to provide these items, services, or approvals.

Detailed contractor tasks. Detailed tasks of the proposed contractor are spelled out and keyed to the work element structure and work element structure dictionary. The request for proposal usually provides a "strawman" work element structure and work element structure dictionary. Figure 5.3 shows a typical work element structure contained in a request for proposal.

Options. More often than not, the contract document or contract schedule will contain procurement options that are contingent upon acceptance and/or successful performance of the proposed work. These options will be described and priced in the responding proposals but may not be placed

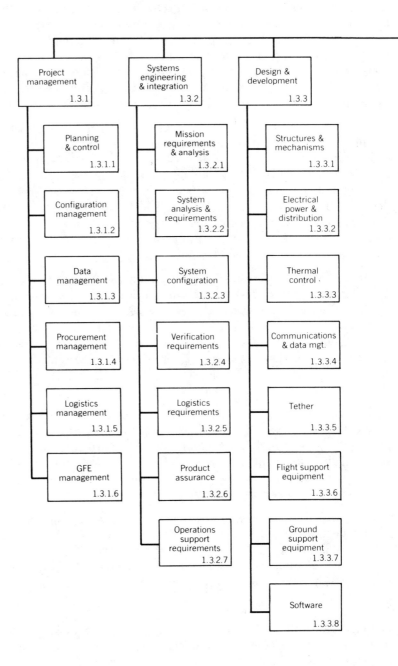

Project management 1.3.1	Systems engineering & integration 1.3.2	Design & development 1.3.3
Planning & control 1.3.1.1	Mission requirements & analysis 1.3.2.1	Structures & mechanisms 1.3.3.1
Configuration management 1.3.1.2	System analysis & requirements 1.3.2.2	Electrical power & distribution 1.3.3.2
Data management 1.3.1.3	System configuration 1.3.2.3	Thermal control 1.3.3.3
Procurement management 1.3.1.4	Verification requirements 1.3.2.4	Communications & data mgt. 1.3.3.4
Logistics management 1.3.1.5	Logistics requirements 1.3.2.5	Tether 1.3.3.5
GFE management 1.3.1.6	Product assurance 1.3.2.6	Flight support equipment 1.3.3.6
	Operations support requirements 1.3.2.7	Ground support equipment 1.3.3.7
		Software 1.3.3.8

86

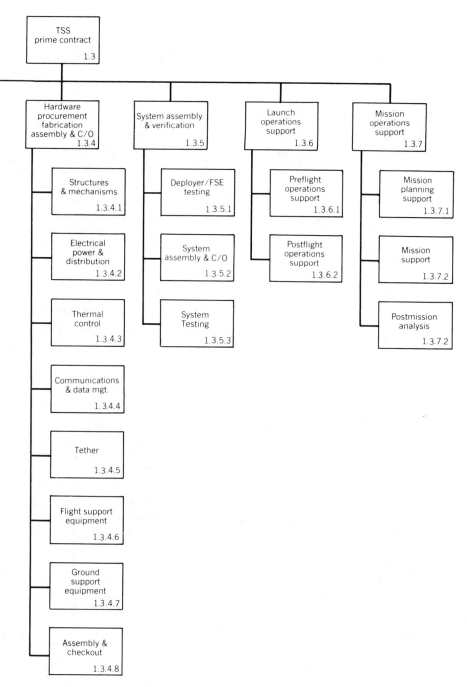

Figure 5.3. RFP work element structure.

under contract at the same time as the initial work. The request for proposal will usually specify a time period within which the option is expected to be exercised, and the customer reserves the right to exercise the option in this time period.

Period of Performance.   The contract document will normally contain a section or "article" on the exact period of performance to be covered under the proposed contract. This period of performance will be used in time-phasing the proposed contract activities and in determining the allocability and acceptability of costs incurred.

Allowable Cost, Fixed Fee, and Payment Provisions.   The overall total contract agreed-to cost and fee will be specified along with the method and timing of payment for the proposed work and for any contract options. The method and timing of payment should be carefully reviewed, understood, and negotiated to assure that adequate cash flow will be available to do the work. For government contracts, it should be recognized that there are delays in payment because of unforeseen legal and procedural obstacles, and that yearly incremental funding for a multiyear contract is often delayed because of failure to enact budget legislation of continuing funding resolutions on a timely basis.

Special Fee Structure and Fee Payment Provisions.   Increasingly, government and industrial contracts are incorporating more complicated fee structures and fee payment provisions. These more complex fee structures are brought about by the desire to motivate the contractor to stay within cost, to stay on or exceed schedule requirements, and to adhere to or surpass performance requirements. Various contract forms such as fixed price incentive fee, cost plus incentive fee, and cost plus award fee are used in these fee payment structures. Incentive fees are usually based on a mathematical or schedule relationship between contracted and actual work performance and can often be complex in structure with varying increments of fee allocated for various increments of increase or decrease in cost, schedule, or performance.

Award fee provisions are usually monitored and controlled by a customer "performance evaluation board" which reviews the contractor's work at uniform intervals during contract performance. The proposed resources must include sufficient labor-hours, materials, and travel costs to participate in these reviews, to prepare "self-evaluation" reports required by the customer, and to make corrections in the next performance evaluation period in the event that it becomes evident that performance improvement is necessary to earn a higher award fee. The customer's determination of the percentage of award fee to be approved during a given contract period is principally subjective in nature but can be a result of qualitative evaluations used to glean a qualitative composite measure of performance excellence.

Except in cases of extreme or obvious inequities, it is difficult to change the award fee decision of the performance evaluation board. Therefore, fee expectations stated in the proposal should be based on realistic anticipations of performance. Award fee is usually paid on a provisional basis based on the percentage of completion of work as determined by the contracting officer. Award fee structures usually include a "base-fee" that is paid regardless of the level of contract performance excellence and an "award-fee" that can range from zero to a prestated maximum figure. A complete understanding of the award fee structure is necessary before starting the proposal preparation process; therefore, it is necessary to fully understand and evaluate this part of the request for proposal before starting to develop detailed text, schedule, or costing information for the proposal.

Technical Direction and Management.   Requests for proposal contain, in their contract document or contract schedule, specific information concerning how the proposer will receive technical direction and management under the proposed contract. In government contracts, "technical direction" is a function that is separated from the "contracting officer" function, and the contract document spells out in detail just what direction the proposing company can receive from the "technical manager" and what direction it can receive from the contracting officer. The technical manager can provide direction *within* the contract scope of work, while the contracting officer must approve changes *outside* the scope of work. Technical direction is defined as a directive to the contractor which approves approaches, solutions, designs, or refinements; fills in details or otherwise furnishes guidance to the contractor. Technical direction includes a process of conducting inquiries, requesting studies, or transmitting information or advice by the technical manager, regarding matters *within* the definitions and requirements of the statement of work. Any company proposing to a government agency should find out as much as possible about the personality, policies, attitudes, and management techniques of the person or persons who are most likely to provide technical direction of the work because the actions of the technical manager and his staff can lead to expenditure of more work than had been anticipated, proposed, or negotiated at the outset of the project. Overruns can result from excessive technical direction or involvement from the customer unless the technical manager has the interests of the cost control and harmonious working relationships at heart. Conversely, a cooperative and understanding technical manager can make it easier rather than harder to meet program commitments by exercising flexibility and understanding in developing and approving program trade-offs.

In addition to specifying duties of the customer technical manager and contracting officer, most government customers and some industrial customers require that the contractor designate one person to act as the project manager and that this person be delegated complete authority to decide all technical matters related to the contract. This project manager is the counterpart of the customer's technical manager and is usually expected to stay on as project manager throughout the duration of the project. The contract document often requires not only that the project manager and other key personnel be named but that the company certify that these key personnel will stay with the project unless approval for a change is granted by the customer. This contract article is designed to discourage the bidding of a job to be managed by experienced personnel and then subsequent replacement of these personnel with a less experienced staff.

Contract Changes.   Because contract changes can be troublesome areas that cause overruns and program slippages, the contract document usually contains considerable verbiage that addresses how changes will be handled. The main changes clause of the contract is in the "general provisions," to be discussed later. The changes clause in a government contract allows the contracting officer to make changes within the *general scope* of the contract. If the change results in an increase or decrease in the cost or time required to do the job, then an "equitable adjustment" is made in the estimated cost, delivery schedule, or other contract provisions. It is in the area of defining and agreeing on what an "equitable adjustment" is that causes an adversarial relationship between the customer and supplier unless the work scope and the change are sufficiently defined. Almost any work activity that is changed while in process will cost more to accomplish unless the change involves the removal of a large part of the work activity itself.

The contractor usually has sixty days to file a claim of increased costs or slipped schedule due to the change. Occasionally, for very large contracts, both parties will agree in advance to specify that a certain dollar value increase or decrease will not give rise to an "equitable adjustment." The purpose of this agreement is to allow small changes to take place that balance out to a zero or minimal change in total contract costs or delivery dates. Also, articles are included in the contract schedule that permit no-cost engineering change proposals to be submitted by the contractor and approved by the customer's technical manager. Other articles include information and potential contract clauses on the notification procedure for changes (how the customer is notified and responds to contract changes) and the method of tracking and accounting for contract changes. These contract schedule articles are also important to read thoroughly and understand before initiating detailed proposal preparation activities. They may affect how much is put into the "allowance for cost growth" when making the proposal cost estimate and establishing a contract bid price.

Facilities and Property Clauses or Articles.   If customer-provided facilities or equipment is to be used in performing the work, the contract schedule will contain agreements as to how the facilities, equipment, or property will be cared for, accounted for, disposed of, or transferred from location to location. These articles may cause additional paperwork, inspection, packaging, shipping, accounting, and/or disposal costs and time to be incurred in the performance of the proposed work; therefore these articles presented in the request for proposal should be read carefully and understood fully. If certain existing assets are required to be used, allowances must be made where appropriate for the inspection, upgrading, and refurbishment of these assets if required prior to their use. A proposal will have to include a complete listing of all facilities, supplies, and equipment expected to be received from the customer to accomplish the work. The proposal must also specify the time duration of use, and certify that the condition of these assets will be acceptable to the customer as they are returned upon completion of the work.

Miscellaneous Articles. A number of miscellaneous articles are also included in the contract schedule included in the request for proposal. These are listed below along with a brief phrase on what each is designed to accomplish.

Total sum allotted. Specifies the limitation of the customer's financial obligation for the work.

Place of performance. Specifies where the work will be performed.

Inspection, acceptance, and free-on-board (FOB) point. Specifies the location of interim inspection and interim acceptance of the services and/or deliverable items called for under the contract.

Reports distribution. Specifies the number of copies required and the distribution location for all reports.

Packing, packaging, identification, marking, and preparation for shipment. Specifies the method of shipment and calls out specifications for packing, packaging, identification, marking, and preparation for shipment.

Designation of special representatives. Designates special representatives of the customer who are charged with the responsibility for special areas, such as patents and new technology reporting.

Information releases and publications. Specifies customer review of material to be presented orally or in written form in the public or professional media.

International System of Units. Specifies whether or not the international system of units will be used in all documentation under the contract. (Watch out for this one—it can be expensive if it is not expected.)

Rights to proposal data. Specifies which pages in the proposal the customer cannot duplicate, disclose, or have others do so for any purpose.

General Provisions

The general provisions of the proposed contract, often called "boiler-plate," is the fine print that defines all of the legal implications of going into business with a specific customer. In a large government request for proposal, this fine print can occupy fifty to one hundred pages (an average of seventy pages) many of which have very fine print and a very high word count per page. One agency has forty-one general provisions with an added thirty-nine special provisions in each contract. Although those who are experienced in working with the government have become accustomed to living under these provisions, mostly imposed because of enactment into legislation by Congress but including some agency-imposed provisions, others who are new to large-scale contracting for industry and government must learn the significance (or insignificance) of each of these provisions before starting in earnest to prepare a proposal.

Most of the general provisions, at least for government contracts, are reflected as required "representations and certifications" discussed earlier. Many have little or no effect on a company that is doing business in an honest and straightforward manner. Neither space nor prudence permits the duplication of the general provisions in this book. Copies may be obtained by writing the customer or agency to be contacted for new business. But the legal department of any proposing company should thoroughly read and understand these general provisions before proposal preparation starts.

OTHER TECHNICAL AND PROGRAMMATIC DATA INCLUDED IN THE REQUEST FOR PROPOSAL

In addition to the above information, many requests for proposal include detailed technical reports, drawings, specifications, and "strawman" plans for the work activities or work outputs being proposed. This is often done to assure that all bidders receive the same information on which to base their proposals, because much of this information may have been provided by the bidders themselves, or it is in the public domain or in business or scientific literature openly available to the public. These documents provide an in-depth insight into at least the customer's understanding of the complexity, content, and timing of the work to be proposed and, therefore, are helpful in preparing the technical portions of the proposal.

OTHER TYPES AND SIZES OF REQUESTS FOR PROPOSALS

The request for proposal just described is perhaps one of the most complex and demanding since it is for a very large procurement, probably for the acquisition of a major system, product, or facility or major subsystem thereof. There are other sizes and types of proposals—as many as there are items to be procured. The following adjective descriptions (used earlier in part) are assigned to classify requests for proposal by size:

Adjective	Number of Pages
Very small size	0–75 pages
Small size	75–150 pages
Medium size	150–500 pages
Large size	500–750 pages
Very large size	750–1,000 pages
Giant RFP	over 1,000 pages

The content of the request for proposal will also vary with the subject matter of the procurement. Many of the request for proposal elements described in the first part of this chapter will disappear, and others will be added when proposals for service-type activities are requested. Content changes and is dependent on whether a process, product, project, service, or combination of these is being requested. Typical types of requests for proposal other than that discussed earlier in this chapter are described below.

Standard Products or Supplies

Requests for proposal are more often called requests for quotation (RFQ) where a price and delivery date for standard products or supplies are concerned. These requests for quotation are classified as very small or small in size and usually only contain a standard part number or series of part numbers, a desired delivery date, and any special packaging, shipping, and handling conditions. The more the product or supply item deviates from standard, the more detailed the request for quotation will be because special accessories, features, and associated services required by the customer must also be described. This type of request for quotation seldom exceeds fifteen or twenty pages plus a letter of transmittal and normally includes a sketch or drawing of the completed item; a parts list or work element structure dictionary; and delivery dates, quantities, and conditions.

General Support Service Contracts

Requests for proposal for general support service contracts usually fall into the "medium" size category. This type of RFP includes a description, map or plan of the facility or equipment to be serviced, and other elements that appear in the larger requests for proposals such as general background information, proposal format and content requirements, evaluation of proposals, reporting instructions, and a detailed statement of work. If the general support service contract is to be a government procurement, the request for proposal will also include the socioeconomic provisions such as equal opportunity provisions, buy-American act provisions, clean air and water act compliance, small business utilization reporting, and so forth. General support services contracts for the government are often directed to small businesses or small minority-owned businesses because they do not require a large financial investment or business base to successfully accomplish the work.

Usually required in proposals responding to these requests for proposal are a management plan and organization; a staffing plan giving staff numbers, certifications, sources, availability, and flexibility; and a section on key personnel. A cost proposal is required, as is a section on experience and past performance. Since contracts resulting from these requests for proposal can consist of "time-and-materials" contracts or "mission-type" support contracts, the method of costing and the amount of cost detail required varies considerably. A minimum requirement is a cost breakdown by calendar period and element of cost (labor, materials, overhead, general and administrative [G & A], and fee). As in larger requests for proposal, the relative importance of the various evaluation factors and criteria will also be described to allow the proposer to place proper emphasis on the various aspects of the procurement. The method of contractor evaluation and fee award, as well as the method of technical supervision and direction by the customer, will also be provided.

Base Maintenance Support Services for a Large Plant or Facility.   Requests for proposal for activities such as base maintenance and support services for a large plant or facility will normally fall into the "large" category. This type of contact differs from the general support services in that a large number of activities are required; more documentation, inspection, and evaluation of results is required; and more personnel and equipment are needed. The additional request for proposal size is brought about by the need for more detailed descriptions of the task or tasks involved. In general, the complexity of the request for proposal is in proportion to the complexity of the job itself which is, in turn, associated with the complexity of the plant or facility being supported. Checklists, procedures, property lists, facilities descriptions, and past maintenance and operation requirements normally form a part of this type of request for proposal. Most of the contract boilerplate, general provisions, evaluation guidelines, proposal formulation instructions, and scope of work provisions that are in a major procurement, will also show up in the large request for a base maintenance support services proposal.

A FINAL COMMENT ON REQUEST FOR PROPOSAL QUALITY

One characteristic that is noticeable in many large requests for proposal, particularly some of those received from government departments or agencies, is the absence of consistency in the quality of writing, publication, and production. This characteristic is understandable because requests for proposal, like proposals, are usually put together in an inordinately short time frame with a limited staff. Inputs are sometimes received from various organizations, in the process of the request for proposal preparation, and little time is available for correlation, coordination, and synthesis of inputs into a cohesive, readable, and attractive document. It will be observed in some requests for proposal issued in the past that page numbering is difficult to follow, various styles and sizes of type are used seemingly at random, format is not consistent, and editorial work has not been thoroughly accomplished. *These characteristics in a request for proposal do not give license to the same characteristics in the responding proposal.* Improvements are constantly being made to the request for proposal preparation process. Many industrial and government organizations are turning to the use of word processors to speed the preparation of requests for proposal and to improve their readability, ease of reference, and attractiveness. At this writing, however, much remains to be accomplished in this area. Some day all requests for proposal will be equal in quality to that of the proposals they expect in response. Nevertheless, the burden will always lie with the potential bidder to respond with a high quality, editorially excellent, attractive, neat, readable, easily referenced, and convincing proposal no matter what condition the request for proposal arrives in.

GOVERNMENT RFP'S: EVOLVING REQUIREMENTS

Federal government requests for proposal are undergoing significant evolutionary changes (as is the entire federal government procurement process) that will measurably simplify the request and its required response. The President signed executive order number 12352 in March 1982 which requires all government agencies to eliminate unnecessary procurement regulations, paperwork, reporting requirements, solicitation provisions, contract clauses, certifications, and other administrative procedures. At this writing, a plan is being considered that will permit annual certifications and representations by each firm working with the United States government. These annual certifications and representations will take the place of the equivalent documents now required with each new proposal. Many other specific actions have been proposed and are being implemented to carry out this recent presidential executive order. To provide the reader with an idea of the scope and importance of these potential future changes in requests for proposal and in the procurement process itself, the presidential order is quoted in its entirety below:[5]

EXECUTIVE ORDER 12352
On
FEDERAL PROCUREMENT REFORMS

By the authority vested in me as President by the Constitution and laws of the United States of America, and in order to ensure effective and efficient spending of public funds through fundamental reforms in Government procurement, it is hereby ordered as follows:

Section 1. To make procurement more effective in support of mission accomplishment, the heads of executive agencies engaged in the procurement of products and services from the private sector shall:

(a) Establish programs to reduce administrative costs and other burdens which the procurement function imposes on the Federal Government and the private sector. Each program shall take into account the need to eliminate unnecessary agency procurement regulations, paperwork, reporting requirements, solicitation provisions, contract clauses, certifications, and other administrative procedures. Private sector views on needed changes should be solicited as appropriate;

(b) Strengthen the review of programs to balance individual program needs against mission priorities and available resources;

(c) Ensure timely satisfaction of mission needs at reasonable prices by establishing criteria to improve the effectiveness of procurement systems;

(d) Establish criteria for enhancing effective competition and limiting noncompetitive actions. These criteria shall seek to improve competition by such actions as eliminating unnecessary Government specifications and simplifying those that must be retained, expanding the purchase of available commercial goods and services, and, where practical, using functionally-oriented specifications or otherwise describing Government needs so as to permit greater latitude for private sector response;

(e) Establish programs to simplify small purchases and minimize paperwork burdens imposed on the private sector, particularly small businesses;

(f) Establish administrative procedures to ensure that contractors, especially small businesses, receive timely payment;

(g) Establish clear lines of contracting authority and accountability;

(h) Establish career management programs, covering the full range of personnel management functions, that will result in a highly qualified, well managed professional procurement workforce; and

(i) Designate a Procurement Executive with agency-wide responsibility to oversee development of procurement systems, evaluate system performance in accordance with approved criteria, enhance career management of the procurement work force, and certify to the agency head that procurement systems meet approved criteria.

Sec. 2. The Secretary of Defense, the Administrator of General Services, and the Administrator for the National Aeronautics and Space Administration shall continue their joint efforts to consolidate their common procurement regulations into a single simplified Federal Acquisition Regulation (FAR) by the end of calendar year 1982.

[5] Executive Order No. 12352: Federal Procurement Reforms. March 17, 1982.

Sec. 3. The Director of the Office of Personnel Management, in consultation with the heads of executive agencies, shall ensure that personnel policies and classification standards meet the needs of executive agencies for a professional procurement work force.

Sec. 4. The Director of the Office of Management and Budget, through the Office of Federal Procurement Policy as appropriate, shall work jointly with the heads of executive agencies to provide broad policy guidance and overall leadership necessary to achieve procurement reform, encompassing:

(a) Identifying desirable Government-wide procurement system criteria, such as minimum requirements for training and appointing contracting officers;

(b) Facilitating the resolution of conflicting views among those agencies having regulatory authority with respect to Government-wide procurement regulations;

(c) Assisting executive agencies in streamlining guidance for procurement processes;

(d) Assisting in the development of criteria for procurement career management programs;

(e) Facilitating interagency coordination of common procurement reform efforts;

(f) Identifying major inconsistencies in law and policies relating to procurement which impose unnecessary burdens on the private sector and Federal procurement officials; and, following coordination with executive agencies, submitting necessary legislative initiatives for the resolution of such inconsistencies; and

(g) Reviewing agency implementation of the provisions of this Executive Order and keeping me informed of progress and accomplishments.

S/R. Reagan
President of the United States

6

THE TECHNICAL PROPOSAL

Through wisdom is a house built; and by understanding it is estab-
lished; and by knowledge shall the chambers be filled with all precious
and pleasant riches.
Prov. 24:3, 4

The most important part of a proposal is the technical proposal volume. It
is the major basis for performing a good work activity or for providing a
good work output. The technical proposal tells exactly how, when and
sometimes why the work will be performed in a certain manner. Hence the
technical proposal must describe the work in detail: provide discussion,
references, drawings, specifications, schedules, and documented evidence
to show how and when the various phases of the work are going to be
completed. It must contain enough substance to demonstrate competence
and technical expertise in the field being proposed, it must demonstrate
understanding of the requirement, and it must provide assurance to the
customer that the job will be completed in a manner that meets all technical requirements.

As discussed in preceding chapters, the objectives, ground rules, constraints, and requirements of the work must be spelled out in detail to form
the basis for a good proposal. A thorough knowledge of the requirements of
the request for proposal and the company's capability and approach to the
work activity are essential. Cooperation and coordination of the entire
proposal team is required to produce the technical volume. The members of
the proposal team preparing the technical volume are the most likely
source of a detailed definition of the work required by the request for
proposal. These work descriptions usually take the form of detailed specifications, sketches, drawings, materials lists, and parts lists. More detailed
designs will invariably produce more accurate cost estimates, and the
amount of detail itself produces a greater awareness and visibility of
potential inconsistencies, omissions, duplications, and overlaps.

It is important for the technical proposal team to be aware of project ground rules concerning production rate, production quantity, and timing of initiation, production, and completion of the job before starting the technical volume. Factors such as raw material availability, labor skills required, and equipment utilization often force a work activity to conform to a specific time period. The technical team must, therefore, obtain or establish the optimum time schedule early in the proposal preparation process, verify key milestone dates, and see that the overall work schedule is subdivided into identifiable increments that can be placed on a calendar time scale. This time schedule must coincide with that required by the request for proposal.

The technical proposal is the basis for the organizational and management arrangements spelled out in the organization and management volume and for the resources estimates upon which the cost or price proposal or cost volume is based. The technical proposal volume should be prepared in advance of the organization and management and cost or price volumes. Since time for proposal preparation is usually short, however, the three volumes are often prepared concurrently, with the technical proposal feeding periodically into the other two volumes.

The essence of a successful technical proposal is responsiveness. This means far more than merely parroting the words contained in the request for proposal or request for quotation. It demands that the proposer comprehend and accurately describe the requirement and the proposed solution.

This dimension of responsiveness is seldom appreciated and frequently neglected in the preparation of the technical proposal. The proposal manager must accept responsibility for: (1) the development of complete "understanding" in the mind of the customer, and (2) establishing the fact that the bidder also has a complete understanding. To accomplish this, he or she directs the team in such a manner that they deliberately share the responsibility and structure their output to foster customer comprehension and technical credibility. A practical, simple device for ensuring customer "understanding" is to have each member of the preparation team write out a brief comment as to what he or she, the writer, would like to have the listener express after reading the section. This will tend to structure the writing of the technical proposal toward the intended result.

The intended result of the technical proposal is, of course, the acceptance and implementation of the proposed solution. Sales in technical and industrial markets are made by supplying pertinent and usable information upon which the customer can base plans or future actions. Pertinent and useful information can generally be reduced to a few simple terms or relationships. If these relationships are clearly defined and then firmly established in the reader's mind, the technical proposal volume will provide a solid basis for the remainder of the proposal.

THE WORK STATEMENT: BASIS FOR
THE TECHNICAL PROPOSAL

The basis for the technical proposal is the proposed contract statement of work, which is normally provided in the request for proposal. The contract statement of work should be correlated as closely as possible with the work element structure (1) to organize the work and divide it among the available performers and (2) to estimate and collect resources required to do the job. (See Chapter 7, "The Organization and Management Proposal," for details on the development of the work element structure.) If feasible, the work statement and work element structures should be closely correlated with schedule elements. In some proposals it is feasible to correlate the statement of work, work elements, and schedule elements on a "one-on-one" basis. This correlation will permit a better understanding of the proposal by the reader and will greatly enhance the process of developing resource estimates of the technical tasks to be performed.

THREE BASIC FUNCTIONS OF THE TECHNICAL PROPOSAL

Technical proposal preparation is accomplished within the framework of the proposed contract work statement and its respective work element structure and schedule, and comprises three basic functions: (1) it describes the work activity or work output; (2) it describes the means of accomplishing the work; and (3) it demonstrates an overall understanding of the job in relation to requirements.

Description of the Work

The work to be accomplished is described through the effective presentation of sketches and drawings, photographs, flow diagrams and schematics, written specifications, material lists or drawing trees, and development plans. All of these methods of presentation are effective in presenting technical data, but their use must be orchestrated by skillful mixing and combination of pictorial, graphic, photographic, and text material to provide an understandable, readable, and easily evaluated technical proposal. It is in the combination of these presentation techniques or methods that the proposal comes the closest to resembling a sales brochure. Although elaborate and expensive artwork and photography are not required or desired, judicious use of these presentation techniques can do much to make a proposal more understandable, attractive, and technically credible.

Sketches and Drawings. The sketches and drawings in a proposal can range from a simple reproduction of a conceptual sketch of a principal investigator to an elaborate photograph-like air brush rendering of the activity or product being proposed. Rough sketches are seldom acceptable for use in a proposal unless they are exact copies of an original scientist's notes on an important discovery or invention. In these instances they can be used to lend credibility to the originality of design or concept. The most acceptable and most cost-effective approach to technical proposal illustrative material is to include reduced, photographically or manually enhanced copies of actual engineering or architectural drawings or computer generated drawings from computer-aided design equipment. The use of computer-aided design techniques will speed the proposal preparation process considerably because computer-aided design equipment is capable of producing isometric drawings, cutaway views, exploded views, and perspective drawings. Through computer-aided techniques, the legends, dimensions, and notes on computer generated drawings can be increased in size to permit legibility when the drawing is reduced to standard proposal page or foldout size.

Although special isometric, cutaway, and exploded views require highly competent technical artists if computer-aided design techniques are not available, the use of selected special views will do much to enhance the reader's understanding and comprehension of a proposed product or project configuration. If engineering or architectual drawings are included in a proposal, only the top level drawings—backed up by sufficient detailed drawings to illustrate that in-depth design has been completed—may be desired. For large architectural projects and fixed-price manufacturing activities, however, it is desirable to present or at least agree with the customer on all drawings down to the lowest level of detail available.

Photographs.   Although large numbers of photographs should be avoided in the technical proposal volume, there is no substitute for a photograph when it is necessary to demonstrate that a given piece of equipment, model, mockup, component, or facility exists. Photographs do much to show the size, shape, and configuration of physical items that are a part of or will be engaged in the work activity or output. An effective way to use a photograph of a partially completed or prototype item is to combine photography with a skillful air brush technique to develop a realistic picture of the completed product. Although this technique should not be used to mislead the customer into thinking an actual full scale production item has already been completed when it has not been completed, it will help the customer visualize the appearance of the final product and will improve credibility by offering a picture very close to that which will be the desired end product. Photographs are most commonly used in technical proposals to show laboratory breadboards, prototype models, mockups, and test equipment identical or similar to that which will be used in the proposed project.

Flow Diagrams and Schematics.   If relatively simple and straightforward in nature, line or shaded drawings or artist renderings of flow diagrams and schematics are effective tools to be used as necessary to illustrate a technical proposal. Shading can be used to indicate various fluids or pressures in hydraulic or pneumatic devices, and sequential flow diagrams can show flow or pressures in various modes of operation. Electrical and electronic schematics can be presented either in block diagram form or in wiring diagram form showing each electrical or electronic component and its interrelationship with the others. Color coding is often useful in flow diagrams and schematics. It should be kept in mind that maintenance-manual simplicity is preferred when presenting complex material in a proposal. The technical proposal should strive to educate rather than to impress or confuse the reader with overly complex technical information. Flow diagrams and schematics must always be accompanied by a description of the symbols, legends, and conventions used in the construction of the illustration. Shaded or colored flow diagrams will show system components, system operational modes, fluid flow and valve action. Block diagrams can be used to show the interrelationship of major components, and the number and complexity of operations.

Specifications: Importance.   The specifications of a work activity or a work output are written statements that depict its principal technical characteristics. Hence, reading and understanding the specifications are the most important parts of any new proposed technical activity. The following words are typical of the types of characteristics that are specified for a work activity or work output:

Acceleration	Length
Braking	Load-carrying capability
Capacity	Maintainability
Cleanliness	Power requirements
Contamination resistance	Range
Cornering capability	Reliability
Density	Square feet
Depth	Take-off distance
Electrical output	Shock resistance
Energy usage	Speed
Fuel economy	Temperature resistance
Height	Tolerances
Human factors	Traction
Humidity resistance	Vibration resistance
Interface requirements	Volume

Landing distance	Weather resistance
Shock resistance	Weight

Since specifications are usually set forth in requests for proposal, it is important to know how to treat these specifications in the work description. Those experienced in proposal preparation insist that the most common pitfall in embarking on a new activity is failure to read and understand the specifications. There are five key steps to meeting the specifications for a new work activity or work output:

1. *Assess relative importance.* In reviewing the specifications for any new work activity or work output, the proposer should *develop an assessment* of the relative importance of each of the specified areas. The relative importance of meeting each area of specified performance in a technical activity is *normally not stated clearly by the requestor!* Therefore, the proposer must make a judgment about which of the specified characteristics are most important and which are the least important. Invariably instances will be encountered when the specified requirements cannot be met and trades must be made to determine where a relaxation in requirements will be the least detrimental to the final output and the least detrimental to being chosen to do the work. Hence, any compromises that must be made in design will be those which will be the least detrimental to the overall project. Usually some trends can be detected in the proposal request, but thorough technical homework is required to fully understand the implications both from a potential work performance standpoint and a contract selection standpoint of compromises made in meeting the specifications.

2. *Point out where requirements are exceeded.* As part of the assessment of relative importance of the specification requirements, it should have also been determined if it is to the proposer's and the project's advantage to *exceed* certain specifications. If the work activity or output being proposed exceeds the specifications in these areas or in any area, it is wise to point out clearly and emphatically that the proposal exceeds specification requirements and indicate in which areas it does so. One must be careful, however, that designers or planners have not "gold plated" the desired output because this may be considered by evaluators as a lack of cost consciousness or of taking excessive technical risk. Exceeding performance requirements may be of such importance to the project that it should not only be discussed in the technical proposal, but it should be mentioned in the letter of transmittal and the proposal executive summary as well.

3. *Explain specification deviations.* If the proposed work activity or work output does not meet the required specifications in any area, the reason for this should be explained in the technical proposal. Perhaps a

better solution to the problem or an innovative approach that eliminates the need to meet certain requirements spelled out in the request for proposal has been developed. If so, deviation from specifications will be considered by the evaluator to be a strength instead of a weakness. Perhaps the stated requirement was unrealistic or unreasonable to begin with. This is another reason that a clear technical description of the reason for deviation will be judged as a strength instead of a weakness. At any rate, a well written explanation of the deviation will be a convincing addition to the measure of credibility that the evaluator(s) attribute to the technical proposal.

   4. Summarize specification adherence information. Information concerning the qualities or performance of the proposed work activity or output that do or do not meet those specified in the request for proposal should be summarized in a clearly visible format. The proposer should not depend on the proposal evaluator to ferret out this information. It is not necessary to wave any red flags that say the job cannot be done because specified requirements have not been met, but the customer should be given an honest look at the capabilities being proposed in relation to what have been requested. A summary of the technical and performance specifications of the project in a tabular format with an indication of which requirements were exceeded or reduced in the proposal is a handy way to summarize this information. It should not be done, however, before calling proper attention to the benefits of exceeding or reducing requirements, else the reader may lose interest before evaluating the full advantages of the proposed plan or design.

Specifications: Types. Specifications fall into five general categories: (1) product specifications, (2) qualification specifications, (3) acceptance specifications, (4) component specifications, and (5) process specifications. It is important for the proposer to recognize the differences and the interrelationship among these four categories of specifications.

   1. Product specifications. Product specifications specify how the product is expected to perform when put to its intended use. These specifications are used in promoting or advertising the item, as performance has been proven or exceeded either by continued use or by laboratory tests. Product specifications should not exceed acceptance specifications or qualification specifications, described below.

   2. Qualification specifications. These are the specifications or requirements that a product must meet in the laboratory before it is placed into general use or marketed as an end item. The proposer must be acutely aware of the qualification requirements because a qualification test program may be required prior to completion of the proposed work activity. Since qualification requirements are usually more stringent than field use requirements to assure a degree or margin of safety when put to use, qualification testing can be expensive and time-consuming to the producer. In many proposals, the supplier is required to describe the qualification test program that demonstrates how qualification requirements will be met.

3. Acceptance specifications. Acceptance specifications are usually applied to a work output (product or project) to identify how the customer will expect the item to perform before he or she will accept it into his or her system for payment. Acceptance specifications are less stringent than qualification specifications but more stringent than product performance specifications. Acceptance specifications state the degree of sampling or inspection, the nondestructive testing that will be performed on the item before acceptance, the tolerances in expected performance, and quality assurance requirements.

4. Component specifications. Component specifications require that components of the final product meet certain qualification, acceptance, and product performance standards, as in the requirement for tire tread thickness or wear on a cargo truck to be purchased by a trucking company. Occasionally the customer will not only require that the product itself meet certain performance requirements, but that the *components* of the product meet a different but compatible set of requirements. Component specifications are used by the supplier of the total product to designate required qualities of the product's subsystems and components.

5. Process specifications. Process specifications are used within a company to specify methods or techniques for treating, handling, assembling, machining, welding, soldering, painting, or otherwise manufacturing a product. Occasionally standardized process specifications are imposed on the supplier by the customer. In these instances, the supplier must either use the customer's specifications in testing for compliance or submit to a customer inspection and process specification review to determine if the supplier's process specifications meet the customer's requirements.

Material Lists and Drawing Trees. A vital part of the description of any new work output or work activity is the material list or parts list. This listing is sometimes tied to the drawing tree or drawing system through the use of a compatible numbering system. The use of part numbers that correspond to the drawing number of that part can eliminate confusion in determining what part belongs to what subsystem. If the part numbering system and the drawing numbering system are both tied to the work statement and work element structure, confusion brought about by the use of several different numbering systems and procedures can be eliminated.

The proposer should be prepared to include a parts list for any product or project supplied and should also be able to explain, in the technical proposal, the material and parts quality control procedures, the material and parts tracking and numbering system, and the drawing tree numbering system if it relates to the material and part numbers. These systems should be organized and documented for submittal as part of the proposal or for its use in maintaining an efficient and effective material and parts inventory, tracking, and reorder system.

The Means of Accomplishing the Work

Every proposer should do some detailed planning and scheduling of the work to be done before submitting a technical proposal and generally such information is submitted to the customer as an important part of the proposal. This information on planning and scheduling submitted with the proposal is sometimes included in the proposal's technical volume and sometimes in the management volume.

The key to providing the best possible work output within a given amount of resources is the timing of work activities to result in as little waste, duplication, overlap, and redundancy of effort and materials as possible. In mass production, a delay in the delivery of a material or part into the process flow or assembly line can hold up the entire work activity. Delays in production can rapidly escalate product costs because many overhead and direct labor costs are constant despite fluctuating work output levels. Too-early delivery of a material or part to a process or assembly line can also cause inefficiencies because of the need for on-line storage and handling of the yet-to-be processed material. In multidisciplined activities or large projects, the timing of application of each unit of resource, whether it be a unit of labor or material, is important because it usually affects another work activity. For example, labor hours cannot be expended on material until the material arrives; manufacturing labor cannot be expended before engineering labor is expended to design the hardware; assembly cannot be completed until the manufacturing is complete; and so on.

These interrelationships of resource elements make timing of work activities a most important factor in the overall development of a competitive technical proposal.

Delivery or Availability Keyed to Need Dates. The most important factor to observe in formulating an estimated schedule of any work activity or work output is to provide the work on the date or dates and at the rate or rates required by the market. The technical scheduler should have on hand the results of the marketing or planning analysis to show: (1) the goals and objectives of the work activity, (2) the action plan of supplying the work output, (3) the requirements of the delivered product or service, (4) and the work elements that make up the overall work activity. The marketing or planning analysis will have future delivery dates and rates that project the most probable future market needs. The technical scheduler will then use the future date of delivery of the work output as an end point and work back in time to the present to develop a detailed milestone schedule.

Developing a Schedule.   Schedule elements are time-related groupings of work activities that are placed in sequence to accomplish an overall desired objective. Schedule elements for a process could be represented by very small (minutes, hours, or days) time periods. The scheduling of a process is represented by the time the raw materials take during each step to travel through the process. The schedule for manufacturing a product or delivery of a service is, likewise, a time flow of the various components or actions into a completed item or activity.

A project (the construction or development of a fairly large, complex, or multidisciplinary tangible work output) contains distinct schedule elements called milestones. These milestones are encountered in one form or another in almost all projects: (1) study and analysis, (2) design, (3) procurement of raw materials and purchased parts, (4) fabrication or manufacturing or components and subsystems, (5) assembly of the components and subsystems, (6) testing of the combined system to qualify the unit for operation in its intended environment, (7) acceptance testing, preparation, packaging, shipping, and delivery of the item, (8) and operation of the item.

Techniques Used in Schedule Planning.   There are a number of analytical techniques used in developing an overall schedule of a work activity that help to assure the correct allocation and sequencing of schedule elements: precedence and dependency networks, arrow diagrams, critical path bar charts, the program evaluation and review technique (PERT), a tool pioneered by the Navy, and program evaluation procedure (PEP) the Air Force version. These techniques use graphic and mathematical methods to develop the best proposed schedule based on sequencing in such a way that each activity is performed only when the required predecessor activities are accomplished. A simple example of how these techniques work is shown in Table 6.1. Eight schedule elements have been chosen; the length of each schedule activity has been designated; and a relationship has been established between each activity and its predecessor activity. The resulting bar chart that is plotted after the analysis is shown on Figure 6.1.

Notice several things about the precedence relationships: (1) some activities can be started before their predecessor activities are completed, (2) some activities must be fully completed before their follow-on activities can be started, (3) and some activities cannot be started until a given number of months after the 100 percent completion date of a predecessor activity. Once these schedule interrelationships are established, a total program schedule can be developed by starting either from a selected

TABLE 6.1. SCHEDULE RELATIONSHIPS

Schedule Element	Title of Schedule Element	Time Required for Completion	Percent Completion Required[a]
A	Study and Analysis	6 months	33 1/3%
B	Design	8 months	50%
C	Procurement	8 months	50%
D	Fabrication	12 months	66 2/3%
E	Assembly	12 months	100% plus 2 months
F	Testing	8 months	100%
G	Delivery	4 months	100% plus 4 months
H	Operation	36 months	100%

[a] Percent completion required before subsequent activity can be accomplished.

beginning point and working forward in time until the completion date is reached, or by starting from a desired completion date and working backward in time to derive the required schedule starting date. If both the start date and completion date are given, the length of schedule elements and their interrelationships must be established through an iterative process to develop a schedule that accomplishes a job in the required time. If all schedule activities are started as soon as their prerequisites are met, the result is the shortest possible time schedule to perform the work.

Most complex work activities have multiple paths of activity that must be accomplished parallel with each other. The longest of these paths is called a "critical path," and the schedule critical path is developed by connecting all of the schedule activity critical paths. Construction of a schedule such as that shown in Figure 6.1 brings to light a number of other questions. The first of these is, "How is the length of each activity established?" This question reflects on the cost estimate that will be included in the cost volume, since many costs are incurred simply by the passage of time. Costs of an existing work force, overhead (insurance, rental, and utilities), and material handling and storage continue to pile up in an organization whether there is a productive output or not. Hence it is important to develop the shortest possible overall schedule to accomplish a job and each schedule element in the shortest time and in the most efficient method possible. The length of each schedule activity is established by an analysis of that activity and the human and material resources available and required to accomplish it. The labor and material estimating techniques described in Chapter 8 are used extensively by the estimator in establishing the length of calendar time required to accomplish a schedule activity as well as the labor-hours and materials required for its completion.

A second question is, "What can be done if there are other influences on

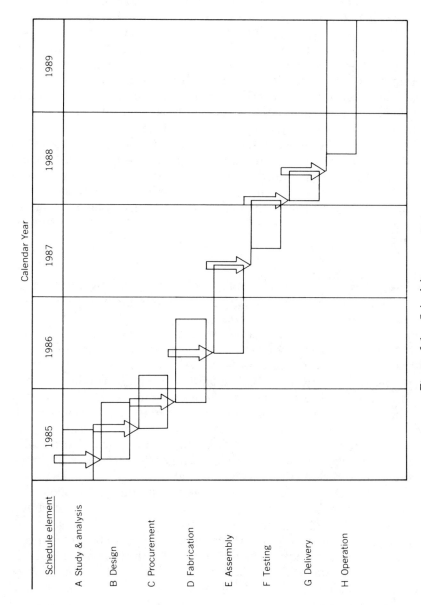

Figure 6.1. Scheduling a project.

the schedule such as availability of facilities, equipment, and labor?" This is a factor that arises in most proposal situations. There are definite schedule interactions in any multiple-output organization that must be considered in planning a single work activity. Overall corporate planning must take into account these schedule interactions in its own critical path chart to assure that facilities, manpower, and funds are available to accomplish all work activities in an effective and efficient manner. A final question is, "How is a credible 'percent complete' figure established for each predecessor work activity?" This is accomplished by breaking each activity into subactivities. For instance, "design" can be subdivided into conceptual design, preliminary design, and final design. If the start of the procurement activity is to be keyed to the completion of preliminary design, then the time that the preliminary design is complete determines the percentage of time and corresponding design activity that must be completed prior to the initiation of procurement. Scheduling activities performed during technical proposal preparation will have a significant bearing on the cost-effectiveness of the work and the competitive ranking of the resulting cost proposal.

Schedule and Skill Interactions. Four factors established by the technical proposal team and by company management determine the optimum time phasing of skills for any given work activity: (1) the attrition rate or "turnover" rate for each skill category, (2) the overall company or shop growth rate in numbers of personnel, (3) the merit salary increases (above inflation or cost of living increases), and (4) the initial and final mixture of skill categories and skill levels. A company with a high attrition rate or a high overall growth rate will have ample opportunity to add skills at lower salary levels to keep its labor costs low despite inflation, and it can provide room for advancement of its total work force through merit salary increases and promotions. A relatively static organization with a stable work force and continuous merit increases and promotions will find it difficult to stay competitive because of "salary-creep" and "skill-level-creep." The only solution to staying competitive in this environment is to seek out other complex and difficult tasks that can be accomplished by a highly skilled, competent, and mature work force.

Any organization that is preparing a proposal must observe and consider the interactions of the job being estimated with other jobs that are in various stages of completion. Optimum planning and scheduling of work activities within an organization will result in full utilization of all available technical personnel. As the more difficult early phases of a project are completed, it is desirable to "off-load" the experienced, highly paid individuals to other projects that are just entering their early phases. This "macroscopic" view of an organization's workload must continue to be considered when planning, scheduling, and estimating technical work activities.

Treatment of Long Lead-Time Items. Because of reduced raw material availability, and long transportation times, it is often necessary to place the order for materials, parts, and supplies long before the appropriate predecessor activity is completed. Often a company must take a calculated risk that the material, parts, or supplies possess the right composition, shape, size, and performance to meet the job specifications suitably; and it has to order these items far in advance of expected delivery just to be sure that the subsequent milestones can be met. It usually pays to have a stock of scarce materials and parts on hand to avoid undue delays. The proposed work schedule should take into account the use of existing material stocks as well as the lead-times required for their procurement and replenishment.

Make or Buy Decisions. When formulating a technical proposal, it is necessary to determine which items will be built in-house (make) and which items will be purchased or subcontracted (buy). The best way to arrive at the make or buy structure is to (1) do a cursory analysis of the in-house workload, (2) compare vendor capabilities with equivalent in-house manufacturing capabilities, and (3) select the most attractive alternative. The amount of work a company subcontracts is a function of its expertise and skill in the required disciplines, its internal workload, and its overall company policy regarding subcontracted work. Generally, it is not effective to subcontract more than sixty percent of an organization's work because the amount of technical management and direction for guiding and instructing subcontractors exceeds that required for that part of the project that remains in-house.

Establishing Schedule Elements. If the overall milestone schedule for a work activity is considered as a level one schedule, the schedule elements listed earlier in this chapter (study and analysis, design, procurement, fabrication, assembly, testing, delivery, and operation) can be considered as level two schedule elements. These level two schedule elements can be further subdivided and described as follows:

Study and analysis. Establishing even the simplest operation will require some study, planning, analysis, scheduling, and estimating before the activity is started. Often, the careful planning and scheduling that has been done during the proposal preparation process must be redone once the contract is negotiated because ground rules have changed, personnel and equipment may have been updated, and resources available may have changed. It is during this initial phase of a schedule that the proposer studies the requirements of the work output, analyzes alternative approaches for accomplishing the objectives of the work, and selects the most effective approach. This study and analysis phase includes definition of the technical, schedule, and cost aspects of the work and usually includes development of a preliminary concept of the process, product, project, or service. The preliminary concept could be represented by a block or flow diagram, sketches or artist's concepts, listings of requirements, preliminary specifications, and process or service plans. Each of these schedule subelements (which could also be duplicated as work elements or cost elements) represents a level three schedule element and can be depicted on a bar chart.

Design.   The second element of a schedule is usually the design of the process, product, project or service. Design is usually subdivided into conceptual design, preliminary design, and final design. In large projects these subelements are distinctly separated and are usually interposed with design reviews at the end of each design phase. In smaller projects the subdivision is less clear, yet present. Conceptual design usually starts during the study and analysis phase, and completion of preliminary design is usually when orders can be placed for long lead-time raw materials. Initiation of fabrication activities (if it is a product or project that is being estimated) must usually await the completion of the detailed design phase.

Fabrication, construction, and assembly.   Fabrication, construction, manufacturing, and assembly of tools, parts, components, structures, and subsystems must start in time to have the appropriate hardware elements ready for testing and subsequent delivery. Part of the scheduler's task is to determine the optimum time to initiate fabrication, construction, or manufacturing and assembly of each hardware or facility item. The scheduler must also plan the best use of company facilities, equipment, and personnel in establishing a fabrication schedule.

The key to fabrication planning is the development of a process plan or operations sheet for each part. This sheet depicts the sequence for all fabrication operations. It shows the materials, machines, and functions required for each step of the fabrication process and will be used later as a basis for the development of the resources estimates of the cost volume. Typical functions included in the fabrication process are annealing, coating, coil winding, cutting, deburring, drilling, encapsulating, forming, heat treating, grinding, notching, milling, printing, plating, processing, punching, riveting, sawing, silk-screening, soldering, turning, welding, and wiring.

In the chemical process industries typical operations that would be performed are atomization, baking, blending, coagulating, condensing, cleaning, diluting, distilling, evaporating, fermenting, filtering, freeze-drying, gasifying, polymerizing, precipitating, pumping, purifying, separating, and settling. The technical proposal should be developed with an awareness of the schedule impacts and implications of each of these activities.

In either the processing of a substance, the fabrication of a product, the conduct of a project, or the delivery of a service, each appropriate work operation or work function must be listed in sequence in the technical proposal or the technical proposal backup material to serve as a basis for resource estimates to be included in the cost proposal or cost volume. Operations sheets for any work activity should consider the flow of materials and parts into the fabrication process, the need for standard and special tooling, and the adaptability of the process or operations sheet to the later application of "standard time" data.

Scheduling of the assembly process for fabricated items or parts is similar to the scheduling of the fabrication process. Operations or planning sheets should be developed for each assembly. Where multiple outputs are planned, it is wise to build a sample unit to verify the operations and times required to assemble the end item. In the planning of the assembly process, the assembly sequence should be itemized in detail, noting the location and method of attaching each part or subassembly and the requirement for design and construction of special jigs, fixtures, tools, and assembly aids. Time cycles of final assembly line work stations should be balanced to provide economical, effective, and efficient flow of the product through each assembly operation.

Testing and inspection. The quality and acceptability of any work output not only will depend on the care and precision with which the total job is performed, but also will be assured and verified through a testing and inspection activity. Simple products, processes, or services may require only a sampling inspection to verify a high-quality work output. The more complex work activities, such as complex high-technology products or projects, will require the planning of several steps or phases in the testing and inspection activity. As mentioned earlier, the three key steps in the testing process are (1) performance or development testing, (2) qualification testing, and (3) acceptance testing. Performance or development testing is done during the early phases of many new product or project's life cycles to prove that the item will fulfill its intended function. Often this development testing is repetitive and interspersed with design and manufacturing changes that make the item work better, perform more efficiently, require less maintenance, and/or cost less to produce. Once the iterative cycle of testing and design is completed, the item is subject to a qualification test program. The final product design is subjected to a prespecified test sequence in which various conditions are imposed on the item to prove that it will work under a wide variety of environments and operational conditions. Qualification testing usually subjects the item to more severe environments than does the next step, acceptance testing.

Once the qualification tests are completed, the end item production is started. As units are completed, they are subjected to acceptance tests to verify that each unit will perform as advertised. Where qualification testing qualifies the design of an item and proves that it will operate under more severe conditions than those expected to be encountered normally, acceptance testing proves that a particular end item will perform at nominal conditions.

In planning any of the categories of testing, it is important first to determine the best overall testing method to demonstrate performance capabilities. It is in test planning that cost targets come strongly into play because the actual verification of many design parameters or goals is time-consuming and expensive. Examples are lifetime testing and reliability testing. It is usually not practical or cost-effective to test an item for two years to demonstrate a two-year lifetime. Methods of accelerated testing and sampling must be proposed to make this type of testing practicable.

Delivery and operation. An often overlooked schedule element during proposal preparation is the delivery schedule. The importance of packaging; preserving; shipping; storage; handling; and supplying of parts, materials, and end items has been recognized recently by the emergence of a whole new profession called "logistics," which is devoted to these activities. There have been many instances of delay, damage, and equipment malfunction brought about by a failure to consider logistics during the delivery and operation phase of a work activity. The best cure for these problems is to obtain the advice and expertise of a qualified logistician when developing the delivery and operations proposal for a work activity. Using the appropriate expertise in this area will cause the proposer to avoid the possibility of unforeseen delays brought about by inadequate consideration of the logistic aspects of the job.

Quality control and reliability functions. Most customers for high technology, complex, or large work activities will either impose a series of requirements to assure product quality control and reliability or will expect the proposer to originate and describe his own systems, procedures, and methods of performing these functions. Frequently, the respondent to a request for proposal will be asked to submit formal or informal preliminary documentation that describes quality control (sometimes called quality assurance) and reliability policies, procedures, and practices to be used in the performance of the proposed work. These documents may take the form of product assurance plans, critical parts control plans, nonconformance review procedures, failure mode and effect analysis plans, contamination control plans, maintainability plans, and others depending on who the customer is and the project's requirements.

Product assurance plan. A brief synopsis of a product assurance plan is usually required to be submitted with proposals as part of the technical or management volume or as an appendix to the proposal; and a final product assurance plan is submitted before the work starts. This plan describes the organization and method for implementing the product assurance program. Customers will be looking for the degree of receiving, in process, and final inspection; the method of identification, treatment, reporting, and correction of nonconformances; the amount and type of inspection and control exercised at vendor and subcontractor plants; and the degree of autonomy and independence of the quality control and inspection functions.

Parts control plan. The method of identification, inspection, and control of critical or prequalified parts or materials will usually be described in the technical proposal volume and then submitted as a plan before the work begins. Some customers have approved only certain vendors for parts and materials that go into their products: the approval having been given after a thorough familiarization with the vendor's own product assurance program and/or qualification of the parts through extensive testing or field use. Identification of parts that will be acquired from qualified vendors, parts selection criteria, parts specifications, parts qualification procedures, parts failure analysis, parts traceability, parts handling and storage, and time cycle and age control are subjects covered in the parts quality assurance program. Critical parts or subsystems are identified with various levels of criticality based on the potential impact of failure of the part or subsystem on mission success or end-item performance.

Nonconformance and resolution reports. The technical proposal should include a description of the method of detecting, reporting, and correcting nonconformances that are identified in the quality assurance, reliability, testing, and/or verification programs. This discussion should include: (1) an indication of which nonconformance and resolution reports will be submitted to the customer for information; (2) a description of the content and format of the reports; and (3) a description of the method of following-up on open discrepancies. If the customer requires any special reports of nonconformances that would indicate a safety or mission hazard on other concurrent programs or projects, the content of these reports should also be described in this section of the proposal.

Failure mode and effect analysis. Various forms of hazard analysis, safety analysis, and failure mode and effect analysis are required by customers who are purchasing complex, high technology hardware or software. The methods, techniques, and procedures that will be used in conducting and reporting these studies should be described in the technical proposal. The customer is usually interested in receiving assurance that failures that could result in fire, explosions, structural damage, personal injury, leakage, shock or mission malfunction are thoroughly investigated as to their potential probability of occurrence and their most probable consequences. It is in this section of the proposal that any preliminary information relative to these hazards is described along with the method to be used in continuing to identify and report them.

The contamination control plan and others.   The contamination control plan is only one of many other plans that may conceivably be required by a potential customer. In complex medical, space, or military applications, cleanliness and contamination control techniques and specifications have been developed to reduce the potential effect of foreign particles and substances on the operators or users of delicate devices as well as their effect on the device itself. Plans for controlling or reducing dust, dirt, moisture, foreign organisms, and other particles during the manufacture, testing, and packaging of the item or items for shipment are described in the technical proposal volume.

Maintainability plan and other "ilities."   Although "maintainability" is not always included under the heading of quality assurance and reliability, it is included in this section as an example of other "ilities" that are often addressed in the technical proposal. (Others may be producibility, manufacturability, operability, etc.) Maintainability is one of the more important "ilities" as it must be considered in the design of the item to be delivered and therefore must be considered at the outset of the project. Ability to maintain the item easily during its lifetime is a major consideration for purchasers who are considering the life cycle cost of an acquisition as an important factor in their purchase decision. As part of the technical proposal, the proposer should describe his or her approach to assuring that product maintainability is designed and built into the item. The proposer's approach to the other "ilities" should also be described in the technical proposal.

Systems engineering.   Most complex, high technology projects employ a discipline known as systems engineering which deals with the application of scientific, engineering, and engineering management skills to the planning and control of a totally integrated project. A multielement discipline, systems engineering includes: (1) transformation of an operational need into a technical description of performance parameters and a configuration through an iterative process of definition, synthesis, analysis, design, test, and evaluation; (2) integration of related technical parameters in order to assure compatibility of all physical, functional, and program interfaces in a manner that optimizes the total project definition and design; and (3) integration of the "ilities" (e.g., maintainability, reliability, producibility) into the total engineering effort. The technical proposal should describe the anticipated systems engineering effort required to deliver the proposed work and should describe how the systems engineering effort will be carried out. Systems engineering includes such disciplinary elements as system and subsystem analysis, dynamic analysis, thermal analysis, electrical power and energy analysis and control, mass properties analysis and control, materials and processes compatibility analysis, and establishing and controlling instrumentation lists.

Usually, all of these disciplines are summarized in a systems engineering plan which is submitted in condensed or preliminary form in the proposal and then fully developed and implemented as the work commences. The proposal should address each of the elements of the systems engineering activity and describe how and by whom they will be accomplished.

Systems and subsystems analysis. Systems and subsystems analysis interrelates and integrates all of the hardware, software, and supporting equipment of the system from an analytical standpoint to provide assurance that the various parts of a system will work together as a whole. Interfaces are identified and analyzed to assure that any adjacent parts, components, subsystems, or elements fit and work well together and that they do not adversely affect each others' performance. Systems and subsystems analysis includes systems trades, stress analysis, fracture mechanics analysis, dynamic analysis, mechanisms analysis, thermal analysis, electrical analysis, data transfer analysis, radiation and magnetic field analysis, maintenance analysis, and operations analysis. Other special analytical studies may be required for specific types of systems such as venting analysis, transportation analysis, environmental impact analysis, and so forth. The proposal should include a description of which of these analytical disciplinary elements will be addressed in the systems engineering activity, the approach to be taken in the analysis, the expected or targeted results, and the methods proposed for verifying the analysis and implementing the results in the project.

Dynamic analysis. The dynamic analysis of the total system may consist of analog, digital, or manual computation of the response and resistance to shock, vibration, and stress under various modes of nominal and unusual operation. Thermal and electrical characteristics of the system as well as mechanical characteristics may also be subjected to dynamic analysis. The proposal should describe the techniques and methods to be used, reference the mathematical or computer models to be employed, and describe the method of verification and correlation with actual test or operational results.

Thermal analysis. If static, dynamic, or steady-state thermal analysis is to be performed to establish thermal interfaces or performance, the mathematical models should be named or the concept to be used in their development should be described.

Electrical power and energy status and control. The systems engineering discipline is usually charged with the job of establishing and tracking electrical power and energy usage budgets. Where multiple power sources or multiple power consumption points exist in a system, trends above power and energy usage budgets are recognized and recorded so that power allocation can be readjusted accordingly. Power and energy utilization timelines are developed to assure that power supplies are commensurate with consumption requirements during system operation. If the system is sufficiently complex to warrant an electrical power budget control activity, the technical proposal should describe anticipated power budgets; provide electrical diagrams, schematics and lists; and describe how the power budget will be tracked and adjusted.

Mass properties (weight) control. If weight or mass is a critically important specification requirement, the technical proposal should recognize this and provide a plan for keeping close track of the projected weight of the system and its components as the work proceeds into final design and production. Some systems are sufficiently complex to require a computerized system that will track the projected design weight of each component as the design proceeds, update this weight as prototypes of the parts are built, and adjust the total weight budget or allocations as appropriate. If such a system is to be used, it should be so stated and described in the proposal.

Materials and process control plans. Often, the materials to be used in the makeup of high technology systems are sophisticated or newly developed, and their interaction with other materials or substances in the system is not well known or defined at the time the system is designed. The systems engineering function may need to establish a method of keeping track of the various types of materials to be used in the system to assure compatibility. This materials control plan is also used for tracking rare or scarce materials and helps assure material availability. Any material and process control plans that are especially established, or existing procedures that are used, should be described in the proposal.

Instrumentation lists. Where there are many channels of instrumentation or measurement required for a complex system, a budget and tracking system may also be established under the systems engineering function to track, establish, and approve instrumentation measurements. Such information as measurement number, name, location, purpose, transmission mode, range of measurement, calibration requirement, bandwidth, etc. will be recorded on a tracking system and measurements will be given a priority within an overall instrumentation budget. The proposal should describe such a procedure if it is to be used in the proposed work or project.

In addition to the above functions, the technical proposal should also describe other activities that are usually performed under the systems engineering discipline. Among these are the development of an engineering requirements document early in the project, and the development of a system description handbook during the final phases of project completion.

If the project requires maintenance or operations handbooks or documentation, the technical content, format, and purpose of each of these documents should be described in the technical proposal along with the method of compiling, reviewing, and assuring the technical accuracy of these documents.

Configuration Management.   When complex systems, products, or projects are undertaken, they invariably generate a large number of interfaces, not only in the hardware or software itself, but between various organizations that are contributing to the work. The abundant interfaces that grow out of these projects must be documented and controlled so each performer will know what the interface is with the adjoining hardware, software, or organization. The discipline that has developed from the need for systematic definition and control of interfaces is termed "configuration management" and it is important to address this subject in either the technical volume or the organization and management volume of the proposal.

Configuration management is treated as part of the technical volume because of its close kinship with systems engineering. In a description of the configuration management function proposed to accompany a new enterprise, the customer may want to know the details of how the function will be performed or the customer may only want to know that the proposer employs a disciplined method to assure hardware and software (and organizational—where appropriate) interface compatibility. The more inquisitive customer will want to know the organizational setup of the configuration management function and how it relates to the project management organization. The customer is interested in the supplier's project manager having maximum control over the end-item's configuration. Other things the customer will want to know are: (1) the methods and documentation (specifications, drawing practices, engineering release systems, etc.) that will be used to establish the system requirements and system baseline; (2) the policies and procedures to be used in controlling changes to the baseline; (3) the configuration accounting system, including the method for making and approving configuration changes; (4) the methods to be used in controlling changes to vendor or subcontractor-supplied items; (5) the major milestones for implementation of configuration management; and (6) the plans that will be (or have been) established for conducting and supporting appropriate configuration management and design reviews.

The configuration management function has charge of the all-important systems specifications and interface drawings, so the customer will want to know how often and by what methods these documents will be updated and if the customer will have a "say" in the approval of changes that may affect external interfaces. If Interface Control Documents (ICDs) are to be used, the method of initiation, control, approval, and issuance of these documents will be important. The customer will also want to know if a Configuration Control Board has been or will be established and who the members are or will be by title and function.

Test Planning and Verification. The test planning and verification program is a vital part of any project where a significant amount of new development work is a part of the activity being proposed. An assembly and verification plan, test plan, or development plan should spell out all of the tests to be performed citing their objectives, conditions, and test limits for subsystem tests, system tests, development tests, qualification tests, and acceptance tests to be conducted during the program. The plan includes all or a part of the following, depending on the complexity of the project and the desires of the customer:

1. A description of the organization, policies, methods, and controls to be implemented. Includes general test requirements, test levels, and durations.
2. Descriptions of the verifications to be performed, including prerequisites, constraints, test objectives, and methods.
3. Test item configuration identification and quantities to be tested.
4. A detailed time-correlated sequence of verification operations from component level through subsystems and systems final acceptance and integration.
5. Description, planned usage, and scheduling of the support equipment, facilities, and tooling necessary to execute the verification activity.

The verification plan is usually accompanied by a test and checkout requirements and specifications document that is prepared after the program work is initiated. This document need not be included in the proposal but its existence and content should be pointed out to the customer at the time of proposal submittal as part of the write-up on verification testing.

The document will identify each test requirement, specification, and constraint applicable to the various functional and environmental tests required for qualification and/or acceptance during the buildup, subsystem, and system test activities. Specifications include allowable tolerance for standards or judgment to be used in determining acceptable performance. Test types, levels, and durations are included. Since qualification test levels are generally more stringent than systems acceptance test levels, the qualification test requirements include test level margins and factors of safety.

On completion of verification tests, most customers will want to know that they will receive a detailed test report.

DEMONSTRATING AN UNDERSTANDING
OF THE REQUIREMENTS

When preparing a technical proposal, the question always arises as to how one can best demonstrate an "understanding of the requirements." This can be done in several ways. First, it is important to demonstrate that one is fully knowledgeable about the work activity or work being proposed. Knowledgeability will become evident to the evaluator as he reads through the description of the work and the description of the means of accomplishing the work. In this review, the evaluator will look for evidence that the firm has a complete understanding of the theory of operation, the disciplines needed to accomplish the job, and the facilities and equipment needed to perform the job efficiently and effectively. The proposing company can convey the fact that it has a thorough understanding of the tasks to be performed by comparing these tasks to those that have been performed successfully by the company in the past, describing any differences, improvements, or similarities. An understanding of the total field of effort can be conveyed by mentioning or discussing what others in the field have done or are doing. An awareness of interfaces with other mating hardware, other activities, and other organizations involved in the project should be demonstrated.

Second, the orderly and logical presentation of the overall schedule, and the depth of penetration into the schedule will help to show that there is a full understanding of the scheduling aspects of the job. Typical detailed scheduling activities down to a lower level in the project can be presented in the technical proposal to demonstrate the fact that this planning has been done and that the schedule interactions and interrelationships are understood. Although it is not always necessary to show *all* detailed schedules, those detailed schedules for the key or critical areas of the work should be included.

Thirdly, an understanding of the job can be demonstrated by accurate and realistic estimates of the *resources* required to do the job. Although the cost estimates are covered in the cost volume, the magnitude of and rationale for these estimates will be an indicator of the technical knowledge of the magnitude of the job and the relative importance of its various parts. It is for this reason that a close coordination and team relationship exist between the technical and cost proposal teams. Since the technical person who is going to perform the work will be making the original labor-hour or material estimates, the size and distribution of these estimates reflect the understanding of the technical team.

DESCRIPTION OF CUSTOMER INVOLVEMENT

An important part of the technical proposal is the description of customer involvement in the work and in the review process. This description can be in a separate section of the technical proposal or it can be interspersed within the various technical work descriptions. The customer will want to know when and what type of technical reviews will be held, the types and frequencies of technical reports, and the means of day-to-day communication between technical counterparts within the supplier's organization and the seller's organization. A description of all technical documentation that will be submitted during the performance of the work, as well as formal and informal technical meetings, should be included in the technical proposal.

DISCUSSION OF PROBLEM AREAS

A frank and open discussion of problem areas is an asset rather than a liability to a technical proposal. The technical approach should discuss any problem areas which might be encountered and their related solutions. These problem areas generally can be described in two ways. The first type of problem is comprised of difficulties that will have to be overcome in the performance of the job. Generally, the discussion of such problem areas addresses itself to a definition of the purpose, scope, and objectives of the program; a discussion of the strengths and weaknesses of alternative approaches; and a generalized description of the results that can be expected from the recommended solution. This section provides an opportunity for discussing the solutions that may be proposed by competitors and diplomatically but logically refuting them in advance.

The second type of problem includes those difficult points that would exist if they had not already been solved by the proposing firm. These solved problems represent a competitive advantage. Assertions that these problems have been solved must, however, be supported by factual evidence of prior performance. Showing the means to avoid pitfalls gives a proposer an opportunity to convince the customer that effort will be expended realistically and that technical accomplishment will be measured accurately.

TYPICAL TECHNICAL PROPOSAL OUTLINES

Since every requesting organization has its own desires about proposal outlines, it is difficult to develop a standarized outline. The request for proposal will usually specify a proposal outline. If not, the bidder is free to choose one. For reference purposes only, two typical technical proposal outlines are included as Figures 6.2 and 6.3. Figure 6.2 is a typical technical proposal outline for a development proposal and Figure 6.3 is a typical technical proposal outline for a hardware proposal. Figure 6.4 illustrates the technical proposal steps in an overall typical proposal flow chart.

I Summary
II Introduction
III Proposed program schedule
    Statement of work
    System design
    Hardware configuration
    Optional equipment
    Operational functions—capabilities
    Production
    Reliability—quality control
    Related services
IV Deliverable items and services
    Reports and documentation
    Equipment
    Optional equipment
    Installation, test, checkout
    Training
V Facilities

Figure 6.2. Development Proposal Outline

I Introduction
II Hardware configuration
    Optional or additional equipment
III Deliverable items and services
    Production items
    Spares
    Quality control
    Testing
    Reliability
    Support equipment
    Related services
    Training
IV Facilities

Figure 6.3 Hardware Proposal Outline.

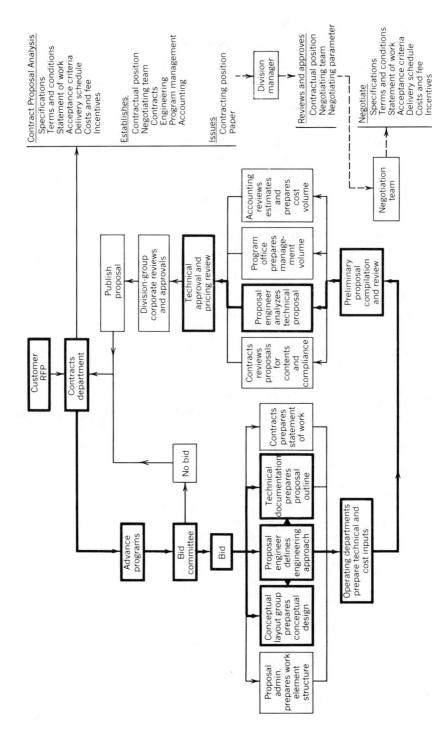

Figure 6.4. Proposal flow chart showing technical proposal activities.

7

THE ORGANIZATION AND MANAGEMENT PROPOSAL

And it shall come about that when the officers have finished speaking
to the people, they shall appoint commanders of armies
at the head of the people.
Deut. 20:9

In the organization and management volume, the evaluator will be searching for the real competence, personality, and character of the proposing company as well as any company or organization that will be supporting it in the work. He or she will be looking for sound, convincing, documented evidence that the organization will perform the work with diligence and dispatch, and that the persons, systems, and structures established for accomplishing the work have a high probability of success. The evidence that will be provided in the organization and management proposal regarding the company's management policies, company organization, project organization, key personnel, plant facilities and equipment, and past experiences and successes is designed to demonstrate the competence, willingness, and capability to manage the job and to keep it on schedule and within cost estimates. This volume of the proposal is essentially a plan of how the company and its supporting contractors will apply organizational resources to carry out the proposed work.

The organization and management proposal addresses itself in detail to the structure of the work and to the company's philosophy of managing the work. This discussion is important because it allows the customer to understand how the organization will support the program. It defines the sources and channels of authority within the organization. It shows how the program manager can use authority and internal alliances to accomplish the program's objectives, and it reveals the rationale behind a company's performance of such management functions as planning, organizing, staffing, directing, and controlling.

THE WORK ELEMENT STRUCTURE
(WORK BREAKDOWN STRUCTURE)

The work element structure (otherwise known as the work breakdown structure), whether specified by the customer or developed by the proposer, is an indispensable feature of a proposal for complex work activities or work outputs. Although it is usually described in the organization and management volume of the proposal, the other two volumes (technical and cost) share the use of the work element structure to interrelate the technical, management, and cost aspects of the work.

The work element structure is correlated with the proposed contract work statement and serves as a framework for managing the work and for collecting, accumulating, organizing, and computing direct and directly related costs. It is also used for reporting technical progress and related resources throughout the lifetime of the work. There is considerable advantage in using the work element structure and its accompanying task descriptions as the basis for organizing, scheduling, reporting, tracking, and managing the project. Hence, it is important to devote considerable attention to this phase of the overall proposal preparation process. A work element structure is developed by dividing the work into its major elements, then breaking these elements into subelements, and subsubelements, and so on.

The purpose of developing the work element structure is fivefold:

1. To provide assurance that all required work elements are included in the work output.
2. To reduce the possibility of overlap, duplication, or redundancy of tasks.
3. To furnish a convenient hierarchical structure for the accumulation of resource estimates.
4. To give greater overall visibility as well as depth of penetration into the makeup of the work.
5. To provide a lower level breakout of smaller tasks that are easy to identify, man-load, schedule, and estimate.

Hierarchical Relationship of a Work Element Structure

A typical work element structure is shown on Figure 7.1. Note that the relationship resembles a hierarchy where each activity has a higher activity, parallel activities, and lower activities. A basic principle of work

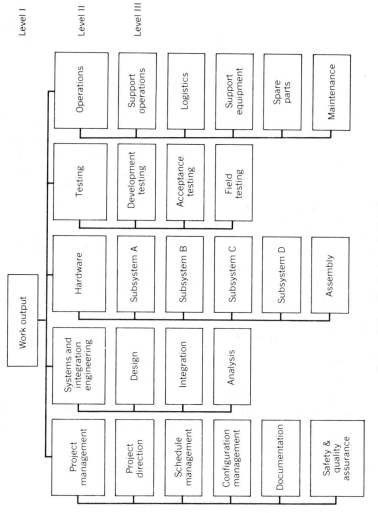

Figure 7.1. Typical work element structure.

element structures is that each work element is made up of a sum of the elements below it. No work element that has lower elements exceeds the sum of those lower elements. The bottommost elements are described in detail at their own level and sum to higher levels. Many numbering systems are feasible and workable. The numbering system shown is one that has proven workable in a wide variety of situations. The "level" is usually equal to the number of digits in the work element block. For example, the block numbered 1.1.3.2 is in level four because it contains four digits.

Functional Elements Described

When subdividing a work activity or work output into its elements, the major subdivisions can be either functional or physical elements. The second level in a work element structure usually consists of a combination of functional and physical elements if a product or project is being proposed. For a process or service, all second-level activities could be functional. Functional elements of a production or project activity can include activities such as planning, project management, systems engineering and integration, testing, logistics, and operations. A process or service can include any of hundreds of functional elements. Typical examples of the widely dispersed functional elements that can be found in a work element structure for a service are: advising, assembling, binding, cleaning, fabricating, inspecting, packaging, painting, programming, projecting, receiving, testing, and welding.

Physical Elements Described

The physical elements of a work output are the physical structures, hardware, products or end items that are supplied to the customer. Starting at level two in the work element structure, the physical elements can be broken down or subdivided into systems, subsystems, components, and parts.

Treatment of Recurring and Nonrecurring Activities

Most work consists of both nonrecurring activities: "one-of-a-kind" activities needed to produce an item or to provide a service; and recurring or repetitive activities that must be performed to provide more than one output unit. The resources requirements (man-hours and materials) necessary to perform these nonrecurring and recurring activities reflect themselves in nonrecurring and recurring costs.

Separation of nonrecurring and recurring activities can be done in two ways through the use of the work element structure concept. First, the two types of activities can be identified, separated, and accounted for within each work element. Resources for each task block would, then, include three sets of proposal estimates: (1) nonrecurring, (2) recurring, and (3) totals. The second convenient method of separation is to develop identical work element structures for both nonrecurring and recurring activities. A third structure which sums the two into a total can also use the same basic work element structure. If there are elements unique to each activity category, they can be added to the appropriate work element structure.

Work Element Structure Interrelationships

Considerable flexibility exists in the placement of both physical and functional elements in the work element structure. Because of this, and because it is necessary to define clearly where one element leaves off and the other takes over, a detailed definition of each work activity block in the form of a work element structure dictionary must be prepared and included in either the organization and management volume or the technical volume. The dictionary describes exactly what is included in each work element and what is excluded; it defines where the interface is located between two work elements, and it defines where the assembly effort is located to assemble or install two interfacing units.

A good work element structure dictionary will prevent overlaps, duplications, and omissions because detailed thought has been given to the interfaces and content of each work activity.

Skill Matrix in a Work Element Structure.   When a work element structure is being constructed, it should be kept in mind that each work element will be performed by a person or group of people using one or more skills. There are two important facets of the labor for each work element: skill category and skill level. Skill categories vary widely and depend on the type of work being proposed. For a residential construction project, for example, typical skill categories would be bricklayer, building laborer, carpenter, electrician, painter, plasterer, or plumber. Other typical construction skill categories are structural steelworker, cement finisher, glazier, roofer, sheet metal worker, pipefitter, excavation equipment operator, and general construction laborer. Professional skill categories such as lawyers, doctors, financial officers, administrators, project managers, engineers, printers, writers, and so forth are called on to do a wide variety of direct-labor activities.

Skill level, on the other hand, depicts the experience or salary level of an individual working within a given skill category. The skilled trades are often subdivided into skill levels and given names that depict their skill level; for example, carpenters are broken down into master carpenters, carpenters, journeymen carpenters, apprentice carpenters, and carpenter's helpers. Because skill categories and skill levels are designated for performing work within each work element, it is not necessary to establish separate work elements for performance of each skill. A work element structure for home construction would not have an element designated carpentry because carpentry is a skill needed to perform one or more of the work elements (i.e. roof construction, wall construction, etc.). The skill *mix* is the proportion of each of several skill categories or skill levels that will be employed in performing the work.

Organizational Relationships to a Work Element Structure.   Frequently all or part of a work element structure will have a direct counterpart in the performing organization. This interrelationship between the work element structure and the organization of the company or project should be described in the organization and management volume of the proposal. In the proposal preparation process, early assignment of work elements to those who are going to be responsible for performing the work will motivate them to do a better job of proposing the work and will provide greater assurance of completion of the work within performance, schedule, and cost constraints because the functional organizations have set their own goals. Job performance and accounting for work accomplished versus funds spent can also be accomplished more easily after the contract is awarded if an organizational element is held responsible for estimating the resources required for a specific work element in the work element structure.

Treatment of Work Elements

Work elements are chosen for a work activity in a way that will make it easy to assign the prime responsibility for a work element to a segment of the organization that will do the work. The work elements conceivably could be identical to the schedule elements. This poses the difficulty that a work element for, say, procurement, would have very little interaction with other parts of the proposed work despite the fact that the procurement function is there to support multiple functions (more than one schedule element).

The interplay among the three factors of schedule, cost, and performance is paralleled by the interplay among schedule elements, cost elements, and work elements. This interplay among the three program factors can be maximized by what is known as a "matrix" of organization and management responsibilities. The choice of different schedule elements, cost elements, and work elements creates a matrix that forces equal attention on all three of the important program factors (schedule, cost, and performance). In a large high-technology project, it is highly desirable to define the elements of schedule, cost, and work *separately* and to have them interact with each other in the form of a three-dimensional matrix.

A work element list that has proven successful for a large number of projects is the following:

Project management

Systems engineering and integration

Subsystems development or acquisition

Assembly and verification

Operations support and logistics

Notice that these work elements can be aligned easily with an organizational structure. For example, the project management activity can be accomplished by the project management organization, the systems engineering and integration can be performed by the systems engineering and integration organization, the subsystems development or acquisition can be performed by the subsystems development or procurement organizations, and so forth. Assignment of work elements to more than one organization is possible but is not good practice unless a lead organization is chosen. Choice of a lead organization for performing a work element provides greater management control of schedule, cost, and performance factors for that work element. Clearly explaining these interrelationships in the organization and management volume of the proposal will do much to lend credibility to the proposal.

THE PROJECT PLAN

The project plan should be defined in detail within the organization and management volume of the proposal. This plan discusses the means available (or to be created) within a company to achieve the objectives of the program. In general, the project plan describes the organizational base from which the program personnel and other resources will be drawn, the schedule to which they will be required to perform, and the manner in which funds and effort will be controlled to ensure accomplishment of program goals. The overall project plan is based on the technical schedule developed as part of the technical proposal. To win contracts (or even get a chance to bid) in today's competitive market, these descriptions must be based on existing capability—the inherent strength of the company. Organizational arrangements may be described under the name of several management philosophies, such as matrix management, project management, or divisional management. The inherent capabilities of the company, regardless of how they are described, must include the ability to create and staff the program organization.

In the organization and management proposal, established policies and procedures which constitute the proposer's means of direction should be summarized. These means should be condensed in the proposal to illustrate the way in which the management plan will be implemented. Items such as the work element structure, master schedule, work authorization, production orders, sales orders, purchase orders, and indeed all of the directive means which will be called upon by the program manager, should be discussed and their application defined.

The organization and management proposal should address itself to the resources available to control effort within the organization. Effort is described in terms of cost, time, personnel, and technical achievement. Control discussions are more fruitful if they concentrate on providing the customer with hard facts which prove that the proposer can respond to requirements and to newly discovered needs of the program, and that controls ensure traceability of decision making. The customer needs assurance that the controls provide a means of identifying expenditure, effort, and other outputs of the plan. The planning discussion for the project should include the means of using information generated by these controls. These include detailed descriptions of reports, liaison, and interchange which will be accomplished for and with the customer. These measures naturally must include, at a minimum, all those reports and liaison efforts described in the request for proposal. Frequently, one can create a very favorable impression on the customer by describing additional means which will be used to inform the customer and to ensure that his or her influence can be brought to bear as the program develops.

Financial, technical, and performance measurement reports normally directed to the project manager(s), line management, and customer's program office are, of course, vitally important to effective management of the program. As such, the plan for submitting them internally to the bidder's management and to the customer should be shown. This feedback of information provides data upon which decisions are made concerning the program.

It must be kept in mind that the objectives of employing a planning, scheduling, and progress tracking or performance measurement method during work performance are *to achieve optimum skill and equipment use throughout the duration of the work, to level off peaks and valleys in workload, and to develop an optimum interface with other ongoing or proposed work*. Optimum skill and equipment use will be a deciding factor in making a proposal cost-competitive and will provide evidence to evaluators that forethought has been given to achieving efficiency in performing the work. Leveling off peaks and valleys in workload will prevent the inefficiencies that could occur through the requirement for rapid fluctuations in the work force. Interphasing of the proposed work with other ongoing or proposed work will permit shared use of equipment, facilities, and personnel between work activities, minimize cross-project interferences, and facilitate contingency planning based on the capture potential of the proposed work and of other pending or uncertain acquisitions.

Visibility

Planning, scheduling, and progress tracking or performance measurement must be proposed in a way that maximum visibility is provided to decision makers in the performing organization during planning and performance of the work. Visibility can be provided in one or more ways as long as the material is presented in a manner that will provide "at-a-glance" status. An overly complex format will only confuse the observer. PERT (Program Evaluation and Review Technique) diagrams that have thousands of events and activities interrelated by a seemingly endless web of intricate interconnecting lines, although they may be effectively used for internal planning, do not impress customers or proposal evaluators. They are of little value in the proposal because they require detailed study to bring about an understanding of project planning and progress even though they may be of value to planners. The most understandable and quickly observed format is the time-oriented bar chart that shows both events and activities on a calendar background. (See Chapter 6.) For simple scheduling situations, a listing of planned and actual dates is sufficient.

With the advent of video graphics display systems, both monochrome and color, there are many ways that planning and scheduling status can be provided to managers and supervisors as well as to selected individuals involved in the planning and scheduling process. These systems are rapidly supplementing and occasionally replacing the more traditional reporting and display media (hard copy, charts, display panels, slides, and projected transparencies). The types of systems to be used for internal and external management visibility should be described in the organization and management proposal. The characteristic of visibility should also be used as appropriate to provide the *customer* with planning, scheduling, and progress information

Those who have been in the business world very long have undoubtedly observed that some organizations establish planning, scheduling, and performance measurement or progress tracking systems but fail to keep these updated properly. These systems are sometimes elaborate and expensive, and it may be their sophistication that prevents their effective updating and use. Ease and speed of update are second only to visibility as important characteristics of planning methods or systems. A proposal should state *how frequently* planning and progress status information will be updated and provide some rationale for that update frequency. Frequency of update and the time required to update the information should be functions of the time period required to correct deficiencies after they are observed.

Competency in rescheduling work to correct for deviations from a plan is dependent upon the scheduling system characteristic that visibly compares actual progress or status with planned progress or status. Whether or not schedule status information will actually be reported periodically to the customer, the customer must be aware that the proposer has a means of tracking actual versus planned work and will constantly take actions to assure that the total job will be completed on time and within the resources proposed.

THE COMPANY'S ORGANIZATION

The potential customer will want to know what specific organizational arrangements have been made to perform the work within the company, what capabilities the company possesses, which of these capabilities will be committed to the proposed work, and how deeply the company's management is committed to a successful outcome. These subjects are normally addressed in the section on the company's organization and capabilities: specifically those related to the proposed work.

Relationship to Corporate Headquarters and Resources

Frequently, a source selection is influenced significantly by the reputation of the proposer in the appropriate field of work. If this reputation is not well known, a considerable amount of detailed information may be required in the organization and management proposal. This information should include personnel, facilities, and equipment that are available at the corporate level to support the project and to assure that overall management and backup capability is available for the project organization. It should provide a discussion on how the project is expected to draw on corporate capabilities during day-to-day operation or during emergencies, and what degree of management and control will be exercised over the project by corporate entities.

An organizational chart of the corporation should be provided and a description of how the proposed project relates to the corporate organization should be included. If there are one or more corporate division levels between the parent company and the project, these should be shown to clarify the position of the work within the overall company framework. Assurance of periodic personal attention by company officials to the work's performance, quality, and timeliness, should be provided.

Interdivisional Relationships

If parts of the work are proposed to be performed by other divisions within a company, the relationships of the project organization to these divisions should be described and the means of managing and transferring the work should be detailed. Information should be provided on the capabilities, organization, location, and resources available to these other company divisions. The method of approval, funding, and transmitting interdivisional work authorizations should be worked out in advance of the proposal submittal date, but need not be included in the proposal unless specifically required or requested in the request for proposal.

Other Internal Company or Division Support

Assuming that the work is to be accomplished in a matrix-type organization, company and division elements other than those in a direct line project organization will be involved in supporting the proposed work. The organization and management proposal should show how the project or work manager is to direct, control, or manage the work of those elements which may be outside of his or her direct supervisory control. The degree of control that the project manager has over these company support elements in the areas of resources, schedules, and performance should be stated, and the method of control of these internal elements should be clearly established.

Relationship with Associates and Subcontractor(s)

If associate contractors or major subcontractors are to be involved in the performance of the proposed work, the prime contractor's relationship with these associate contractors and subcontractors should be addressed in brief. Existing or past working relationships, geographical proximity, and established lines of communication should be pointed out to show that a smooth and cooperative relationship will exist during the performance of the job. Since a complex subcontractor and sub-subcontractor arrangement can cause schedule delays and cost increases if not properly managed, these arrangements should be as simple and straightforward as possible. Since subcontractor responsiveness is a key factor in staying on schedule and within costs, evidence of past or current ties that improve or enhance teamwork between the prime contractor and subcontractor should be provided.

Indirect, General and Administrative, and Fee Rates

The company organization portion of the organization and management proposal is a convenient place to explain the company's policy on indirect, general and administrative costs, and fee or profit; and to describe the rationale and basis for establishment of factors, percentages, or amounts that will later be used in pricing the proposal in the cost volume. (Some companies place this rationale and discussion in the cost volume, but it is discussed here because it is conveniently tied to the company's organization, policies, and procedures.) As discussed later in this chapter, indirect costs are of significant concern both to the performer and to the customer because they are sometimes difficult to control. Since indirect costs are there only to support the direct activities of the company that represent marketable work activities or work outputs, any sudden reduction in the workload will cause a corresponding jump in indirect percentages or rates unless management action is taken to reduce or control the indirect costs. Continual monitoring of overhead expenditures within each department, division, overhead center, or profit center is necessary to keep overhead costs in line. This process should be described to the customer's satisfaction in the organization and management proposal.

An important feature of a sound indirect cost management system should be the methods whereby the disciplines for control are established with the divisional or departmental manager. The divisional or departmental manager should be held responsible for coordinating requirements with other operating activities and setting the original indirect cost targets of the department. Once a departmental budget is agreed upon, he or she then has the continuing responsibility for justifying to top management variances of actual performance from budget objectives. This is a day-to-day responsibility and one that requires continuous interfacing with company operational elements. Variances from budget are not uncommon, but should not automatically be eliminated by routinely adjusted budgets. Variances should be thoroughly examined and investigated for cause before embarking on target revisions. If the cause can be corrected by improvement in the department operations, top management should enforce austerity on the operation causing the problem to bring the indirect costs back in line. If the cause of variance is due to major business volume fluctuations, a management directed, overall revision in indirect cost budgets may be necessary.

The purpose of indirect cost variance analysis is to disclose the causes of indirect cost overruns so that corrective action can be taken. To direct that action to the source of the problem, it is necessary that each plant-wide variance be traced to the specific cost centers where the variance originated.

The goal of department heads and supervisors at lower tiers of the organization is to minimize unfavorable variances in their respective control areas. Hence, a line supervisor should receive performance reports on labor and other significant costs at least weekly; daily labor reports might be justified in some instances. Prompt information will enable the supervisor to detect the occurrence of a variance early enough to correct a cost overrun that otherwise might become irreversible. Generally, company management will receive overhead reports monthly. Any longer period would not permit timely identification of problem areas, while a shorter period could be considered impracticable.

In normal circumstances, there should be no significant business volume variance from predictions over a short period, such as the budget year. Most companies can project production volume realistically from their backlogs and from statistical patterns on such new business as spare parts and components. Anticipated volume on new proposals for major programs or projects cannot be forecasted accurately, but the impact of those potential work activities is often not severe during the first year regardless of a company's success or lack of success in winning them.

The principal impact on the projected volume for a short period comes from the sudden *decrease* in an ongoing major work activity through partial or total cancellation or deferment of delivery. When that action occurs, all projected costs, whether classified variable or fixed, should be reevaluated. For example, the designation of some administrative staff or supervisory personnel as fixed costs at the previously projected volume range may have been a valid decision for the flexible budget within that range. However, no fixed costs, and especially no manpower costs classified as "fixed," should be immune from cost reduction procedures when there is a substantial drop in volume.

In summary, the company should establish and maintain an indirect cost control procedure and should describe this procedure in the organization and management proposal volume when required by the request for proposal or when prior marketing feedback has indicated that this area may be of significant concern to the customer. The proposal discussion should include but not be limited to the following:

First, top management must recognize the need for controlling and accurately estimating indirect costs in order to maintain a competitive posture. Without this top management support, the indirect cost estimate becomes meaningless.

Next, the indirect cost control and estimating function must be placed high enough in the company organization to permit effective dealing with all levels of management. It should be a part of the finance or comptroller organization, assigned sufficient authority to request and receive account accumulations compatible with an effective program, and to make reductions in indirect budgets where appropriate.

Company accounts should be clearly segregated to categories that will easily identify the operating responsibility with respect to expenditures. Budgets should be established and then negotiated. Revisions should be made as changes in volume or overall business trends dictate. Revisions should not be made merely for cosmetic reasons. Each negotiation of the indirect cost budget should seek improvement in criteria and techniques for establishing this important element of the company's performance.

General and administrative costs should be treated in a like manner if requested by the request for proposal or if advance marketing information has shown that undue customer concern exists in the area of general and administrative expenses.

Exposure of both indirect cost and general and administrative costs is appropriate mainly for cost-reimbursable type negotiated procurements. Many firm fixed price bid situations will not require exposure of these factors in a proposal, indeed, it may be detrimental to the company's competitive posture to do so.

In either the organization and management volume, the cost volume, or the letter of transmittal, it may be appropriate to provide rationale and supporting data for the fee structure to be used in performance of the work. In certain situations the fee structure is proposed by the customer in the request for proposal rather than by the proposer. In any case, the fee negotiations may make up a considerable part of the contract negotiations. Therefore, fee rationale must be carefully generated and made available *within* the company and exposed in the proposal only to the degree that would be necessary to support a strong company front and position relative to the establishment of a fair and equitable profit or fee for performing the work.

THE PROJECT ORGANIZATION

In proposals for smaller work activities, there may be no need to establish a project manager, project coordinator, or project office. Generally, however, even in small jobs there is one person designated in the company to see that the work is accomplished on time and within costs. This person may manage more than one job at a time, or may be exclusively assigned to the proposed work. The customer usually wants to know the identity, capability, authority, and responsibility of this person and how he or she will communicate and work with the customer in accomplishing the job. In larger projects, where much hinges on the abilities and authority of the project manager, much more information should be provided about the project manager and about other key project and company team members. The capabilities of key personnel will be revealed in a résumé or biography.

Inherent in the project organization description should be the relationship of the project manager with the company management and the relationship of the project office elements with the company divisional or line elements that support the project. Most customers want to know that the project manager has direct access to company management and company resources. In other words, the project must be closely knit to the company structure in a way that company resources can be activated or put to work on the project on short notice to solve unexpected problems in management, schedules, personnel, or other resource commitments. The customer would also like to know that the company line organizations that are supporting the project, although not directly responsible to the project manager in a supervisory sense, will be cooperative and responsive to the needs of the project. Particularly important functions in any project organization will be the ones that report on and control technical changes, the ones that control costs, and the ones that review, revise, and establish schedules. The project organization, then, must have a good mix of business, financial, and technical skills. The proposal should show how these skills are interrelated and integrated to provide a cohesive, efficient, and effective management structure.

The project organization discussion should emphasize responsiveness, timely reporting, and effective communications and interfaces with the customer's organization. If there are counterparts in the proposer's and customer's organizations in specific disciplines, the method and degree of communication between these counterparts should be addressed. If extensive documentation is to be provided in the proposed contract, those functions in the project office that are responsible for preparing or coordinating each item of documentation should be singled out to provide the supplier as well as the customer the assurance that all vital areas of documentation are covered. The project organization portion of the organization and management proposal volume is also the place to discuss any special management, organizational, or programmatic ground rules, assumptions, or guidelines that will be followed during the management of the project. The overall philosophy of project management, as well as specific policies, should be spelled out and clarified here.

Specific areas that affect product quality, reliability, or cost-effectiveness should be discussed in the project organization section. Methods of inspection, quality assurance, reliability assurance, and other forms of work monitoring should be described as well as means and methods that the project office will use in taking corrective actions to overcome deficiencies. If the company uses techniques such as quality circles or other special interdisciplinary teams to assure high productivity and innovative solutions to problems, the relationship and input of these teams to the project organization should be described. Other checks and balances, whether they be administrative policies, organizational arrangements, or special project procedures should be discussed along with their anticipated and demonstrated benefits. Some of the principal functions of the project organization which should be described in the organization and management volume are listed below:

Project Direction

The project direction function of the project management organization integrates all of the other project management functions while providing day-to-day management direction of the project. Project direction is usually accomplished by a project or program director or manager and is sometimes assisted by one or more deputy or assistant project managers or directors. In the project direction discussion of the organization and management volume, the proposer should describe how the project or program manager or director will integrate the work of the personnel and organizations who are supporting the project. This should include how task assignments are made, how internal review and tracking of progress is accomplished, how priorities are set, how decisions and conflicts are settled, and how appropriate corrective measures are determined and assigned to someone for action. The participation of the project manager and the project staff in design reviews, management reviews, and project staff meetings should be described; and the frequency, format, attendance, and follow-up procedures for these meetings should be explained. If formal task assignments are made, the method of making these assignments as well as the means of tracking their progress and completion dates should be outlined. This discussion should include the procedure for establishing required completion dates and for the conduct of periodic reviews to assure that progress is on schedule for completion on these dates. The methods to be used by the project manager in reviewing and checking on progress and status of the work activity should be shown. If management control centers with schedule or network displays are to be used, these should be described along with the procedure for their periodic updating. The method used for setting priorities as the work progresses should be established and described, and the responsibilities for changing these priorities should be spelled out.

The discussion on project direction should explain how the project manager gets inputs relative to deficiencies and problems, who on the staff is available to help resolve these problems, and how corrective action is assigned to resolve them. The customer will want to be assured in this discussion that all anomalies will be addressed and corrected at the earliest possible time and in the most efficient manner. In this and the following sections on program office functions, any procedures, forms, systems, or policies that are to be used should be described to show what tools the project manager and project staff will have available to aid in making decisions among alternate paths and to assist the project manager's judgment in settling disputes and conflicts.

Project and Cost Control Management

Project and cost control management refers to those actvities which assure the integrated planning, scheduling, budgeting, work authorization, and cost accumulation of all tasks performed during the project. It provides project performance planning, including preparation and maintenance of a project management plan, project schedules, resource status reports, and cost forecasting. Also included are the establishment of project performance criteria, the control of change parameters, and the analysis and summary of measured data. Continuous monitoring of all functional management disciplines is provided for central direction and control of the overall project, including timely resolution of problem areas to ensure that established schedules are met. Establishment, operation, and maintenance of a management information system is a portion of this element. Other task elements include interface with the customer, contract administration, and proposal administration. The following are specific areas included under project and cost control management:

1. Updating of the work element structure(s) dictionary.
2. Preparation and maintenance of a cost allocation, tracking, and reporting system.
3. Monitoring of costs versus budget allocations.
4. Identification of technical performance measurement parameters and values, and technical achievement planning including preparation, submittal, and maintenance of technical performance reports.
5. Maintenance of surveillance of cost accounts in order to assure reasonably accurate accrued charges.

Information Management (Documents and Data)

Information management refers to the overall management process and activities required to ensure proper control of documents and data. Services are included to identify, control, and monitor the preparation of and maintain status of the documentation for the project. Establishment, implementation, and maintenance of a data management plan and procedures are included. Monitoring and preparation of documentation and data required by task orders, agreements, or directives are included, as is the establishment, operation, and maintenance of a project level information file.

Procurement Management

Procurement management includes management and technical control of interdivisional work, subcontractors, and vendors. Tasks included are the providing of contractual direction to other divisions within a company, subcontractors, and vendors; authorizing subcontractor tooling and equipment; analyzing subcontractor reports; conducting subcontractor and vendor reviews; and on-site coordination and evaluation of procurements. Also included are the maintenance of records and submission of any required reports relating to the geographic dispersion of minority and small business participation in procurements.

Logistics Management

Logistics management includes:

Spares management
Inventory management

Repair and overhaul policy
Propellants, gases, and fluids forecasts and usage reports
Warehousing and storage policy
Transportation analysis and planning

The logistics management activity provides the effort required to implement, operate, and maintain a logistics management activity for support of the project. Included are the preparation and maintenance of:

1. *Systems support and logistics plans*
2. *Recommended spare parts lists*
3. *Maintenance analyses*
4. *Analysis of support requirements*

Safety Management

Safety management consists of the definition, direction, and monitoring of a safety program that will assure the development of a safe product, prevent accidents and incidents, and minimize hazards to personnel and property. Safety is an integral part of design, development, manufacturing, testing, handling, storage, and operation. Safety management is accomplished through training, analysis, safety program assessments, and preparation of a project hazard summary; development and implementation of procedures, controls, reviews, audits, safety analyses, and safety design; and a safety plan which covers the safety program and its implementation.

Other Management Areas

Other management areas that are sometimes assigned at the project organization level are configuration management, quality and reliability assurance, and the "ilities" (maintainability, producibility, etc.). (See Chapter 6 for a discussion of these areas. Since these areas are considered to fall in the category of engineering management rather than project management, they are included in this book under the technical proposal volume.)

PROJECT LABOR RATES AND FACTORS

Either the organization and management proposal volume or the cost proposal volume should include a section providing backup and rationale for the current and projected labor rates used in the proposal for all skill categories and for skill levels within these categories. This information will support the pricing figures used in the cost volume. Any factors to be used for escalation or inflation should be described along with their method of application. If different overhead pools are applied to different categories of labor rates, these should be described. Labor rates for overtime, percentages of overtime, labor rate variations for different work shifts, and other labor rate factors should be backed up by suitable rationale, historical data or statistical analysis. Methods of keeping the labor rates and factors current throughout the job performance should also be described, along with any provisions that can or will be implemented for the control of these amounts.

THE MAKE OR BUY PLAN

The "make-or-buy" plan is a description of what parts of the work will be done within the company and what parts will be done by organizations other than the proposing company. The most convenient outline for the make or buy plan is the work element structure outline. Each activity or product in the work element structure can be assigned to a given "in-house" or "out-of-house" organization. When out-of-house organizations are used, the customer may want to know not only who these organizations are but how much of the work will be given to them. Use of a large subcontract for a major portion of the work will arouse interest in the customer as to the subcontractor's company and project organizations and key personnel. In some procurements a bidder may be asked to supply as much information on the subcontractor's company organization, project organization, key personnel, and management philosophy as is provided for the proposing company.

The make or buy plan will give the customer an overall view of the mixture of planned in-house and out-of-house effort. Available with this make or buy plan should be a description of the rationale or reasons for the identification of each work activity or output as either a "make" item or a "buy" item, and the reasons for selecting a specific subcontractor if it is a "buy" item. Although this information may or may not be required for submittal to the customer, it is essential that it be in company records to satisfy management and to provide an information base for make or buy decisions on subsequent proposals. As mentioned in Chapter 2, the marketing decisions and bid/no bid decision may have been made based on a specific make or buy analysis. The results of this earlier analysis should be kept available during the proposal preparation, negotiation, and initial contract period to help substantiate earlier decisions and to serve as a basis for making changes in the make or buy structure if it becomes necessary to do so.

KEY PERSONNEL AND RÉSUMÉS

Key personnel résumés are often not given the attention they deserve in the proposal preparation process. As pointed out in Chapter 10, source evaluation boards usually assign a significant weight to the education, experience, and "track record" of key personnel. The tendency of most proposal preparation teams is to draw its key personnel résumés from a supply of standard résumés at the last minute and include these résumés in the proposal with little or no modification. It is a serious strategic mistake to fail to interview the person in question to make sure that the résumé is up to date, that it carries with it *all* experience applicable to the proposed work, and that it has been purged of irrelevant or inapplicable information. The important areas to emphasize in this careful and deliberate rework and tailoring of key personnel résumés are discussed in the following paragraphs.

Education

The educational level of key personnel is often a scored criteria for high technology, multidisciplinary, or complex work activities or work outputs. Merely listing the degree type and title, a common practice with even high level engineering and scientific personnel, is not always enough to convey educational background. A paragraph that provides information on the academic *level* of achievement; the specific areas of study included; and the subject matter of any special theses, dissertations, papers, or publications that were a part of the educational process will enhance the proposal reader's in-depth knowledge of the individual's educational accomplishments. With advancing technology, the importance of continuing education and updating knowledge within a field has increased markedly. Accomplishments in post-baccalaureate areas should be listed in terms of subject, depth, and achievement level. Other forms of recognition by the academic community such as honorary degrees or teaching fellowships should also be included.

Experience Categories

Proposal evaluators usually divide experience into at least two categories: specialized experience and general experience. In evaluating an individual proposed for a key position in a major proposed contract or subcontract, they look not only at the *length* of specialized and generalized experience but the *depth* of this experience in areas similar or identical to the proposed work. Depth of experience can only be adequately conveyed by a good detailed description of the duties, responsibilities, and activities of the individual in previous positions. Specialized experience is either identical to or very closely related to that required for the proposed work. General experience is experience within the same field, discipline, or area of endeavor as the proposed work. Specialized experience rates highly with evaluators and is a significant factor in the selection of key scientific or engineering personnel. In the case of key management personnel, general management experience is often more important than experience in managing the specific work activity being proposed. A broad, rather than restricted, background is looked for in the résumés of the project managers and other key managers. Varied work experiences such as a term of employment with major competitors, the customer or the "customer's customer" are usually regarded as important by the teams that evaluate organization and management proposals.

In describing specialized or generalized experience, it is desirable to state or quote specific evidence of the *quality* of the work that was produced during the tenure of employment. This can be done by citing specific achievement of goals at or before their required dates, cost reductions, innovative accomplishments, and special recognition by the company or the customer for specific outstanding work accomplishments.

Awards, Honors, and Other Outside Activities

Awards, honors, and recognition by external organizations can add a convincing climax to a well-written résumé that matches the person to a specific job. Since the proposing company rather than the individual is writing the proposal, there is no need to be overly modest when quoting actual results of outstanding individual performance. This information should be accompanied by evidence of continued efforts toward professional education and advancement.

Skill Mix Among Key Personnel

Not only should each résumé be updated and emphasis provided to adapt it to the specific task or tasks at hand, but the *mix* of skills and experience provided by all of the key personnel collectively should be a subject of discussion and positive reinforcement within the organization and management proposal. For example, key personnel in a multidisciplinary scientific project should not all have chemical engineering backgrounds. Evaluators will look closely at this skill mix of key personnel to be sure it closely matches the discipline mix of the work activity or work output itself.

Staffing

The staffing section of the organization and management proposal should be used to correlate the organization block with the functions of each position. The functions, as described in the position description, and the capabilities of the person tentatively assigned to this position should be clearly related. In most instances, four to eight people constitute the key individuals. Discussions of specific individuals should normally be limited to those key people. Their staffs can then be described in more general terms.

PLANT FACILITIES AND EQUIPMENT

Another area of company capability too often taken for granted or described in an offhand manner in small or major proposals alike is the description of the company's facilities, testing and manufacturing equipment, tools, fixtures, utilities, and other capital assets. Here too, is a place where some updating, editing, and selectivity in presentation will be fruitful. It should be recognized that the customer/evaluator is principally interested in how well the job will be done, not how many facilities the proposing company has to perform all of its jobs. Highlighting the characteristics that make facilities specifically useful and attractive for performing the job at hand will economize on presentation space and present a more convincing argument that one indeed has and will fruitfully use the facilities, equipment, and other real assets required to do the job.

The customer is normally fully aware that a bidder *may not* have in existence all of the facilities necessary to perform the job. When this is the case, it should be stated frankly. Then the steps should be outlined that will be taken to obtain the facilities. In this way a seeming disadvantage may be turned into a positive advantage by demonstrating how well management solves its problems.

Specialized Equipment and Facilities

As in the case of the experience of key personnel, equipment can be placed into two categories. For equipment, these categories are specialized equipment and facilities and general purpose equipment and facilities. Specialized equipment is that which is directly and specifically applicable to performing the job. This equipment could have been designed and built or acquired for a previous job, or it may have been developed specifically for the proposed work as an aid to enhancing a competitive posture. Specialized equipment includes special tooling; special electrical, electronic, or mechanical test equipment; special manufacturing equipment; or special microprocessors or computers. Since this type of equipment is itself expensive and time consuming to design, build, test, and operate, on-hand availability of the equipment at the beginning of the contract activity could provide a significant competitive advantage.

General Purpose Equipment and Facilities

General test, manufacturing, tooling, or inspection equipment and facilities need not be described in detail in the proposal but can be included in a referenced document. Particular general purpose equipment or facilities that will be used on the job can, however, be included in the organization and management proposal. The customer should be provided with the knowledge, however, that a proposing company is fully equipped not only to do the job but to take on almost any unforeseen emergency that would keep the job from getting done in a timely and cost-effective way. This discussion should include the policy on providing backup equipment to be used in the event of primary equipment failure. If one does not have adequate facilities and equipment in-house to meet unforeseen circumstances, evidence should be provided to the customer that a subcontractor or vendor is readily available who can absorb negative slack caused by unforeseen problems. Methods of updating and maintaining equipment capabilities should also be described and any planned equipment or facility modifications, acquisitions, or improvements should be disclosed.

Compatibility of Equipment with Personnel Skills

The customer must be convinced that the proposer not only has the proper specialized and general purpose equipment and facilities to do the job, but that he or she has skilled personnel to operate and maintain the machines, test equipment, computers, and related facilities. These skills must be continually updated and modified as new, more advanced equipment becomes available. The best evidence that can provided here is the tabulation of the number of skilled operators and maintenance personnel available for the items scheduled for use in the project, and an indication how and on what schedule these persons will be applied to the job. The first part is provided in the organization and management proposal, and the second part is included in the cost proposal (covered in Chapter 8).

High Technology, Advanced Equipment

The use of high technology, advanced equipment may have played heavily in the marketing plan and decision to bid. If it did, the organization and management proposal should provide the company's rationale for using this high technology equipment and should give a commitment to keep this equipment well maintained and continually updated to conform to the latest state-of-the-art.

COMPANY PAST EXPERIENCE AND SUCCESSES

The organization and management proposal should do a thorough job of describing a company's past experiences and successes in (1) identical work (if any), (2) similar work, and (3) related work. In addition it should give as much information as possible on the record of performing quality jobs within cost targets and on schedule. An overall company management and financial report, condensed for the specific proposal, is a valuable constituent of the organization and management proposal. Figure 7.2 is an outline that can be used as a checklist for company data that may be desirable or requested to be included in the proposal. Needless to say, the disclosure need not be as extensive as that implied in Figure 7.2 unless RFP requirements so dictate.

The most convincing evidence that can be provided about a company's ability to do a good job of management is an actual cost/performance/ schedule track record on a similar job. This type of documented evidence, accompanied by a letter of commendation or letter of recommendation from the previous customer can be an essential ingredient in a winning proposal. Further, listings of the contracts held over the past several years, names of key personnel dealt with in the customers' organizations (for reference purposes), and a narrative evaluation of each contract's success will help the evaluator recognize competence and broad-based experience.

METHODS OF ACHIEVING EFFICIENCY, ECONOMY, AND EFFECTIVENESS

It is in the organization and management portion of the proposal that one has the greatest opportunity to show how a company can, through innovative, aggressive, and competent management, provide greater efficiency, economy, and effectiveness in performing the work than competitors.

In this part of the proposal, a proposing company should tell the customer how it plans to:

1. Attract high quality personnel to accomplish the job.
2. Combine skills in the right mixture to achieve optimum skill utilization.
3. Time-phase work and account for real time rescheduling of work if required to meet changing conditions.
4. Motivate employees to provide a high quality work output.
5. Adjust skill levels for economy as the work progresses.
6. Evaluate progress in real time and correct errors quickly.
7. Adopt new procedures, methods, and equipment as they become available.
8. Keep employees well trained and updated in their skills throughout the project.
9. Provide management attention and control of indirect (overhead and burden) costs.

1 Company

Outline of company's history
Existing plants
Directors and share distribution
Listings of bankers, solicitors and auditors
Resumes of principals and key management personnel

2 Products (existing and proposed)

Sales history (month, region, product–3 year)
Description (product brochures)
Patents (pending and issued)
Competitive advantages (e.g. design, service, modification, technology)
Research and development (description)

3 Market

Size, share, location (existing and projected)
List of principal competitors
Potential competitor's reaction

4 Marketing Plan (first 3 years)

Sales estimates
Verification of sales estimates (e.g. letters of intent from potential customers)
Marketing organization (management, experience)
Advertising and sales promotion
Buyers, distributors, end users

5 Manufacturing

Raw materials (sources, volumes, advantage)
Manufacturing processes and technologies
Production layout
Quality control
Plant (location, site requirements)
Buildings (plans, specifications, construction estimates or quotes)
Equipment (new and existing; cost estimates or quotes)
Employment (first 3-year projection by numbers, skill, wage and salary rates)

6 Financial

Three-year audited financial statements (including affiliates if a company is in existence or if shareholders own one or more other companies)
Capital requirements of project (estimate of land, building, equipment, working capital and start-up costs)
Sources of financing of capital requirements financial projections:
1. Proforma *balance sheets* and *income statements* for first 3 years
2. Cash flow: monthly year 1; yearly for years 2 and 3
3. Return on equity/return on investment

(Continued)

7 Other information should also be included if appropriate, such as:

Appraisal reports (equipment)

Franchise agreements

Grant approvals or applications

Lease agreements

Feasibility studies

Timing of project (start-up)

Present or threatened litigation affecting the company
or major principals

Figure 7.2. Company Data Checklist for Organization and Management Proposal.

Attracting and/or Retaining High Quality Personnel

The ability to attain excellence and to maintain this excellence in providing a work activity or work output will depend to a large degree on the quality of personnel a proposing company has attracted or plans to attract to do the work. The personnel management hiring and promotion policies of the company need not be described in detail in the proposal, but key points of this policy may be valuable in stating one's case. What is the policy on the encouragement of versatility and cross training of personnel? Does the company have a policy of hiring at the bottom end of salary scale and promoting from within the company or of gaining supervisory and management personnel from the outside? Does the company plan to use "contingency hiring" (job offers contingent upon winning the contract) for the proposed task? What are the sources of new personnel planned for the job? How can the company be assured that the skill categories and skill levels needed can be located, hired, and retained?

Combining Skills in the Right Mixture
to Achieve Optimum Skill Utilization

Are multiskilled employees to be used for more than one job? Will the mixture of skill categories and skill levels be changed as the job progresses? If so, how? These questions should be addressed to show the customer that the company is skillful in managing the human resources that are to be employed in doing the work.

Motivating Employees to Produce High Quality Work

Does the company have specific policies that motivate employees to do high quality work? Are incentive awards, bonuses, and performance awards used? Are these awards sufficient in size to trigger substantial employee contributions or are they merely routine programs with little or no monetary or recognition benefits? What evidence exists of high employee morale? low turnover? low absenteeism? few employee grievances?

or high productivity? What is the documented record of work quality over the past several years? Proposal recipients will be more convinced of the ability to achieve a high quality work output if some of these specifics are provided.

Adjustment of Skill Levels as the Work Progresses

Are there plans or methods to shift higher skilled workers onto the project if difficulties needing their services occur? Are means provided to *reduce* skill levels in later phases of the program by transferring lower paid employees to the job when the higher skills are no longer needed? Are other existing or anticipated projects available that will absorb higher paid skills when they are no longer needed for ongoing work under the proposed contract? The answers to these questions will give an indication of a company's flexibility and adaptability to changing conditions throughout the project or work activity.

Evaluating Progress and Making Corrections

What systems, methods, techniques, or policies not already described in other parts of the proposal are there for evaluating progress and making corrections in work output? How is a day-to-day account of progress versus estimates in cost, schedules, or performance kept? What methods are used to rapidly identify deviations from planned or expected performance and to quickly make corrections in work methods, materials, or procedures? Assurance of closely monitored work performance will demonstrate an adherence to the principles of high quality and timely performance.

Adoption of New Procedures, Methods, and Equipment

What is the company policy regarding upgrading and advancement of procedures, methods, equipment, and facilities? Is there an ongoing research activity funded with overhead or profit that continually seeks to improve the tools available to do the job? Does the company have a history of willingness to adopt new procedures, methods, and equipment as soon as they are proven workable? What is the company's record of accepting and adopting employee suggestions that enhance efficiency, economy, and effectiveness? A good record in these areas should be exposed and advanced as proof of a company atmosphere of continued improvement in management and capital assets.

Employee Training

Are internal or external training programs used to keep employees' skills up-to-date and up-to-quality? Is sufficient feedback given to the employee to give him or her a knowledge of his or her shortcomings and areas of needed improvement? Does the company provide any other means for continued employee improvement?

Control of Indirect (Overhead and Burden) Costs

It is more than likely that at least half of every dollar that is paid to a company will be spent for overhead or overhead-related items. Because overhead is such a large budget item in any company's business, it must be constantly monitored and controlled to keep the company in a competitive posture for new work. As part of every proposal preparation process, a company should and must take a hard look at its overhead amount, analyzing its overhead expenditures and overhead elements in detail, and adjusting its business practices (if required) in order to propose its new work based on a competitive overhead. As maintained earlier in this chapter, the company's approach to analyzing and controlling overhead and burden costs should be described in the organization and management volume of the proposal. Because overhead costs are company controlled, the proposal preparation team must be given support by the corporate, company, and/or division management in describing this large cost factor and in explaining how it will be kept under control. In the review, analysis, and control of overhead costs, the proposal team must recognize that there are some overhead cost elements that are difficult or impossible to control, and there are some that are more subject to control.

Labor Burden. Of the three categories of overhead costs, labor burden is the most difficult to control. Some labor burden elements, such as social security and unemployment compensation taxes are established by law, and therefore cannot be changed unless the law is changed. Other labor burden cost elements such as paid vacations, paid holidays, and sick leave are the subject of union-management agreements or contracts. Only in recent years has there been a trend toward *reduction* of some of these fringe benefits through labor negotiations, and these have been counterbalanced by job security provisions in union contracts that require employee retention even in times of decreasing workload. Some of this labor burden or fringe benefit amount consists of employer-granted benefits like bonuses, retirement plans, and profit sharing plans designed to increase employee motivation and improve job performance. Reduction in these benefits is possible but may be accompanied by decreased employee morale and reduced worker efficiency. Most proposers, therefore, consider labor burden as a relatively fixed amount and are often obligated to project increases rather than decreases in labor burden due to the continuing competition for skilled professionals and skilled workers.

Material Burden. Material burden is more subject to cost control and cost reduction than labor burden because high technology systems can be used

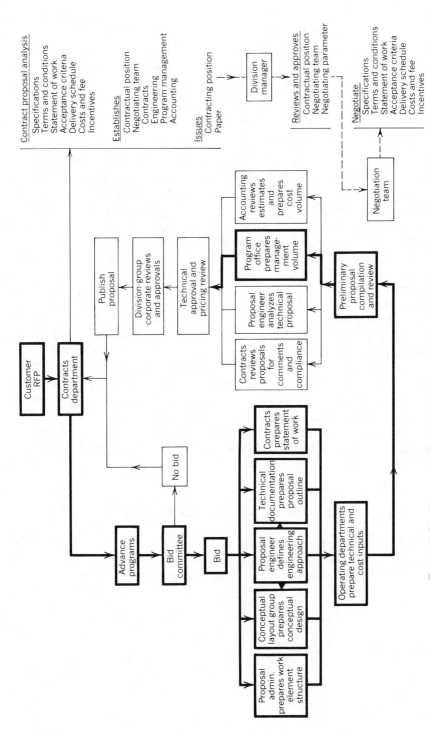

Figure 7.3. Proposal flow chart showing organization and management activities.

to reduce the costs of purchasing, inspecting, handling, storing, packaging, protecting, shipping, and disposal of materials. Although material burden is sometimes the smallest of all of the three categories of overhead costs, significant gains in competitive posture can be made by describing how advanced technology, cost-effective techniques will be applied in this area.

Overhead Costs. By far the largest part of a company's overhead consists of the wide range of activities listed under "Indirect/Overhead Costs." Heat, light, water, and rental are only a few of the costs the company must pay to stay in business. Companies of all sizes have been continually hit with increasing overhead costs. Despite the continual increase in overhead cost elements, much room exists for innovative ideas and methods of combining, reducing, and/or eliminating some of these costs. Some of the solutions stem from high technology approaches to business and industrial management, but others are simply innovative management arrangements that use existing resources to their fullest rather than expending new resources. These subjects should be briefly discussed in the organization and management proposal volume to provide the customer an insight into the methods, procedures, and techniques that will be used to keep overhead costs under control.

In summary, the organization and management volume should show principally how the job will "be carried out with all diligence." It should reflect the capability, experience, and personality of the company and the team that is expected to do the job and should offer persuasive arguments that the proposing company or firm can manage the job well and carry it through to a successful completion on schedule and within cost constraints.

ORGANIZATION AND MANAGEMENT PROPOSAL FLOW

Figure 7.3 shows the position of the organization and management activity in the overall proposal flow. Note that the organization and management volume uses inputs from all previous activities.

8

THE COST PROPOSAL

A false balance is an abomination to the Lord, but a just weight is
His delight.
Prov. 11:1

CREDIBILITY: A KEY OBJECTIVE

Whether a fixed price quote or a detailed cost proposal for a negotiated procurement is being submitted, a detailed cost and price estimate or volume will be required either by the management in the first case or by the customer in the second. The most important characteristic of the proposal's cost volume is its *CREDIBILITY!* Webster defines "credible" as "offering reasonable grounds for being believed; plausible."[1] The major difficulty many proposers have encountered in establishing a proposal's credibility resides in the distinction between "cost" and "price." Price is the amount at which transactions take place in the market. It is a value set by a company officer with the appropriate authority. It is the dollar amount that he decides to propose to win a specific contract. The price of a work activity or work output is based on many factors. Two important ones are the estimated cost of producing the work and the desired profit. Other factors that help establish the price deal with competition, business plans, product line maturity, customer importance, possibilities of follow-on work, and many others. In specific instances where it is desired to introduce a product or service into the marketplace or to capture a certain segment of the market, price can be less than estimated costs. But costs must be predicted or forecasted with the highest degree of accuracy possible in order to determine the profit of the venture (or the amount of profit foregone).

[1] *Webster's New Collegiate Dictionary.* Springfield, Mass: Merriam, 1981.

It must be remembered that the profit of a venture is its price minus all of the expenses incurred in performing the work or: *profit = price − cost.* The difficulty most often encountered in establishing price credibility is that some organizations have either deliberately or unknowingly quoted an unrealistic price in order to acquire the work. That is, they have stated a *price* that is less than the sum of the desired profit and estimated cost. This has resulted in an undue suspicion by customers that a quoted price may not be achievable. To counteract this suspicion, it is necessary to take a systematic, deliberate approach to the establishment of credibility in the cost proposal. Assuming that a positive and quantifiable profit is desired, this means that both cost credibility and price credibility must be established in a proposal.

Credibility Area 1: Matching the Work Content to the Resources Available

As skills in resource estimating have increased over the past several years, it has become evident that the resources (labor-hours and materials) to do a job can be linked to the job in a methodical and systematic way. The cost estimating techniques, methods, and procedures that are now available to proposers will permit the proposer to establish a cost for each portion of the work which, with good management of each job task, will permit successful completion of the work. The proposer must first define the job in detail; second, estimate the resources required to do the job; third, add the cost estimate to the desired profit to determine the desired sales price; fourth, compare the desired sales price with the required market price; fifth, adjust the cost or profit to fit market price goals; and sixth, *readjust the work content to fit any modifications to the cost.* This last step, matching the work content to the resources available or established by the market price, is the step most often overlooked in pricing a proposal. The techniques and tools described in this chapter will allow this adjustment to be accomplished, thereby improving credibility.

Credibility Area 2: Appropriate Time-Allocation of Resources

One fault or flaw in a proposal that could cause more damage to the potential of capturing the work than any other is failure to allocate realistically resources (skills, materials, equipment, and funds) to the various elements of the proposed work. Presumably, the customer will have at least some technical knowledge of at least certain portions of the work to be performed. If so, the evaluation of the credibility of the cost proposal will center on the proposer's understanding of the requirement as evidenced by careful and meticulous distribution and application of skills, materials, equipment, and funds to each element of the work. This allocation process will be scrutinized in two ways: first, in the time-allocation of the various the overall job; second, in the distribution of these resources to each work element.

Credibility Area 3: Labor-Hour Estimates

The cost of labor, wages, and related fringe benefits is a large element in any cost proposal. Often this cost element exceeds any other single cost element. Many times, labor costs will exceed the costs of all other cost elements combined. Because of this, credibility in establishing labor-hour estimates and their associated labor rates is not only desirable but essential. The preparer of the proposal cost volume must be familiar with the various methods of estimating labor hours and must employ these methods to improve proposal credibility. Labor-loading methods, shop-loading methods, industrial standards, parametric estimating, learning curve methods, and "direct" labor estimates are summarized in this chapter.

Credibility Area 4: Traceability of Resource Estimates

Whether company management or a customer is evaluating the cost proposal, the evaluator will be interested not only in the bottom-line price, but in the *derivation* of this price. The cost proposal volume must clearly expose and explain the steps that were taken to build up the total cost and resulting price. The thread of methodology from the basic man-hour estimates through the application of rates and factors and assembly of the total cost from its elements must be observable and easily followed by an evaluator. An obscure or incompletely described methodology will often injure credibility as much as an incorrect estimate or mathematical error. Traceability of buildup of the resources required to do the job, and an ability to *describe* the flow of resource element assembly into a final price are important factors in establishing proposal credibility.

Credibility Area 5: Supporting Data and Backup Material

Another name that encompasses the supporting data and backup material that accompanies a cost proposal volume is *rationale*. Merely providing a large volume of statistics, historical costs, or written backup will not improve proposal credibility; but in-depth backup *rationale*, supplied in an organized manner and keyed to specific resource values, will firmly undergird proposal credibility. Skill in providing the best possible backup data within proposal page limits and volume size constraints will enhance selection potential.

Important things to be remembered in the reading and study of this chapter are (1) a cost estimate usually involves fitting the resources to the detailed work description and (2) a price estimate usually includes fitting the work to the resources available or the established competitive market price. Restating the earlier equation as "cost = price − profit" shows that, when price or profit (a "negative profit" being a loss) are established or adjusted; the cost must be established or adjusted by altering work content, delivery schedules, quantities, specifications, or skill levels used to match the resources allocated or available.

By far the most appropriate and most effective cost estimating method to use for cost proposal preparation is the industrial engineering type, labor-hour and material based cost estimate. Otherwise known as a "ground-up" cost estimate, this type of estimate will address all of the five areas needed for proposal cost credibility. Experience has shown that an in-depth analysis of the work and estimating of work elements will create the most credible, supportable, usable, and accurate cost estimate. This estimate can then be compared with an independently derived parametric cost estimate developed from one of many available cost models. This in-depth cost estimating procedure usually consists of the following phases of activity:

1. Preparation of a complete list of all drawings, documents, publications, materials, and parts required to perform the job; and analysis of these items to establish a make or buy decision on each.

2. Detailed manufacturing or process planning, including a preliminary or conceptual design of each major tool or piece of special equipment, and a complete description and analysis of the manufacturing or process flow.

3. Application of work standards and adjustment to account for expected performance against these standards.

4. Definition of each administrative, engineering, manufacturing, assembly, testing, shipping, and support task by discipline; and the use of standard industrial engineering methods, labor-loading techniques, judgment of skilled personnel, and historical experience to arrive at a detailed estimate.

5. Application of standard catalog prices, recent purchase order data, vendor quotations for materials and parts, and the competitive solicitation of quotations for subcontracts.

6. Use of the latest available information on labor rates, travel costs, fringe benefits, overhead costs, and general and administrative expenses.

    Through the use of these techniques, sufficient detailed data can be accumulated to convince both the performing organization and the customer that the job can be performed within the estimated and proposed resources.

THE COST PROPOSAL CONTENT

The cost volume of the proposal consists of eight sectons: (1) the introduction—a brief comprehensive statement of the scope of work to be performed; (2) the ground rules used for the formulation of the estimate; (3) a program summary of the cost estimate, and the total program cost by work element structure; (4) the cost estimate by work package—a summary of cost at major work package and sublevels of the work element structure (WES) including task description and estimating rationale; (5) the cost summary by elements of cost—sublevels of work element structure showing functional cost elements such as direct labor by category, overhead, material; and other direct and indirect cost; (6) cost and pricing supporting information—the composition of rates and factors by projected fiscal years, economics, escalation, and sources of rates; (7) incremental costs—the computations for selected increments of procurement (where applicable); and (8) backup material, rationale, and supporting data. All of these elements are not necessarily included in every cost proposal since the secret to a competitive posture may thereby be revealed. However, in a cost-reimbursable contract, the agency charged with reviewing the bids and managing the contract will take full advantage of any detail presented to them by the bidder. In these instances the bidder will find that it will be advantageous to provide adequate estimate rationale in the cost proposal. Providing much more detail than the request for proposal asks for is not a good practice because it may result in increased evaluation and negotiation times. However, to be competitive in the environment of negotiated versus advertised procurements, full disclosure, innovation, and cost efficiency are infinitely more successful than obscure pricing and estimating techniques and methods.

THE PROPOSAL ESTIMATING PROCESS

The proposal estimating process, used in the preparation of the cost volume, is comprised of parallel and sequential steps that flow together and interact to culminate in a completed pricing structure. Figure 8.1 shows the anatomy of the proposal estimating process. This figure graphically depicts how the various resource ingredients are synthesized from the basic labor-hour estimates and material quantity estimates. Labor-hour estimates of each skill required to accomplish the job are combined with the labor rates for these skills to derive labor dollar estimates. In the meantime, material quantities and purchased parts are estimated in terms of the units by which they are measured or purchased, and these material quantities are combined with their costs per unit to develop direct material dollar estimates. Labor overhead or burden is applied to direct

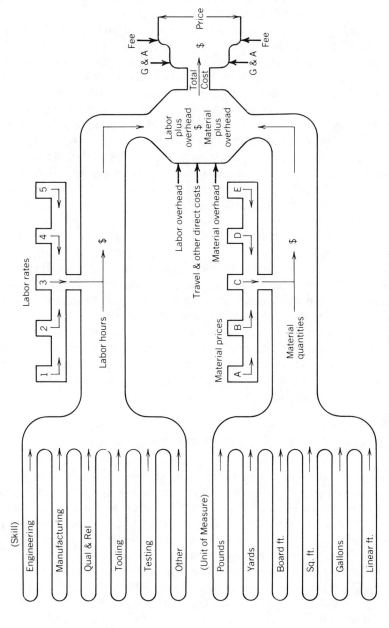

Figure 8.1. The anatomy of an estimate.

material costs. Then travel costs and other direct costs are added to produce total costs; general and administrative expenses and fee or profit are added to derive the proposal "price."

Labor rates that are applied to the basic labor-hour estimates are usually "composite" labor rates; that is, they represent an average of the rates within a given skill category. For example, the engineering skill category may include skill levels such as draftsmen, designers, engineering assistants, junior engineers, engineers, and senior engineers. The number and titles of engineering skills vary widely from company to company, but the use of a composite labor rate for the engineering skill category is common practice. The composite labor rate is derived by multiplying the labor rate for each skill by the percentage of man-hours of that skill required to do a given task and adding the results. For example, if the six skills have the following labor rates and percentages, the composite labor rate is computed as shown in Table 8.1. In this above example, the engineering composite rate would be $(8.13 \times .07) + (10.31 \times .03) + (13.56 \times .10) + (19.15 \times .20) + (25.19 \times .50) + (32.10 \times .10) = \$21.87$ per hour.

Another common practice is to establish separate overhead or burden pools for each skill category. These burden pools carry the peripheral costs that are related to and are a function of the labor-hours expended in that particular skill category. Though the mathematics consists only of multiplication and addition, multielement work activities or work outputs greatly increase the number of these mathematical computations. It becomes readily evident, therefore, that the computations required for a cost proposal are so complex that computer techniques for computation are essential for any cost proposal involving more than the simplest tasks.

Estimating Based on the Work Element Structure

The entire cost estimate is developed using the framework of the work element structure for collection, correlation, computation, and display of costs. Most companies have their own work-element-structure-based

TABLE 8.1 COMPUTING COMPOSITE LABOR RATE

Engineering Skill	Labor Rate ($/Hour)	Percentage in the Task	Multiplier
Draftsman	$ 8.13	7	.07
Designer	$10.31	3	.30
Engineering assistant	$13.56	10	.10
Junior engineer	$19.15	20	.20
Engineer	$25.19	50	.50
Senior engineer	$32.10	10	.10
		Total 100	

automatic data processing system that performs all of the mathematics needed to compile a complete multiskill, multiyear, and multielement estimate. Frequently the cost estimate will be developed at a lower level than that which will be included in the cost proposal. A customer may request pricing down to level three in the work element structure, where the company will elect to go down to level five in its own estimating process. This practice reduces the amount of costing material that must be provided in the cost proposal but causes lower level backup material to be generated that can be used later in supporting negotiations. The work element structure is the framework upon which the work elements, cost elements, and schedule elements are based and correlated.

THE PROPOSAL COST ELEMENTS

The major cost elements of a proposal can vary considerably and depend on the work activity being estimated. Generally, however, the costs for any activity can be subdivided into labor costs, labor overhead costs, subcontract costs, material and material overhead costs, travel costs, computer costs, other direct costs, general and administrative expenses, and profit or fee. Labor cost elements are derived by estimating labor hours for each skill category and each skill level and multiplying the labor rates for each skill by the hours for each. The proportions of each skill category and level required to do a total job and the related overhead materials and supplies, will assist in the development of overhead rates for each major skill category. For example, "an engineering overhead pool" includes the overhead costs for a category that includes a predetermined mix of engineering skill levels. Along with an overhead pool, the composite engineering labor rate can be developed based on the same mix of skill levels. When composite labor and overhead rates are used, proposal estimates can be reduced to estimates of the hours required by several major skill categories, and labor costs can be computed using a composite labor and overhead rate for that skill category.

Labor Costs

Labor costs, when developed for proposals, are generally completed using broad composite skill categories, such as: project management; engineering; manufacturing; tooling; quality, reliability, and safety; and testing. Another category, simply labeled "other" provides a means for costing labor hours that do not fall into any of these categories. The seven skill categories are described in the following sections. (Other major composite skill categories can be developed to fit a company's wage, salary, and organizational structure.)

Project Management Labor.   Project management labor includes the overall administrative effort of planning, organizing, coordinating, directing, controlling, and approving the work activities required to accomplish the program objectives. The subelements of project management are project direction, cost control management, logistics management, procurement management, configuration management, information management, and safety management.

Engineering Labor.   Engineering labor includes the study, analysis, design, development, evaluation, and redesign for specified subdivisions of work. This skill category includes the preparation of specifications, drawings, parts lists, wiring diagrams; technical coordination between engineering and manufacturing; vendor coordination; test planning and scheduling; analysis of test results; data reduction; and engineering report preparation.

Manufacturing Labor.   Manufacturing (or manufacturing and assembly) labor includes such operations as fabrication, processing, subassembly, final assembly, reworking, modification, experimental production, and installation of parts and equipment. Included is the preparation and processing of material of any kind (metal, plastic, glass, cloth, etc.). Preparation and processing includes but is not limited to flashing operations, annealing, heat treating, baking, refrigeration, anodizing, plating, painting and pretest, and production services. Fabrication (the construction of detail parts from raw materials) includes the hours expended in the cutting, molding, forming, stretching, and blanking operations performed on materials of any kind (metal, wood, plastic, cloth, tubing) to make individual parts. Experimental hours spent in construction of mock-up models, test articles, testing, and reworking during the test program should be considered as direct manufacturing labor-hours, as should machine setup time when performed by the operator of the machine.

Tooling Labor.   Tooling labor includes planning, design, fabrication, assembly, installation, modification, maintenance. It also includes rework of all tools, dies, jigs, fixtures, gauges, handling equipment, work platforms, test equipment, and special test equipment in support of the manufacturing process. This skill includes effort expended in the determination of tool and equipment requirements, planning of fabrication and assembly operations, maintaining tool and equipment records, establishing make or buy plans and manufacturing plans on tooling components and equipment, scheduling and controlling tool and equipment orders, and programming and preparation of tapes for numerically controlled machine parts. It also includes preparation of templates and patterns.

Quality, Reliability, and Safety Labor.   Quality, reliability, and safety labor includes the development of quality assurance, reliability assurance, and safety assurance plans; receiving inspection, in-process inspection, and final inspection (of raw materials, tools, parts, subassemblies, and assemblies); and reliability testing and failure report reviewing. It includes the participation of quality, reliability, and safety engineers in design reviews and final acceptance reviews.

Testing Labor.   Testing labor includes the skills expended in the performance of tests on all components, assemblies, subsystems, and systems to determine and unify operational characteristics and compatibility with the overall system and its intended environment. Such tests include design feasibility tests, design verification tests, development tests, qualification tests, acceptance tests, reliability tests; also tests on parts, systems, and integrated systems to verify the suitability in meeting the criteria for intended usage. These tests are conducted on hardware or final designs that have been produced, inspected, and assembled by established methods. Skills expended in test planning and scheduling, data reduction, and report preparation are also included in this category.

Other Labor Costs.   Other labor costs include categories of labor and skills not included in the foregoing five categories. These other labor costs can include direct supervision and management, direct clerical costs, and miscellaneous direct labor activities.

Materials and Subcontract Costs

Where there are a large number of buy items (items or services to be procured from outside organizations), the "subcontracts" cost element is usually subdivided into major subcontracts and other subcontracts. Major contracts are usually established by setting up a cost value above which the contract is considered a "major subcontract." The reason that major subcontractors are singled out is that their performance has a significant effect on the conduct of the overall prime's work activity. Cost and financial reporting, schedule reporting, and performance reporting are usually required to a higher degree from major subcontractors than from other contractors. This greater depth of reporting and visibility into the work of major subcontractors gives the prime performing organization better management control of the work progress.

The "materials" cost element includes tangible raw materials, parts, tools, components, subsystems, and assemblies needed to perform the work. Service contracts are not usually covered under materials, but there are grey areas in the definitions of materials and subcontracts that result in some possible overlap. An organization's accounting system normally will specify clearly under which category each procurement falls. This relationship should also be described in the organization and management volume or the cost volume of the proposal.

TREATMENT OF OTHER NECESSARY GROUND RULES

Since the preparation of a cost estimate often brings up questions about the work that have not been asked or discussed, the cost proposal team must often define or force the definition of other general ground rules that have not been developed by other members of the proposal team or by the company's management. These ground rules and assumptions can include areas such as the policy for providing spares, spare parts, warranties, maintenance manuals, repair manuals, optional equipment and services, and customer services. The ever-present areas of scrap, waste, and human error allowances in themselves can cause large errors in estimating and must not be overlooked when formulating estimates of each work element.

Spares and Spare Parts

In the proposal for a product or project, it is important to determine the degree of manufacture, distribution, stocking, warehousing, and sales of spare parts. In virtually every product manufactured today, there are certain subsystems, components, or parts that have a limited lifetime. Items such as batteries, gaskets and seals, drive belts, and illumination devices invariably have to be replaced before the useful lifetime of the overall product is expended. These so-called "expendable" items must be periodically replaced by the owner or user, and must be readily available to keep the product in an operational condition. The business organization that is interested in maintaining growth or expansion through satisfied customers must include the logistics system to provide these spare parts in the cost proposal. To a similar degree nonexpendable parts must also be stocked to replace those damaged because of wear, malfunction, or misuse. The best procedure for developing and pricing an initial spare parts list is to review the complete list of parts, subassemblies, and assemblies, and to make a decision concerning the spares level for each based on an anticipated or assumed failure or use rate. This completed spares list, can be used in developing the total quantities needed, the manufacturing rate, and the resulting resource estimate. The method of estimating spare parts costs as well as the reasons and supporting data for this method should be included in the cost proposal.

Maintenance and Repair Manuals

Virtually every work activity or work output is accompanied by some sort of assembly, maintenance, repair, or instruction manual. Assembly instructions, maintenance manuals, and repair manuals usually take a significant amount of time and effort to develop because their content must be extracted, condensed, simplified, and clearly described based on more complex engineering and manufacturing documentation. In establishing initial cost proposal ground rules, then, specific assumptions must be made as to the quantity, quality, number of pages, types of illustrations and artwork, and distribution of these instructions and manuals. These ground rules should be included in the proposal.

Optional Equipment and Services

In industries where products are standardized to reduce production costs and to increase the benefits of mass production, there are few options provided, but the trend toward customization, individuality, and adaptability of a work output to a specific individual's or company's taste or circumstances has resulted in numerous products that have optional extra equipment or services. In some products the list of options is even longer than the list of parts in the original item. For this reason it is important to consider carefully what optional equipment and services are to be included in the inventory, to develop a resources policy and resource estimate for these items and services, and to state these resources and their rationale in the cost proposal.

ESTIMATING MATERIAL COSTS

The pounds, cubic or square yards, board feet, square feet, gallons, or linear feet of the required materials are usually obtained by determining or computing quantities directly from a "bill of materials" or parts list; or from detailed drawings and specifications of the completed item with added sufficient allowance for waste or scrap. The next step is to apply the appropriate material unit price or cost to this quantity to develop the final material costs. The costs of procuring, handling, storing, and maintaining materials stocks and supplies can be included in the material costs or may be included in material overhead costs. Usually, materials are classed as those items purchased rather than made by an organization.

Drawing Takeoff (If Detailed Drawings Already Exist)

The most precise means of determining the actual quantity of materials required to do a job is the extraction or calculation of material quantities from drawings of the item or specifications for the process or service if these detailed drawings already exist. Calculation of material quantities involves such considerations as the anticipated method of manufacturing the item, conducting the process, or delivering the service; the size or quantity of uniform purchase lots; and the anticipated scrap, waste, boil-off, or leakage. Since the term "materials" covers a wide range of substances varying from raw materials to completed parts, there is often a delicate balance between the type, shape, and kind of material purchased and the labor to be performed on it *after* it is purchased.

Careful analysis of any existing drawings and specifications of the work output is required to determine (1) the best state or condition in which to purchase the material; (2) the optimum size or quantity of material bought; (3) the method of fabrication that will best use the full quantity of puchased material; and (4) the expected quantity of scrap or waste resulting from successful manufacture of the product. A certain amount of waste can be expected because the material sizes do not usually conform to the shape of the completed part. Good manufacturing design, however, will make maximum advantage of available material sizes and shapes to minimize waste. It should be pointed out in the proposal how the careful analysis and estimating of these factors have saved resources in the overall work output or work activity. If detailed drawings and specifications for the work do not exist, then the estimator must forecast the labor-hours and materials required to produce these drawings and specifications.

Material Handbooks and Supplier Catalogs

Once material quantities have been developed from drawings, specifications, and parts lists; costs can be derived from material handbooks, supplier catalogs, or supplier quotes. The most highly refined catalogs and handbooks are available for architectural building construction, but ample catalogs are available for the manufacturing and process industries; and catalogs and handbooks are continually becoming available for high-technology industries such as aerospace industries. It is always desirable to use the latest available catalog prices.

A good estimator will obtain and keep a complete file of catalogs and handbooks containing descriptions and prices of materials, parts, supplies, and subsystems and components of the major product or products being estimated and will reference the handbooks used in deriving cost estimates in the cost proposal.

Quantity Buy and Inventory Considerations

The quantity or number of supplies or parts purchased or stocked strongly affects the materials costs. The study of materials, supplies, and goods, and their handling, transportation, packaging, shipping, and storage is called logistics. To stock just the right quantity of materials or supplies, a logistics study must be done of the economics of inventory systems.

The basic decision that faces a company in developing materials costs for a proposal is whether to take advantage of the lower costs of materials made possible by buying materials in large quantities and saving these materials until they are needed, or to wait until the materials are needed before purchasing them. The benefits of buying materials in large quantities are fourfold: suppliers and producers can offer these materials at lower prices when larger quantities are purchased because of the production economies of scale; the buyer can avoid future cost or price increases for the purchased material due to inflation or escalation; the ready availability of vital materials can often serve as a cost avoidance in producing a work output where there is a fluctuating demand; and the purchase of larger quantities of needed materials at one time rather than in separate lots reduces the procurement and transportation costs per unit of material.

These four benefits of buying and stockpiling quantities of materials larger than those needed immediately for the work activity are counteracted by other costs associated with the storage, maintenance, handling, and use of the larger quantities of materials; and by the "opportunity cost" of having capital tied up in inventory. The real "out-of-pocket" costs of carrying an inventory include insurance and taxes on the stockpiled material and the land or building it is stored in; breakage, deterioration, and pilferage of the material; and heating, light, and security for the warehouse or storage area.

Scrap and Waste Considerations

The most important thing that can be said about scrap and waste in material estimating is that these factors must not be forgotten or omitted in the estimator's analysis of the job to be done. A normal amount of waste or scrap is encountered in almost every manufacturing or production process because materials must be changed in form, shape, or volume in some manner to arrive at a final product. In this process of converting the shape or form of a material, scrap material is produced by the machining process, by-products are formed, and the inspection process will reveal and cause rejection of a certain portion of the work. Standard sizes or quantities of material should be proposed wherever possible.

The estimation of scrap and waste factors can be done most effectively by reviewing the actual manufacturing or production process, observing actual scrap and waste factors on previous projects, by judiciously applying these factors to the activity being proposed, and by referencing the factors used and the method of application of these factors in the proposal itself.

Bills of Material

When a product is first designed, a key part of the design documentation is a bill of material. A bill of material or parts list is usually included in or with the initial detailed design drawings of an item, and it is updated as the design changes. This bill of material is a valuable source of material quantity information on which proposed material costs can be based.

Subcontracts

In proposing an overall category of purchased items for a given work activity, the term "materials" sometimes includes the use of subcontracts to produce partially finished materials, parts, or components. Since subcontracts and materials are both procured items, they are sometimes categorized together in a cost proposal. More often, however, subcontracts (specially major subcontracts) are costed separately with a full range of documentation, cost estimates, and supporting rationale to be provided for each major subcontractor.

TREATMENT OF DOCUMENTATION

In these times of high technology and sophisticated projects, products, and services, a large part of a company's resources is spent in formulating and writing specifications, reports, manuals, handbooks, engineering orders, and product descriptions. The complexity of the engineering activity and the specific document requirements are important determining factors in proposing the labor-hours required to prepare documentation.

The hours required for documentation will vary considerably depending on the complexity of the work output; however, average labor hours for origination and revision of documentation have been derived based on experience, and these figures can be used as average labor hours per page of documentation. (See Tables 8.2 and 8.3.) These tables are also handy in determining the amount of time to prepare a proposal, as a proposal is essentially a form of technical documentation.

TABLE 8.2   NEW DOCUMENTATION

Function	Labor-Hours per Page
Research, liaison, technical writing, editing, and supervision	5.7
Typing and proofreading	0.6
Illustrations	4.3
Engineering	0.7
Coordination	0.2
Total	11.5 hrs
(a range of 8 to 12 labor-hours per page can be used)	

Source: R. D. Stewart, *Cost Estimating*. New York: Wiley, 1982.

TABLE 8.3.   REVISED DOCUMENTATION

Function		Man-Hours per Page
Research liaison, technical writing, editing and supervision		4.00
Typing and proofreading		0.60
Illustrations		0.75
Engineering		0.60
Coordination		0.20
	Total	6.15 hrs
(a range of 4 to 8 labor-hours per page can be used)		

Source: R. D. Stewart, *Cost Estimating.* New York: Wiley, 1982.

THE PROCESS PLAN

A key to successful proposal costing of manufacturing or construction activities is the process plan. A process plan is a listing of all operations that must be performed to manufacture a product or to complete a project, along with the labor hours required to perform each operation. The process plan is usually prepared by an experienced foreman, engineer, or technician who knows the company's equipment, personnel, and capabilities, or by a process planning department chartered to do all of the process planning. The process planner envisions the equipment, work station, and environment; estimates the number of persons required; and estimates how long it will take to perform each step. From this information he or she derives the labor hours required. Process steps are numbered and space is left between operations listed to allow easy insertion or omission of operations or activities as the process is modified. A typical process plan is shown on Figure 8.2.

MANUFACTURING ACTIVITIES

The most common method of estimating the time and cost required for manufacturing activities is the industrial engineering approach whereby standards or target values are established for various operations. The term "standards" is used to indicate standard time data. All possible elements of work are measured, assigned a standard time for performance, and documented. When a particular job is to be estimated, all of the applicable standards for all related operations are added together to determine the total time. Then major adjustments are made to the estimate of time and resources by applying a "realization factor" which is derived by dividing actual experienced time by the "standard" time for a given series of manufacturing activities.

Drawing No. D21216   Part No. 1D21254
Title: Cylinder Assembly (Welded)

Operation Number	Labor Hours	Description
010	—	Receive and inspect material (skins and forgings)
020	24	Roll form skin segments
030	60	Mask and chem-mill recessed pattern in skins
040	—	Inspect
050	36	Trim to design dimension and prepare in welding skin segments into cylinders (two)
060	16	Locate segments on automatic seam welder tooling fixture and weld per specification (longitudinal weld)
070	2	Remove from automatic welding fixture
080	18	Shave welds on inside diameter
090	16	Establish trim lines (surface plate)
100	18	Install in special fixture and trim to length
110	8	Remove from special fixture
120	56	Install center mandrel—center ring, forward and aft sections (cylinders)—forward and aft mandrel—forward and aft rings—and complete special feature set up
130	—	Inspect
140	24	But weld (4 places)
150	8	Remove from special fixture and remove mandrels
160	59	Radiograph and dye penetrant inspect
170	—	Inspect dimensionally
180	6	Reinstall mandrels in preparation for final machining
190	14	Finish OD—aft
	10	Finish OD—center
	224	Finish OD—forward
200	40	Program for forward ring
220	30	Handwork (3 rings)
230	2	Reinstall cylinder assembly w/mandrels still in place, or on the special fixture
240	16	Clock and drill index holes
250	—	Inspect
260	8	Remove cylinder from special fixture—remove mandrel
270	1	Install in holding cradle
230	70	Locate drill jig on forward end and hand drill leak check vein (drill and tap), and hand drill hole pattern
290	64	Locate drill jig on aft ring and hand drill hole pattern
300	—	Inspect forward and aft rings
310	8	Install protective covers on each end of cylinder
320	—	Transfer to surface treat
340	24	Remove covers and alodine
350	—	Inspect
360	8	Reinstall protective covers and return to assembly area

Figure 8.2. Process Plan. (Source: R.D. Stewart, *Cost Estimating*, New York: Wiley, 1982.)

The use of standards produces more accurate and more easily justifiable estimates. Standards also promote consistency between estimates as well as among estimators. Where standards are used, personal experience is desirable or beneficial but not mandatory. Standards have been developed over a number of years through the use of time studies and synthesis of methods analysis. They are based on the level of efficiency that could be attained by a job shop producing up to 1,000 units of any specific work output. Standards are actually synoptical values of more detailed times. They are adaptations, extracts, or bench mark time values for each type of operation. The loss of accuracy occasioned by summarization and/or averaging is acceptable when the total time for a system is being developed. If standard values are used with judgment and interpolations for varying stock sizes, reasonably accurate results can be obtained. Sources of the standards, as well as the rationale for the application of these standards, should be included in the proposal.

CONSTRUCTION ACTIVITIES

One of the most structured, documented, and well-thought-out activities that proposers deal with is construction. In a construction proposal, it is important to recognize and to include adequate labor hours and materials for each step in the construction process, and to meticulously lay out and identify each construction activity.

The need for on-site physical access to the construction element being performed at a given time dictates a general flow of activities for the construction process. The unique feature of an integrated on-site manufacturing and assembly process performed by diverse skills, makes it particularly important to lay out the construction flow sequence as a prerequisite to and an integral part of the estimating of labor hours and materials. In the fields of residential and industrial construction alone, there are nearly 3,000 categories of material and labor. Many construction labor standards are tied to the item being installed or material being used. Construction estimating manuals usually include average wage rates for various construction skills and trades, wage modification factors that adapt these wage rates to various geographical areas, and material and labor costs associated with each construction activity. Any construction manuals used in the proposal rationale should be listed or referenced.

IN-PROCESS INSPECTION

The amount of in-process inspection performed on any process, product, project, or service will depend on the cost of possible defects in the item or scrappage of the item as well as the degree of reliability required for the final work output. In high-rate production of relatively inexpensive items, it is often economically desirable to forego in-process inspection entirely in favor of scrapping any parts that fail a simple "go, no-go" inspection at the end of the production line. On the other hand, expensive and sophisticated precision-manufactured parts may require nearly one hundred percent inspection. A good rule of thumb is to add ten percent of the manufacturing and assembly hours for in-process inspection. This in-process inspection does not include the in-process testing covered in the following paragraph.

TESTING

Testing usually falls into three categories: (1) development testing, (2) qualification testing, and (3) production acceptance testing. Rules of thumb are difficult to come by for estimating the resources required for development testing because testing varies with the complexity, uncertainty, and technological content of the work activity. The best way to estimate the cost of development testing is to produce a detailed test plan for the specific project and to cost each element of this test plan separately, being careful to consider all skills, facilities, equipment, and material needed in the development test program. Again rationale should be included in the cost proposal.

Qualification testing is required in most commercial products and on all military or space projects to demonstrate adequately that the article will operate or serve its intended purpose in environments far more severe than those intended for its actual use. Resources required for this qualification testing and the estimating rationale should be included in the cost proposal.

Receiving inspection, production testing, and acceptance testing can be estimated using experience factors and ratios available from previous like work activities. Receiving tests are tests performed on purchased components, parts, and/or subassemblies prior to acceptance by the receiving department. Production tests are tests of subassemblies, units, subsystems, and systems during and after assembly. Experience has shown, generally, that test labor varies directly with the amount of fabrication and assembly labor. Rationale for estimating receiving and production testing resources should be included in the cost volume along with the rationale for the resources required for other forms of testing.

SPECIAL TOOLING AND TEST EQUIPMENT

Special purpose tooling and special purpose test equipment are important items of cost because they are used only for a particular job; therefore, that job must bear the full cost of the tool or test fixture. In contrast to the special items, general purpose tooling or test equipment is purchased as capital equipment and costs are spread over many jobs. The type, quantity, rationale, and resources required for special purpose tooling and equipment should be included in the proposal cost volume.

COMPUTER SOFTWARE PROPOSAL COST ESTIMATING

Because of the increasing number and types of computers and computer languages, it is difficult to generate overall ground rules or rules of thumb for computer software cost estimating. Productivity in computer programming is greatly affected by the skill and competence of the computer analyst or programmer. Usually, a company will have some experience base for estimating the systems analysis and computer program coding time required for various types of machine languages and high order languages. It is important to include this historical base and rationale in the cost proposal since software costs are becoming an ever-larger part of proposal costs for many high technology projects.

LABOR ALLOWANCES

Standard times assume that workers are well trained and experienced in their jobs; that they apply themselves to the job one hundred percent of the time; and that they never make mistakes, take breaks, lose efficiency, or deviate from the tasks for any reason. This, of course, is an unreasonable assumption because there are many legitimate and numerous unplanned work interruptions that occur with regularity in any work activity. Therefore, labor allowances must be added to any proposal estimate that is made up of an accumulation of standard times. In most instances, these labor allowances can accumulate to a factor of 1.5 to 2.5. The total standard time for a given work activity, depending on the overall inherent efficiency of the shop, equipment, and personnel, will depend on the nature of the task.

Standard hours vary from actual measured labor hours because workers often deviate from the standard method or technique used or planned for a given operation. This deviation can be caused by a number of factors ranging from the training, motivation, or disposition of the operator to the use of faulty tools, fixtures, or machines. Sometimes shortages of materials or lack of adequate supervision are causes of deviations from standard values. These variances can add five to twenty percent to standard time values.

Another type of variance from standard time is called personal, fatigue, and delay (PFD) time. Personal times are for personal activities such as coffee breaks, trips to the restroom or water fountain, unforeseen interruptions, or emergency telephone calls. Fatigue time is allocated because of the inability of a worker to produce at the same pace all day. Operator efficiency decreases as the job time increases. Delays include unavoidable delays caused by the need for obtaining supervisory instructions, equipment breakdown, power outages, or operator illness. PFD time can add ten to twenty percent to standard time values.

Although normal or routine equipment maintenance can be done during other than operating shifts, there is usually some operator-performed machine maintenance activity that must be performed during the machine duty cycle. These activities include adjusting tools, sharpening tools, and periodically cleaning and oiling machines. In electroplating and processing operations, the operator maintains solutions and compounds, and handles and maintains racks and fixtures. Tooling and equipment maintenance can account for five to twelve percent of standard time values.

The overall direct labor hours derived from the application of the preceding allowance factors to standard times must be increased by additional amounts to account for normal rework and repair. Labor values must be allocated for rework of defective purchased materials, rework of in-process rejects, final test rejects, and addition of minor engineering changes. Units damaged on receipt or during handling must also be repaired. This factor can add ten to twenty percent direct labor hours to those previously estimated.

For projects where design stability is poor, where production is initiated prior to final design release, and where field testing is being performed concurrently with production, an engineering change allowance should be added. Change allowances vary widely for different types of work activities. Even fairly well defined projects, however, should contain a change allowance.

The labor hours required to produce an engineering prototype are greater than those required to produce the first production model. Reworks are more frequent, and work is performed from sketches or unreleased drawings rather than production drawings. An increase over first production unit labor of fifteen to twenty-five percent should be included for each engineering prototype.

COST GROWTH ALLOWANCES

Occasionally a cost proposal will warrant the addition of allowances for cost growth. Cost growth allowances are best added at the lowest level of a cost estimate rather than at the top levels. These allowances include design growth allowances; reserves for possible misfortunes, natural disasters, and strikes; and other unforeseen circumstances. Reserves should be used to account for design growth since cost growth with an incomplete design is a certainty, not a reserve or contingency! The cost proposal should include a discussion of the above labor allowances and cost growth allowances along with the computation method and rationale for their application.

ESTIMATING SUPERVISION, DIRECT MANAGEMENT, AND OTHER DIRECT CHARGES

Direct supervision costs will vary with the task and company organization. The cost estimator must carefully analyze the staffing plan prepared in the organization and management portion of the proposal to identify all direct management and supervisory personnel who will be charging their time directly to the project. Labor costs for all other management and administrative personnel will be accumulated under indirect costs or allocated as part of general and administrative expenses.

Two cost elements of "other direct costs" that are becoming increasingly prominent are travel and transportation costs. A frequent check on public and private conveyance rates and costs is mandatory. Most companies provide a private vehicle mileage allowance for employees who use their own vehicles in the conduct of company business. Rates differ and depend on whether the private conveyance is being used principally for the benefit of the company or principally for the convenience of the traveler. Regardless of which rate is used, the mileage allowance must be periodically updated to keep pace with actual costs. Many companies purchase or lease vehicles to be used by their employees on official business, and sometimes personal travel. Per diem travel allowances or reimbursement for lodging, meals, and miscellaneous expenses must also be included in overall travel estimates. These reimbursable expenses include costs of a motel or hotel room; food, tips, and taxis; local transportation and communication; and other costs such as laundry, mailing costs, and on-site clerical services. Transportation costs include the transport of equipment, supplies, and products, as well as personnel, and can include packaging, handling, shipping, postage, and insurance charges. Rationale for travel and transportation costs should be included along with their corresponding resource estimates.

COSTING IN THE PROPOSAL FLOW

As shown in Figure 8.3, when technical and cost inputs are completed by the operating departments, the accounting or finance department assembles the cost proposal or cost volume. The accounting department uses predeveloped labor rates for the various skills that will be used in performing the job; applies labor burden, material burden, and overhead costs; calculates cost-of-money; and proposes a fee structure. The forms shown on Figures 8.4 through 8.13 are typical forms used by the accounting, finance,

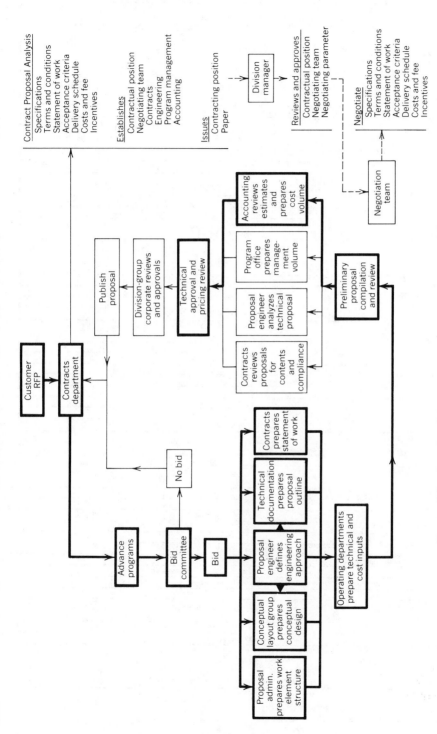

Figure 8.3. Proposal flow chart showing cost volume preparation.

177

	PAGE NO.	NO. OF PAGES
This form is for use when *(i)* submission of cost or pricing data *(see ASPR 3-807.3)* is required and *(ii)* substitution for the DD Form 633 is authorized by the contracting officer.		

NAME OF OFFEROR	SUPPLIES AND/OR SERVICES TO BE FURNISHED
HOME OFFICE ADDRESS *(Include ZIP Code)*	

DIVISION(S) AND LOCATION(S) WHERE WORK IS TO BE PERFORMED	TOTAL AMOUNT OF PROPOSAL $	GOVT SOLICITATION NO.

DETAIL DESCRIPTION OF COST ELEMENTS

	EST COST ($)	TOTAL EST COST[1]	REFER-[2] ENCE
1. DIRECT MATERIAL *(Itemize on Exhibit A)*			
a. PURCHASED PARTS			
b. SUBCONTRACTED ITEMS			
c. OTHER - *(1)* RAW MATERIAL			
(2) YOUR STANDARD COMMERCIAL ITEMS			
(3) INTERDIVISIONAL TRANSFERS *(At other than cost)*			
TOTAL DIRECT MATERIAL			
2. MATERIAL OVERHEAD 3 *(Rate % X $ base =)*			

3. DIRECT LABOR *(Specify)*	ESTIMATED HOURS	RATE/ HOUR	EST COST ($)		
TOTAL DIRECT LABOR					

4. LABOR OVERHEAD *(Specify department or cost center)3*	O.H. RATE	X BASE =	EST COST ($)		
TOTAL LABOR OVERHEAD					

5. SPECIAL TESTING *(Including field work at Government installations)*	EST COST ($)		
TOTAL SPECIAL TESTING			

6. SPECIAL EQUIPMENT *(If direct charge) (Itemize on Exhibit A)*			
7. TRAVEL *(If direct charge) (Give details on attached Schedule)*	EST COST ($)		
a. TRANSPORTATION			
b. PER DIEM OR SUBSISTENCE			
TOTAL TRAVEL			

8. CONSULTANTS *(Identity - purpose - rate)*	EST COST ($)		
TOTAL CONSULTANTS			

9. OTHER DIRECT COSTS *(Itemize on Exhibit A)*			
10. TOTAL DIRECT COST AND OVERHEAD			
11. GENERAL AND ADMINISTRATIVE EXPENSE *(Rate % of cost element Nos.)3*			
12. ROYALTIES 4			
13. TOTAL ESTIMATED COST			
14. FEE OR PROFIT			
15. TOTAL ESTIMATED COST AND FEE OR PROFIT			

This proposal is submitted for use in connection with and in response to *(Describe RFP, etc.)*

and reflects our best estimates as of this date, in accordance with the instructions to offerors and the footnotes which follow.

TYPED NAME AND TITLE	SIGNATURE
NAME OF FIRM	DATE OF SUBMISSION

DD FORM 1 APR 68 **633-4**   REPLACES EDITION OF 1 JAN 67, WHICH IS OBSOLETE.

EXHIBIT A - SUPPORTING SCHEDULE (Specify. If more space is needed, use blank sheets)

COST EL NO.	ITEM DESCRIPTION (See footnote 5)	EST COST ($)

HAVE THE DEPARTMENT OF DEFENSE, NATIONAL AERONAUTICS AND SPACE ADMINISTRATION, OR THE ATOMIC ENERGY COMMISSION PERFORMED ANY REVIEW OF YOUR ACCOUNTS OR RECORDS IN CONNECTION WITH ANY OTHER GOVERNMENT PRIME CONTRACT OR SUBCONTRACT WITHIN THE PAST TWELVE MONTHS?

☐ YES ☐ NO If yes, identify below.

NAME AND ADDRESS OF REVIEWING OFFICE (Include ZIP Code)	TELEPHONE NUMBER/EXTENSION

. WILL YOU REQUIRE THE USE OF ANY GOVERNMENT PROPERTY IN THE PERFORMANCE OF THIS PROPOSED CONTRACT?

☐ YES ☐ NO If yes, identify on a separate page.

I. DO YOU REQUIRE GOVERNMENT CONTRACT FINANCING TO PERFORM THIS PROPOSED CONTRACT?

☐ YES ☐ NO if yes, identify: ☐ ADVANCE PAYMENTS ☐ PROGRESS PAYMENTS OR ☐ GUARANTEED LOANS

V. DO YOU NOW HOLD ANY CONTRACT (or, do you have any independently financed (IR & D) projects) FOR THE SAME OR SIMILAR WORK CALLED FOR BY THIS PROPOSED CONTRACT? ☐ YES ☐ NO If yes, identify

. DOES THIS COST SUMMARY CONFORM WITH THE COST PRINCIPLES SET FORTH IN ASPR, SECTION XV (See 3-807.2 (c) (2))?

☐ YES ☐ NO If no, explain on a separate page.

INSTRUCTIONS TO OFFERORS

. The purpose of this form is to provide a standard format by which the offeror submits to the Government a summary of incurred and estimated cost (and attached supporting information) suitable for detailed review and analysis. Prior to the award f a contract resulting from this proposal the offeror shall, under the conditions stated in ASPR 3-807.3, be required to submit a Certificate of Current Cost or Pricing Data (see ASPR -807.3(e) and 3-807.4).

. As part of the specific information required by this form, the fferor must submit with this form, and clearly identify as such, ost or pricing data (that is, data which is verifiable and factual and otherwise as defined in ASPR 3-807.3(e)). In addition, e must submit with this form any information reasonably required to explain the offeror's estimating process, including:

a. the judgmental factors applied and the mathematical or other methods used in the estimate including those used in projecting from known data, and

b. the contingencies used by offeror in his proposed price.

3. When attachment of supporting cost or pricing data to this form is impracticable, the data will be specifically identified and described (with schedules as appropriate), and made available to the contracting officer or his representative upon request.

4. The format for the "Cost Elements" is not intended as rigid requirements. These may be presented in different format with the prior approval of the contracting officer if required for more effective and efficient presentation. In all other respects this form will be completed and submitted without change.

5. By submission of this proposal, offeror, if selected for negotiation, grants to the contracting officer, or his authorized representative, the right to examine, for the purpose of verifying the cost or pricing data submitted, those books, records, documents and other supporting data which will permit adequate evaluation of such cost or pricing data, along with the computations and projections used therein. This right may be exercised in connection with any negotiations prior to contract award.

FOOTNOTES

Enter in this column those necessary and reasonable costs which in the judgment of the offeror will properly be incurred n the efficient performance of the contract. When any of the osts in this column have already been incurred (e.g., on a etter contract or change order), describe them on an attached upporting schedule. Identify all sales and transfers between our plants, divisions, or organizations under a common control, which are included at other than the lower of cost to the riginal transferror or current market price.

When space in addition to that available in Exhibit A is equired, attach separate pages as necessary and identify in his "Reference" column the attachment in which information upporting the specific cost element may be found. No standard format is prescribed; however, the cost or pricing data must e accurate, complete and current, and the judgment factors sed in projecting from the data to the estimates must be stated n sufficient detail to enable the contracting officer to evaluate he proposal. For example, provide the basis used for pricing aterials such as by vendor quotations, shop estimates, or nvoice prices; the reason for use of overhead rates which depart significantly from experienced rates (reduced volume, a anned major rearrangement, etc.); or justification for an increase in labor rates (anticipated wage and salary increases, tc.). Identify and explain any contingencies which are included n the proposed price, such as anticipated costs of rejects and efective work, or anticipated technical difficulties.

3 Indicate the rates used and provide an appropriate explanation. Where agreement has been reached with Government representatives on the use of forward pricing rates, describe the nature of the agreement. Provide the method of computation and application of your overhead expense, including cost breakdown and showing trends and budgetary data as necessary to provide a basis for evaluation of the reasonableness of proposed rates.

4 If the total royalty cost entered here is in excess of $250 provide on a separate page (or on DD Form 783, Royalty Report) the following information on each separate item of royalty or license fee: name and address of licensor; date of license agreement; patent numbers, patent application serial numbers, or other basis on which the royalty is payable; brief description, including any part or model numbers of each contract item or component on which the royalty is payable; percentage or dollar rate of royalty per unit; unit price of contract item; number of units; and total dollar amount of royalties. In addition, if specifically requested by the contracting officer, a copy of the current license agreement and identification of applicable claims of specific patents shall be provided.

5 Provide a list of principal items within each category indicating known or anticipated source, quantity, unit price, competition obtained, and basis of establishing source and reasonableness of cost.

Figure 8.4. Contract pricing proposal.

RFP. No. _____
Offeror _____

Yearly Cost Summary

	Precontract Costs	First Year	Second Year	Other Years	Total
Labor hours					
"Productive" (hands-on labor)					
"Nonproductive" (other direct labor)					
Total straight time					
Overtime					
Total labor hours					
Costs					
Direct labor—straight time					
Direct labor—overtime					
Direct labor—shift premium					
Total labor cost					
Payroll additives					
Fringe benefits					
Overhead					
Other direct costs					
Subtotal					
G&A expense					
Total estimated cost					
Fee/profit					
Cost of facilities capital (cost of money)					
Total estimated cost & fee/profit					

Figure 8.5. Yearly cost summary.

180

RFP No. _____

Offeror _____

ST = Straight time
OT = Overtime

Labor Costs

□ Prime
□ Subcontract

□ Exempt
□ Nonexempt, Nonunion
Precontract □
Year □ #1 □ #2

Labor Classification	Avg. Headcount	Shift	Labor Hours		Labor Rates		Labor Costs			
			ST	OT	ST	OT	ST	OT	Shift Premium	Total
Totals										

Figure 8.6. Labor costs.

Labor Costs Summary

RFP No. _____

Offeror _____

☐ Prime
☐ Subcontract

Labor Classification	Avg. Head-count	Labor Hours		Labor Costs			
		Straight Time	Overtime	Straight Time	Overtime	Shift Premium	Total
Precontract							
Exempt							
Nonexempt, Nonunion							
Nonexempt, union							
Total							
First year							
Exempt							
Nonexempt, nonunion							
Nonexempt, union							
Total							
Second year							
Exempt							
Nonexempt, nonunion							
Nonexempt, union							
Total							
Remaining years							
Total							

Figure 8.7. Labor costs summary.

182

	Payroll Additives				Prime ☐ Subcontract ☐
RFP. No. _____ Offeror _____					
Element	Base	Rate	Cost	Labor Hours	Cost per Hour
Precontract & First year Federal insurance compensation Act Federal unemployent insurance State unemployment insurance Workmen's compensation Other (specify)					
Total					
Second year Federal insurance compensation act Federal unemployment insurance State unemployment insurance Workmen's compensation Other (specify)					
Total					
Other Years					
Grand total					

Figure 8.8. Payroll additives.

RFP No. _____
Offeror _____

Fringe Benefits
☐ Prime
☐ Subcontract

☐ Exempt
☐ Nonexempt, nonunion
☐ Nonexempt, union
Year ☐ #1 ☐ #2

Element	Base	Rate	Cost	Labor Hours	Cost per Hour
Priced fringe benefits Group insurance Retirement Savings plan Education assistance Other					
Total priced fringe benefits					
Fringe benefits included in labor costs Sick leave Civic and personal leave					
Fringe benefits not priced Severance entitlement Other (identify)					
Total fringe benefits					

*Exclude vacation and holidays

Figure 8.9. Fringe benefits.

184

RFP No. _____	Overhead and G&A	
		☐ Prime
Offeror _____	Expense Summary	☐ Subcontract

Offeror's fiscal year begins _____ , and ends _____

Description of burden distribution bases
Overhead
G & A

Proposed Rates (Percentages)		First Year	Second Year	Third Year	Fourth Year	Fifth Year	Total
Overhead	Pricing						
	Ceiling						
G & A	Pricing						
	Ceiling						

Costs (Dollars)

Overhead	Amount proposed						
	Amount at ceiling rate						
G & A	Amount proposed						
	Amount at ceiling rate						
Allocation base (amount)	Overhead						
	G & A						

Historical information (Percentages)		Recorded rate	DCAA* audited rate	Final negotiated
Overhead	Most recent year 2nd most recent 3rd most recent 4th most recent 5th most recent			
G & A	Most recent year 2nd most recent 3rd most recent 4th most recent 5th most recent			

*Defense contract audit agency

Figure 8.10. Overhead and G&A expense summary.

185

RFP No. _____

Offeror _____

Overhead Expense Forecast

First contract year ☐   Prime   ☐

Second contract year ☐   Subcontract   ☐

_____Account_____   _____Amount_____

Total overhead expense pool   _____

Distribution base (identification and amount)

Overhead rate

For indirect personnel included in the expense pool, specify functions
included and the staffing and rates within each function.

Figure 8.11. Overhead expense forecast.

RFP No. _____

Offeror _____

G & A Expense Forecast

First contract year ☐   Prime ☐

Second contract year ☐   Subcontract ☐

Account   Amount

Total G & A expense pool   _____

Distribution base (identification and amount)

G & A rate

If local indirect personnel are included in the expense pool, specify functions included and the staffing and rates with each function.

Figure 8.12. G&A expense forecast.

187

RFP No. _____
Offeror _____

Other Direct Costs

☐ Prime
☐ Subcontractor

Element	Precontract	First Year	Second Year	Other Years	Total
Travel Relocation Recruitment Training—contract related Other (list)					
Total					

Figure 8.13. Other direct costs.

or pricing organization in accumulating costs for the cost volume. Figure
8.4 is the contract pricing proposal that accompanies proposals to the
government. (Recently, a more simplified version has been developed but
it requires backup information of the same type as shown on this earlier
version of the form.) The other figures shown can be used for yearly cost
summaries, labor costing backup, labor cost summary, description of payroll additives and fringe benefits (labor burden), overhead, general and
administrative costs; and other direct costs such as travel, relocation,
recruitment, and training. The priced proposal, after management review
and approval, is forwarded to the proposal publishing activity along with
backup rationale, appendices, and supporting data for incorporation into
the published proposal.

9

PROPOSAL WRITING AND PUBLICATION

Write the things which you have seen, and the things which are, and the things which shall be hereafter.
Rev. 1:19

Great was the company of those that published it.
Ps. 68:11

The culmination of the proposal preparation activity is the writing and publication of the data, information, and backup material that has been collected, organized, and iterated during the proposal preparation process. Since the written and published word is being used in the proposal as the means of communication to the reader or evaluator, the choice, organization emphasis, and interrelationship of these words is of vital importance. Proper selection of the right amount of text, illustrations, tables, and graphs; and the presentation of this material in an attractive, readable, easily referenced format is the key to stimulating the reader/evaluator's positive reaction to a proposal. All of the material presented in the proposal must be useful to the reader or evaluator, and this material should work together in a synergistic way to depict clearly and concisely that: (1) the proposer has a thorough understanding of the job requirements, (2) the proposer has the capability and experience required to perform the work in a successful manner, and (3) the job will be carried out on schedule and within cost constraints in a high quality manner.

THE PROPOSAL QUALITY AS A REFLECTION
OF WORK QUALITY

At a recent seminar on proposal preparation, the instructor asked the question: "What single thing, in or about a proposal, will most convincingly show the reader or evaluator that the company will provide a high quality work activity or work output?" After much deliberation, and after several good but not profound answers, one student replied, "The quality of the proposal itself!" This answer highlighted a fact that many companies overlook: *the quality of the proposal itself* is an indicator or reflection of what can be expected in the quality of the work to be performed. The quality of writing, organization, illustrations, printing, and even the quality of the paper and cover are important in conveying the overall knowledge to the customer that a company exerts meticulous care in doing its work. Elaborate or fancy proposals without high quality content or technical excellence, of course, are of little value. In-depth quality can be easily observed and readily recognized by the experienced proposal evaluator.

THE WRITER'S ROLE IN PROPOSAL PREPARATION

Synergism in Proposal Writing

Unfortunately, many proposals fail to present a cohesive, integrated flow of material from start to finish. This is usually caused by the fact that several or many individuals, organizations, or departments contribute to the proposal, often making inputs just prior to the publication date, and that insufficient effort and time is applied by the proposal writer and proposal manager in tying together the entire package into a consistent and interrated "story" of how the company can and will do the work.

Writing a proposal is much like baking a cake. Each ingredient in and of itself would be rather tasteless and uninteresting. But when the ingredients are combined in a precise manner and allowed to interact and unite into one entity, the whole becomes attractive, palatable, and highly desirable. The combination of ingredients under the right interactive conditions has formed a whole new product. This "synergistic" approach *must* be used in proposal writing if a high potential of capture is expected. The proposal writer must avoid having his proposal appear as merely a group of ingredients that have been collected from several sources and have not been correlated in writing style, content, mathematical consistency, or technical content. When inputs are derived from several sources, the information must be thoroughly digested and reconstituted into a total cohesive package through the proposal consolidation review and reconciliation process. This reconstituted information must then be put into words by a skilled writer or team of writers who have an overall appreciation for the importance of the work to the company and a positive and almost aggressive optimism related to acquisition of the new work. All of this must also be presented in a manner which meets good writing practice in the areas of style, grammar, punctuation, spelling, and word usage.

Words Stimulate

The proposal writer must remember that throughout the proposal the objective is to stimulate the reader or evaluator to make a positive decision relative to the company's expertise and ability to do the work successfully and in an outstanding manner. This ability is usually reflected in the writer's words, by an underlying confidence and assurance that the company will win, and by the documentation of convincing and authentic experience. When writing about specific activities or outputs to be provided to the customer, it is usually most effective to use the first person future plural tense in describing work to be done. For example, "*we will* perform the following packaging and handling activities," is a positive, future tense statement that *presumes* that the proposing company will be awarded the contract. Avoid statements like "we would" or "if the contract is awarded to us we would . . ." which imply doubt as to confidence in acquiring the work. The best practice to follow is to write the work statements and plans *as if the contract has already been received.* This writing style reinforces the reader's assurance that a proposing company has both the desire *and* ability to do the work, and that the company has taken a winner's attitude and approach to acquiring and performing the work successfully.

Another example of a positive writing style that will assist in stimulating the reader or evaluator to make a favorable selection recommendation is to use *past tense* statements when it comes to reflecting commitments to the project. For example, "We *have assigned* Mr. Roger Scott as project manager for this work;" or "We *have set aside* 2,600 square feet of our K–10 building shop area for the tooling and equipment described below." Both indicate a degree of company *pre-commitment* to the work. First person singular past tense is best used when describing actual past accomplishments of personnel, equipment, or company. As an example: "Mr. Scott successfully managed the REVAMP and CONTROL projects during 1983. These projects were completed within cost targets and on schedule."

Documenting and Explaining a Record of Success

A proposal is no place to be modest! A proposal is one document in which it is not only desirable but absolutely necessary to document and explain successes in areas directly or indirectly related to the proposal task. Flowery superlatives relative to a company's ability should not be included in the proposal itself. However, they can be used sparingly in the letter of transmittal. A well-documented historical record of successes, along with positive testimonials of third parties, will give a firm the competitive edge over other competitors who have equal technical excellence but who have failed to describe and document their successes.

What about past failures? Abilities and capabilities should be emphasized rather than limitations and weaknesses. Being honest does not mean pointing out one's faults. It does mean being completely *truthful* about capabilities and not misleading the customer into thinking that facilities, personnel, finances, or resources are available to do the job when they do not exist. If a past major program failure does exist, it is desirable to point out the corrective measures that have been taken to preclude recurrence of the malady. But this description must not be overly complex or cumbersome as it will detract from the positive aspects of a company's capabilities.

The Proposal Writer as a Storyteller

The proposal writer must be sufficiently familiar with the request for proposal or request for quotation and the overall project plans to assess and bring into focus the relative importance of each phase of the work and to generate an overall consistency and flow of information in the proposal to make it both interesting and persuasive. The proposal writer is usually responsible for finalizing and coordinating a detailed outline of the proposal's contents, a glossary of terms, and a bibliography of reference books, periodicals, reports, and other documents. The proposal writer is not only the grammarian but the integrator of words and ideas, imparting just the right emphasis and explanation to each part of the written proposal. The writer is the storyteller who makes the proposal stimulating, even exciting, to the reader or evaluator.

PUBLICATION OF THE PROPOSAL

If a company is likely to submit proposals on a periodic basis and not on a "one time only" basis, it is most practical, desirable, and efficient to do proposal publication work *within* the company's organization. In-house publication of proposals, using company personnel and equipment, is desirable because (1) the potential work performers should be involved as closely and as integrally as possible with the publication process; (2) the confidentiality of proposal information should be preserved; and (3) the timeliness of publication should be ensured. Other benefits of in-house publication of proposals are immediate access to the publication staff and proposal material to incorporate changes, and maximum responsiveness of the publication staff to company objectives. In the opinion of the authors neither proposal writing nor proposal publication are appropriate activities to subcontract to another company.

To publish a proposal in-house, personnel, skills, and equipment must be surveyed to determine the methods of composing and reproducing printed text and illustrative matter that are available within the company. Table 9.1 compares various methods of composition commonly used for proposals and Table 9.2 is a comparison of commonly available reproduction methods.

WORD PROCESSING: A BOON TO PROPOSAL PUBLISHERS

By far the most advantageous method of composition for proposals is the use of the word processor or computer text editor. The greatest advantage of computerized text management systems is that the basic text need only be entered once. There is no need of typing and retyping preliminary drafts, rough drafts, final drafts, and final copy. A hard copy draft can be produced rapidly on a high speed printer; edited or modified by the originator, writer, and/or editor; and modified by adding, deleting, moving or changing only those words or sections affected. The high speed printer used for drafts can either be of the dot-matrix type or the letter quality type. The letter quality type is slower but results in more readable print and still is at least twice as fast as a typist. Printers can be given instructions to produce double or multispaced drafts for ease of editing, or single spaced final copy for photocopy reproduction.

Word processing magnetic disks or cassette tapes can be transferred to computer tapes that drive phototypesetting equipment. The most modern computer phototypesetting equipment can provide a wide variety of fonts and type styles. Since most proposals employ computing equipment in deriving the final formats of the cost estimates and resulting price estimates, it is reasonable to assume that the same or compatible automatic data processing equipment can be used for the word processing or text editing functions. Most large companies have computers that will perform the multiple functions of accounting, bookkeeping, computing, and word processing. Small business and personal computers have recently become available which will provide these same functions at a low initial investment cost and a low operating cost.

THE PUBLICATION DEPARTMENT'S ROLE
IN PROPOSAL PREPARATION

The company's publication department usually has responsibility for organizing, publishing, and sometimes even writing the physical proposal document or documents. Of immediate and prime concern to the company publication manager is the planning and scheduling of publication activities and the availability and allocation of personnel. The proposal publica-

TABLE 9.1   METHODS OF COMPOSING

Method	Advantages	Disadvantages
Linotype (hot type) set by typographer	Wide choice of book faces. Automatic justification of columns. May be set in galley form, or pages may be made up by typographer. Excellent quality.	Most expensive method. Changes require re-setting type. Major changes could require entire pages to be reset. Last minute changes are very expensive and could affect schedule. This method is rapidly becoming outdated with the advent of modern computer techniques.
Justowriter (cold type)	Good quality. Assorted book faces. Automatic justification after a master tape is punched. Proportionally spaced characters produce a type-like appearance. About half the price of hot type.	Last-minute changes may be difficult since changes in characters per line may require retyping additional lines.
IBM Executive electric typewriter, Varityper DSJ, or equivalent reproduction typewriter (cold type)	Good quality, fast, and economical. Assorted book faces. Proportionally spaced characters create typelike appearance, provide greater readability, and more characters per inch than standard typewriters. Repro may be typed (1) in galley or page form or (2) direct on paper masters. With method 1, corrections are easily made by covering error with "white-out" and retyping, by stripping in change, or by retyping paragraph.	Justification requires a second typing.
Standard electric typewriter	Fair quality, fast. Assorted faces. Even impression. Repro may be typed in galley form	Standard character spacing does not read as well as proportional spacing, and has less characters per

(Continued)

TABLE 9.1   METHODS OF COMPOSING   *(Continued)*

Method	Advantages	Disadvantages
	or directly on paper masters	inch. Standard characters generally have an "office quality" look.
Word processing	Excellent quality, fast, convenient, typesetting can be done directly from the word processing information on most computer-driven typesetting machines. This is by far the *best* method for proposal preparation because of the inherent ability to make last minute changes without re-inputting large volumes of text.	Most costly of the systems that can be chosen unless the word processing and typesetting already exists within the company or closely available on short notice and quick turnaround. Specially trained keyboard operator is required.

TABLE 9.2   REPRODUCTION METHODS

Type of Reproduction	Advantages	Disadvantages
Photo offset on a Multilith or offset press using film offset negatives and metal plates	Excellent quality. Any type and size repro may be used including paste-up. Line illustrations and halftones reproduce well. Foldouts may be printed and pages may be ganged on larger press. Wide range of papers available.	Highest cost per page. Requires the most time for reproduction, although it is possible to print several hundred pages offset on both sides, including some halftone illustrations, in quantities of 100, in less than 8 working hours. This includes binding 25 copies with plastic comb binding.
Ektalith paper plates on a Multilith press	Good quality. Cheaper than photo offset. Any type repro including paste-up. This is a photographic process.	There are few commercial sources for this process. The equipment is made by Kodak and must be purchased.
Xerox paper plates on a Multilith press	Reasonably good quality. Cheaper than photo offset; Fair range of repro materials. Copy may be	Will reproduce surface imperfections in repro material. Will not reproduce large solid areas

(Continued)

TABLE 9.2 REPRODUCTION METHODS *(Continued)*

Type of Reproduction	Advantages	Disadvantages
	any size. This is a photo electrostatic process.	well (such as bold black type or illustrations). Halftones are difficult to reproduce.
Itek paper plates on a Multilith press	Good quality. Cheaper than photo offset; cost is in the range of Ektalith and Xerox. Equipment is made by Photostat Corp. Any type and size repro up to twice final size can be copied. This is a photographic process.	Since this is a relatively new process, it is comparatively expensive.
Multilith master (direct paper plate)	Fair quality. Cheapest method using Multilith press since repro is also the plate. Text is typed with a carbon ribbon directly on the special paper master, which is then put on Multilith press.	Repro must be final size and very clean. Corrections and erasures often produce poor results. Art work is difficult to prepare on masters. Line art and halftones would have to be reproduced by another method.
Photostats	Good quality. Inexpensive if only a few copies are needed. Any size and type repro may be used. Line and halftone reproduced well. Continuous-tone photostats look like original photo with no screen necessary. Any number of matte positives made from each negative.	Less economical if more than 6 copies are required. Reproduction only on one side of sheet.
Diazo blue or black	Fair quality. Very inexpensive. Text may be typed on translucent vellum. Line art may be drawn on vellum final size. Vellums are run through diazo machine for copies. Diazo equipment is expensive to own, but the commercial	Repro must either be on a final size translucent or intermediate must be made to run through the diazo machine. Changes and corrections to vellum generally show a ghost image. Blue line has an "office quality" look. Halftones require a film

(Continued)

TABLE 9.2   REPRODUCTION METHODS   *(Continued)*

Type of Reproduction	Advantages	Disadvantages
	service is reasonably priced.	negative and film positive before they can be run through the diazo machine.
Xerox copies	Fair quality. Inexpensive. Text and line art may be reproduced on bond paper, translucent paper, or other materials. Xerox translucent intermediate may be used to run through diazo machine.	Same as for Xerox paper plates. Poor on large solid areas.
Mimeograph	Fair quality. Very inexpensive. Stencil typed in typewriter. Corrections can be made easily.	Stencil must be cut perfectly or color is uneven. Line art is electronically copied from good original. Halftones must also be copied electronically, producing very coarse, poor results.
Spirit duplicator	Fair quality; very inexpensive. Easy to operate. Office equipment.	Care must be taken in preparing master or corrections may show. Color is generally purple but may be red, green, or black. Line art is limited if prepared on master. Halftones impossible.

tion leader must be a person who is fully acquainted with all phases of publications work; who is available to devote full time to the effort, if required, during the publication phase; and who can work under pressure. Above all, this person must be one who is aware of the magnitude of the work being proposed and appreciates the efforts of, and pressures on, the other members of the proposal preparation team. The publication *leader*, knowing the situation, must be able to obtain cooperation and to meet schedules. The publication *manager* should schedule other department work so that additional people will be available when needed. This usually means that the entire publication department of a small company will be tied up for the last several days of the proposal effort.

Once the publication leader has been selected, he or she should devote full attention to the proposal. In the early stages of planning, only the publication leader and occasionally an illustrator will be needed. The first task of the publication leader is to attend proposal conferences and briefings, and to become acquainted with the other members of the team and their specific responsibilities in the overall effort. During the initial stage of development, only small contributions will be received from individuals preparing the technical and organization/management volumes and, therefore, the publication leader will have the time to prepare background material and to organize outlines, progress charts, and other guide material.

The publication leader, as well as the writer, should become thoroughly familiar with the request for proposal or request for quotation. The RFP/RFQ may specifiy a specific format or other publication requirements. A review of this document will familiarize the leader with the technical aspects of the proposal and will put this person in a position to allocate attention to the various phases of the work being proposed.

The proposal *publication* leader must work very closely with the proposal *processing* leader and a proposal *production* leader to plan the editing and the physical typing, typesetting, or word processing; and printing, binding, and mailing. Proposal production includes preparation of text material, illustrations, tables, graphs, photographs, indices, appendices, bibliographies, tables of contents, summaries, inserts and foldouts, and special covers. To avoid excessive work during the last few days prior to submitting the proposal, lengthy sections can sometimes be printed and held for collation. Once printing costs are established, the publication leader should make every effort to work with the printer in scheduling work to minimize costs and to obtain the best quality finished document possible.

A typing or word processing and editing format sheet should be prepared since final text preparation will probably require additional typists or keyboard operators who may be unfamiliar with the company's or project's format requirements. The format should be based on two precepts: readability and ease of typing or word processor input. Abbreviations must be standardized as soon as possible in the proposal cycle, as should reference symbols, mathematical terms, and format for the preparation of formulas. This guide matter should be distributed to all parties concerned before any final material is prepared.

While preparation of the technical volume or volumes is in its early stages, the publications department can compare such sections as company background and history, experience in similar projects, resumes of key personnel, and facilities descriptions. In a well organized publications department, this material can be lifted from a hard copy or word processor library and tailored to suit the particular proposal. If it is not available as such, it must be gathered from previous proposals or obtained from company management and from other departments. If these sections are voluminous, they can be printed in advance, as can covers, separators, appendices, and indices. By the time these tasks are completed, information will be coming in from the technical and organization/management teams and proposal writers. If it is not being received, a gentle (or not so gentle) prodding may be in order. Methods such as tape recording, dictating, or consultation with a writer may speed things up. It should be explained that the originator of the written material should not spend time polishing up the grammar and syntax, as this can be done in final copy editing of the entire document. Sketches and other material requiring artwork must be pre-scheduled and received on time, and text inputs must be received in time to prepare a final draft for management review prior to final text polishing and printing. Proposal text is most often printed on 8½ by 11 inch white paper.

Tables and Illustrations

Schematic and block diagrams, flow diagrams, charts, and graphs are absolutely essential to understanding how a system or piece of equipment functions. Nothing is more fatiguing to a proposal reader or proposal evaluator than to have to wade through numerous pages of technical data which require the reader to form mental pictures when real pictures would be so much better. The reader can be helped to understand the work activity or work output being proposed by using visual aids frequently. Text should be converted to tabular form wherever possible. (Tables are more easily seen at a glance and allow the reader to find what is being looked for quickly.)

If available, hardware photographs can add a touch of realism that cannot be duplicated with mere words. If photographs are to be used, however, they must be reproduced in such a way as to have the greatest impact. Extraneous material that detracts from the important features of the work activity or work output should be either cropped or retouched. However, retouching should be kept to a minimum to hold down the cost. Excessive retouching actually defeats the realistic impression desired.

Sometimes there is an opportunity to achieve great impact and drama with an illustration. For example, for a piece of equipment or an operation that is not yet built or in process, a good detailed artist's conceptual illustration can never be construed to be unnecessarily elaborate. A detailed rendering, painted or drawn to resemble a photograph, can be very effective since it imparts a feeling of reality that could not be achieved with a line drawing. This type of illustration can be used if it serves the purpose of stimulating reader interest, understanding, or knowledge of the work being proposed. Reproduction of these artforms should be such that will preserve the quality of the original as much as possible. A good illustration should not be ruined by using an inadequate reproduction method.

A full page illustration should not exceed the maximum text area. Illustrations should be prepared larger than the final size whenever possible to take advantage of sharpening the lines when reduced to final size. Ink lines are preferable; but clean, black pencil lines will reproduce well when reduced by fifty percent or less. Pencil art, however, should be reproduced by photo offset in order to produce the best effects. Because they are cumbersome to handle, expensive to reproduce, and difficult for the reader to find, foldout pages should be used sparingly.

Integrating Tables and Illustration into Text

Illustrations and tables should be located as closely as possible to the point of text citation. Cutting the smaller illustrations into the text provides the ultimate in readability. This procedure requires a foreknowledge of illustration sizes in order to plan the pages. Full page illustrations should be avoided if one-sided printing is used since it is desirable to have the referencing text and the figure on the same page. If pages are printed on both sides, however, a full-page (or smaller) illustration can face its text citation. In instances where extremely large flow diagrams, tables, charts, or graphs are required, a foldout page is the only solution. These large pages can be more easily referenced by the reader if an 8½ by 11 inch blank apron is provided on the left margin and the figure is inserted in an appendix at the rear of the volume. These sheets may then be folded out and referenced beside the text in any portion of the proposal volume.

Proposal Covers and Bindings

The cover is most likely the only part of the proposal that will resemble a brochure. The impact value of a good cover may win a significant psychological advantage and a chance to gain points even before the proposal is opened. The most objective evaluator cannot fail to be motivated to read further when confronted with an interesting and well executed cover. The cover will *gain* attention, while the material inside the volume must *hold* attention. The cover, however, need not be overly expensive to be effective. With the imaginative use of stock and two colors, an impressive cover can be produced. A photograph, combined with good color balance and creative typography can often be eyecatching as well as meaningful to the evaluator. The creative nature of the company preparing the proposal will generally reflect in the proposal cover design. The four-color process is usually impractical for proposal covers because the cost and time required for high quality work are usually prohibitive. The cover paper stock will influence the graphic treatment of the cover and vice versa. Paper covers should be of adequate weight to sustain repeated handling. Generally, a 100–pound cover or a double weight (135–pound) cover is used.

Except for proposals of less than fifty pages, the best methods of binding are plastic combs or multi-ring notebooks. For proposals where a large number of volumes and/or copies are required, the former is a more practical binding method. Proposals with few copies required can be bound in multi-ring notebooks. Many interesting styles of notebooks are available, some of which contain clear plastic covers on the front, rear, and binding edge for insertion of a specially printed insert. Some notebooks come equipped with "D-rings" that allow pages to lie with even edges, some have pockets on the inside covers for insertion of supplemental information. Although these notebooks are very attractive and handy for evaluation, they have the disadvantages of high price and a greater possibility of lost, removed, or miscollated pages. Comb-bound proposal volumes may be more than one inch thick, yet their facing pages lie flat when the proposal is opened, just as is the case with the more expensive multiringed notebooks. Pages may be removed and replaced if necessary in comb-bound documents, but are less likely to be inadvertently removed. Pages may be printed separately, collated, then bound. Plastic combs come in an assortment of colors, sizes, and lengths to adapt to almost any binding situation. This binding method can be accomplished in-house with relatively inexpensive equipment. Proposals of less than fifty pages may be printed in signatures and bound like a brochure. A one-piece cover is used and the pages are wire or thread-stitched, or stapled to the cover. This method, however, is not geared to the rapid, in-house processing demanded by most proposals.

THE PROPOSAL FORMAT

An outline of a typical multivolume proposal format is shown on Figure 9.1. Whether the proposal is a multivolume proposal or a single volume proposal, it will contain most of the subjects listed on this outline. The first step of overall proposal writing and publication that is taken jointly by the publications leader, writer, and proposal manager is to prepare and approve a *detailed outline*. If the proposal itself is voluminous, this outline could extend in length to as much as ten pages. The proposal preparation, writing, assembly, and publication processes will be much easier if this detailed outline is prepared at the beginning of proposal development and kept up to date as the proposal takes shape. This outline is used as a detailed guide for writing, assembly and integration of all parts of the proposal but can also be used to make a rough estimate of the number of words, pages, illustrations, fold-outs, or tables needed in each section and subsection. This information will allow the publication leader to decide how many volumes and covers are needed and the approximate size of each volume. The detailed outline is the framework of the total proposal and the structure that permits the writer to present proposal information with a common thread of continuity. A prearranged outline numbering and format system should be developed to assure outline numbering or lettering consistency.

The Letter of Transmittal

Although the letter of transmittal of a proposal is often written last, it is probably next in importance to the proposal cover in stimulating the evaluator to read further. The letter of transmittal should, in a one-paragraph opening, describe the work activity or work output that is being proposed. This summary can be further supported by an "Executive Summary," included in a separate volume or at the very beginning or very end of the proposal material itself. The letter of transmittal should convey the fact that the company has an unshakable confidence in its ability to perform and complete the work on schedule, within cost, and in a high quality manner; and that the project has the total support and backing of corporate management. If any superlatives are used in the total proposal package, the letter of transmittal should include them. Statements such as "In view of this company's outstanding past successes in performing similar and identical tasks, as well as our competitive price estimate, it is appropriate and prudent that our firm be employed to perform the work," are not unheard off and often acceptable in a letter of transmittal where they would be overbearing or presumptuous when included in the proposal text material.

The letter of transmittal should also include references to the request for proposal or request for quotation, telephone conversations, or previous correspondence if appropriate, and other important information to be highlighted such as time duration of proposal validity, payment provisions, and any other special stipulations or conditions. For example, if the entire proposal is based on the customer supplying drawings, technical support, parts or materials, facilities, equipment, goods, or personnel on specified dates, this should be clearly stated and the appropriate proposal volume and page should be referenced in the letter of transmittal.

Front Matter

The "front matter" of a proposal volume generally consists of a title page, a "proprietary information" statement page, a foreword, a table of contents, a list of illustrations, a list of tables, and an executive summary (if not included in a separate volume). The title page includes the name of the work activity or work output; the organization to whom the proposal is submitted; the name, address, and telephone number of the organization submitting the proposal; the date submitted; the security classification (if any); and a document or library number. The "proprietary information" statement page states that the proposal information cannot and should not be transmitted to other companies. The foreword is a one paragraph statement serving to identify whether the proposal is internal, external, unsolicited, or responsive to a request for proposal or request for quotation.

If the proposal is in response to a request, the requesting document title and number is referenced.

The table of contents is a "road map" to help the reader determine the major and minor elements of the proposal and their interrelationship with each other. It should include a cross reference list to pages or paragraphs of the request for proposal or request for quotation. This cross reference list will help the evaluator quickly identify which part or parts of the proposal is responsive to which RFP/RFQ requirement, and will assist in determining responsiveness to each requirement. It is sometimes desirable to include the table of contents and cross reference list in all volumes of a multivolume proposal to allow the reader to find material in volumes other than the one he or she is currently evaluating. A list of illustrations and a list of tables are included to permit a rapid scanning of pictorial or graphic material in the proposal. If there are relatively few tables in the proposal, the list may be combined with the list of illustrations.

The Proposal Executive Summary

The executive summary, which can and often does appear in every proposal volume, is a brief presentation containing the desirable results the customer will obtain, how these results will be ensured, and why this particular company should be selected to do the work. It strongly emphasizes the key sales points of the proposal.

It is a tried and true principle of good salesmanship that first impressions are both crucial and persistent. The initial impression gained by the customer from a proposal is derived from the proposal executive summary. The effects of this impression can influence the evaluation of the entire proposal. This is the evaluator's first encounter with the text. This portion of the proposal should be the ultimate in clear, persuasive prose.

The executive summary will be read by individuals at several decision levels. A few of these decision makers will be technical experts. The majority of them are more concerned with basic relationships than technical detail. Major new work acquisitions are of interest to other divisions within the customer's organization. The executive summary can be used by the customer to inform these interested parties about the new work. The proposal executive summary is an ideal vehicle to inform, persuade, and educate this group of people. The summary is simply a capsule version of the new work activity.

Objectives of the Executive Summary. The summary sets the scene. It should convince the customer that it is worthwhile to read, study, and constructively evaluate the proposal. To accomplish this, the client's own self interest should be appealed to by highlighting these key benefits (three or four at most) which will be gained by selecting this firm to perform the program. If these benefits are among the two or three which *the customer has indicated* are the most desirable, they will be doubly effective.

Preparation. The executive summary can best be prepared in the final stages of the proposal preparation process. At this point in the preparation cycle the solution is fully developed and all of the relevant points about the program have been defined. These points form the basis for writing the summary. The proposal writer has been thoroughly indoctrinated during the preparation of the proposal and at this point in the cycle should be free to prepare the executive summary.

The executive summary, being of such crucial importance to the proposal, demands the best writing talent available. The best talent can produce a better job if an organized approach is used. These are some steps which this talent can use in writing an executive summary:

1. The entire document should be read carefully and brief notes made of the important points.
2. These notes should be put on three by five cards, one item per card. Other important items can be added as required. The cards can then be arranged in a logical sequence.
3. With these notes as a guide, the writer can construct sentences which express the ideas put forth in the proposal.
4. Order and sequence should be evaluated and changes made as necessary. Then the sentences can be placed in paragraphs along with connectives and transitions as appropriate.
5. The entire executive summary should be reread to ensure that it contains no statements that are not substantiated by the source. A reader unacquainted with the original should be able to glean the essential facts from the executive summary and form valid conclusions.

Technical, Organization and Management, and Cost Volumes

Detailed content of these volumes is discussed in Chapters 6, 7, and 8 respectively. The writer and publisher must be sufficiently familiar with these three volumes to assure that there are no overlaps, duplications, inconsistencies, or omissions in these three volumes and that all three sections of the proposal are consistent in format; content; grammar; abbreviations and names used; references and cross references; page, figure, and table numbering; and printing style. The writing and publishing team must also assure that these three proposal sections are compatible with other proposal material such as the letter of transmittal, appendices, and any supplemental material requested by and supplied to the potential customer.

Appendices

Appendices are normally used to include a draft (or final) contract document, company financial reports, facilities descriptions, and supplemental proposal backup material. Appendices and referenced documents are often used to avoid exceeding proposal page limitations and can be provided, if desired, only "on request" to reduce the volume of material initially transmitted to the customer. Including a draft or final contract document as an appendix, enclosure, or reference has the tremendous psychological advantage of giving the customer the opportunity to immediately respond positively with a contract award or request for a negotiation session if the customer likes the contract document. The disadvantages of including a proposed contract document are: (1) not enough is usually known about final contract provisions at the end of the proposal cycle, and (2) without sufficient explanatory words, the contract document, even if a draft, may be construed as a final nonnegotiable position when the proposer actually intends to leave the door open to reasonable contract changes.

Tables of Contents, Indices, Lists of Terms and Abbreviations

As mentioned earlier, it is sometimes desirable to repeat the table of contents, index, or lists of terms and abbreviations in each proposal volume if a large multivolume proposal is being evaluated. As shown in Chapter 10, large proposals are usually evaluated by source evaluation boards consisting of several teams. Each team may evaluate its respective volume (technical, organization and management, and cost) and not have an opportunity to view the overall proposal content except in the form of a table of contents or index. Also, terms and abbreviations, which are consistent between all volumes, often appear in more than one volume, necessitating their repeat in *each* volume.

Index Tabs and Figure Positioning

The practice of including index tabs or index tab sheets at major subdivisions within each proposal volume will make the evaluator's job easier and will provide an ability to more quickly and readily flip to a given portion of the proposal for a quick look or in-depth study. Index tabs on major headings and even subheadings should be clearly marked, durable, and color coded if possible to provide a ready visual reference. Tabs should be printed right side up when the proposal volume is rotated one fourth turn clockwise. Positioning of figures or tables, if not on the page vertically, should also be readable right side up when the volume is rotated *clockwise* one fourth turn. Two major irritants to proposal evaluators are: (1) difficulty in finding and cross referencing information and (2) having to turn the book with binding toward them to read illustrations and tables. The above positioning of index tabs and figures will reduce or eliminate these irritants.

PUBLISHING THE GIANT PROPOSAL

The size of a proposal can vary from just a few pages to many *volumes* of pages. (See frontispiece.) Even the best-managed publications department can be completely thrown into disorganization by sudden demand for thousands of pages in a limited number of days. It is not uncommon for proposals for large, complex, high technology projects to require up to fifty *volumes* of proposal material for *each* copy of the proposal. Usually the beleaguered manager of such a proposal cannot hope to reduce the deluge of paper or extend the time. Time can be bought, however, by using every clock hour and by adding manpower: creating a corps of deputies and supporting organizational elements. A large *ad hoc* organization is usually required to meet the demands of a giant proposal. Not every company will produce one of those classic piles of three-ring binders, but whatever the company produces, it should be braced for the day when it is asked to turn out an immense document in a very limited time. Then pages will be calculated and people will be counted and there will not be enough clock hours available for the regular staff in the usual facilities to just pick up and lay down the sheets, to say nothing of reading them, sorting them, or making marks on them.

This company will need help—a giant *ad hoc* organization to cope with a giant assignment. An effective *ad hoc* publication organization can often be created by merely expanding and reinforcing existing publication units. But it should be remembered that all the internal help that is to be concentrated on a special job must be obtained at the expense of the other activities of the company. It may be necessary to resort to a bit of temporary distortion of job descriptions and functions to assure that maximum benefit is extracted from the talent available.

Although proposal preparation, writing, and publication is inherently and necessarily an in-house task because of time and company security limitations, the publication of an immense proposal is an occasion to deviate from an in-house proposal development policy and to use outside help in selected areas and for selected tasks. The most appropriate tasks to subcontract are the physical aspects of proposal publication such as final typesetting, printing, binding, packaging, and preparation for mailing. All writing, editing, and final mailing must be done by company personnel to assure technical and business accuracy and timeliness of mailing. If a vendor is used, security and work quality should be closely controlled by on-site monitoring of the vendor's activities to ensure that publication support is not shared with a business competitor.

Irrespective of the chain of command or the titles bestowed on groups and individuals, activity throughout the *ad hoc* proposal organization will fall into three categories: developing content, processing, and production. The special demands of the giant job on each of these functions can be described without attempting to define any rigid organizational structure.

Developing Content

Required: Strong Editorial Leadership. Heightened interest and involvement on the part of the proposal technical staff will bring new and able people into the act as authors and reviewers. The efforts of the original authors will be reviewed by their superiors at an early stage in the proposal preparation process, and real technical editing, such as lifting out whole sections or combining and redoing illustrations and tables will have been done far upstream in the process. The publication staff must devote itself principally to the mammoth task of editing, sorting out, and checking all the input information. For a giant proposal, it is important that early in the planning stages a top level technical editor work closely with the proposal authors to provide editorial leadership on such things as making the detailed outline, establishing relative emphasis of the various proposal elements, apportioning content among volumes, determining format, and setting ground rules for the graphic material. Poorly conceived instructions to the originating authors can complicate processing operations far downstream. Within the restrictions imposed by the request for proposal or request for quotation, a company should get things off on the right foot mechanically. New and special formats, nonstandard page sizes, special type faces, or anything else that will work a hardship on the group or on vendors should be avoided.

The "Very Detailed" Outline. Developing a very detailed outline down to a low level and "freezing" it early in the proposal preparation process is particularly important for the giant proposal. Starting with a general format outline such as that shown on Figure 9.1, a more detailed outline can be constructed. An overall outline is sometimes indicated by the requesting organization in the request for proposal or request for quotation. Given some freedom in the detailed structure of the outline, most technical people can construct an array of topics and subtopics and apply the prearranged outline numbering structure to show interrelationship and subordination. The challenge for the helpful editor is to supply lively, active-voice titles that in turn challenge the technical author or inputting organization, as well as constrain the subject matter to its specific contribution to the overall proposal. The outline for a giant proposal must give many far flung authors the proper perspective of their individual contributions. The outline is also the basis of checklists and status charts of authors' contributions that will be needed in the processing operations,

Ia   **Letter of Transmittal (sometimes put in each volume)**

A summary of what is being proposed

Company's confidence and support in accomplishing job

References to RFPs, letter requests, phone calls, etc.

When the notice to proceed must be given

Time duration of proposal validity

Payment provisions

Special stipulations and conditions

Ib   **Front Matter: title page, foreword, table of contents,* list of illustrations, list of tables**

II   **Technical Proposal**

Scope of work

Description of work

Schedule for the work

III   **Organization and Management Proposal**

Company organization

Project organization & key personnel duties

Résumés

Experience and past performance

IV   **Cost Proposal**

Resources estimates

Rationale and backup information

Cost summary and pricing information

V   **Appendices**

Draft Contract

Company financial report

Facilities descriptions

Supplemental material

IV   **Executive Summary (optional)**

*Note: Table of contents for all volumes should be in *each* volume.

Figure 9.1.   Proposal Format for Multivolume Proposal.

and the very first outline draft must contain detailed page quotas. Previous proposals on similar subjects and detailed reports on constituent subjects of the giant proposal will provide first cut estimates of page quotas. If this outline is well done and not allowed to fluctuate, at least in its major subdivisions, the publication department can prepare, in advance, the assortment of covers and tabbed dividers that will be required for the multitude of volumes and sections of the proposal.

The Logistics of Handling Large Proposal Inputs.   Although it should be one's intent to avoid including large volumes of support material not needed for complete understanding of a proposal, often the customer requires this data because entities within the customer's organization have requested it. The practice of consigning everything that can be interpreted as support material to appendices, not only helps the reviewer by reducing the amount of material to be waded through to obtain continuity, but facilitates production by allowing transfer of existing materials from previously published documents or word processing files. If extracts or complete issues of reports by a company or by a subcontractor are to serve as appendix material, every effort should be made to use them in their original form and to run them from the original stored information. It is no problem or violation to insert an opening page in the appendix stating that "Appendix C is identical to Section 5 of the June 1982 report on . . . , and the format of the original report is retained."

When providing large quantities of data such as computerized cost printouts, camera copies of these machine-produced plots and tabulations can be included to provide the customer with authentic original information. Considerable time can be saved in producing these sections if patching or mounting of such sheets is resisted. A single lead page can point out what the column heads are and describe the content and sequence of the sheets that follow. Bulk should be reduced and duplication of excessive or repetitive material should be avoided. Sometimes a selected computer run can be followed with a printed table that summarizes its results.

Simplifying Illustrations.   Creators of content for the giant proposal must be made aware early in the proposal development process of the illustrator's requirements. General ground rules such as size, clarity, position on page (horizontally or vertically), labeling, etc. should be provided to all members of the proposal writing team. As the proposal process continues, the illustration department will begin to assess the types, sizes, and complexity of figures, photographs, tables, charts, and graphs that are to be included in the proposal. Standardization of format can be worked to advantage when printing huge numbers of illustrations. Blank forms can be prepared, for example, if many different calendar bar chart shedules are to be produced. If a number of graphs are to be included, standard grids can be established. Mass production of figures can employ many artistic "tricks-of-the-trade" to reduce illustrator man-hours for duplicating routine formats. Modern photocopy techniques can produce neat, clean, legible figures and diagrams using the "cut-and-paste" method without compromising overall proposal quality. Computer graphics outputs can speed the production of figures and charts by at least an order of magnitude and can reduce artwork and drafting times to near zero. Individuals who are preparing inputs to proposals should be cautioned to avoid the practice of placing too much text in a graphic illustration.

Processing the Giant Proposal

The activities that are contained in the conversion of raw content to final copy ready for printing are commonly grouped together under the term *processing*. If the groundwork mentioned earlier has been thoroughly done, processing of the information will be much easier. The huge proposal still imposes some heavy loads on editors, illustrators, typists, and word processor operators. The processing phase not only includes the assembly and integration of the total package and preparation for printing, but also includes the review-correct-and-approve cycle. The approval cycle itself can cause changes and iterations in the proposal material, particularly if last-minute management or technical decisions are made to adjust the company's competitive or technical posture.

Coordinating the Processing Operations. Normal publication operations use editorial groups to guide the technical authors, compile and sort out the pieces, and steer things through the production process. The volume of work in a giant proposal both permits and necessitates the separation of these functions. First, there is true editing, which is the skill of making the words flow together and conform to requirements for accuracy, grammar, and format. Then there is an enormous amount of checking and proofing required, followed by actual transmittal of the material to the production or printing units. This last step requires steady and patient workers adept at screening out the confusion without relaxing the pressure to meet the publication schedule. Mobilizing processing operations, then, will recognize the different qualifications of the existing staff as well as those who have been recruited from other organizations within the company. There may be some editors who can bring order to any pile of paper and some coordinators who can do a good job of copy editing, but it is usually better to have a sharp break between these functions, even to underscore it with a slight separation in physical work location. Reading-writing types can often be found in the library, publications, training, and personnel. The straight coordinators are best recruited from administrative departments.

The Special Style Manual. Every company has its own editorial guide book or style manual, but for the enormous proposal it is worthwhile to reissue it in parts to cover specific editorial problems and procedures. There will be sections of interest only to the editors and originating authors. Others, like the section on format, abbreviations, and special symbols, for example, must go to all typists, word processor operators, and illustrators. This special style manual or group of manuals can contain other detailed editorial guidelines and ground rules that are unique to the proposed work or that have been specified or requested in the request for proposal or request for quotation.

Checklists and Tracking the Processing Schedule.   The separation of processing operations and the possibility of several sequential operators working on any one parcel of manuscript make it necessary to use a covering checklist to assure that everything gets done in the proper sequence. This is true particularly when several shifts are being used to perform the work, a situation which is not uncommon in giant proposal preparation. There needs to be a checklist for the first run of sort-edit operations, and perhaps separate ones for the review-approve cycle and for the final checks before production. The coordinator of processing activities needs every possible relief from explaining things to each worker: work must be parceled out quickly to the next processing operation. Professional scheduling personnel may be available within the company. If so, these people can help in scheduling and tracking the proposal processing activities for a giant proposal. The giant proposal *itself* is a work activity that must be planned, scheduled, estimated, and carried out with split second timing and precision. The processing, as well as the printing function, can use conventional planning and scheduling tools to accomplish this objective. Status and load charts can be used to keep a real-time check on the progress of each proposed element. These charts not only provide visibility of the overall publication effort, but provide a basis for real-time last-minute changes and updates to the publication schedule. The overall proposal outline is the natural base for status charts and checklists. The outline can be listed on the left margin of the checklist or time chart and responsible individual or organization or calendar time frame can be placed along the top.

These checklists and charts can then be used in assuring that all processing operations are done by the appropriate individual or organization and at the required time.

Production Operations

Final typing, photography, and printing work for the giant proposal, as mentioned earlier, may require the use of a vendor or subcontractor for outside help. Although this work can and sometimes must be done outside the company, the existing company personnel responsible for these functions should act as a channel for the work. A company's purchasing department, the regular production supervisors, and those who will process the huge document must select and contract with these vendors well in advance, brief them thoroughly on what is coming, and keep them advised every step of the way. If word processing is used either extensively or exclusively, final typesetting can be done directly from the same basic computer magnetic disks or tapes that were used for the original draft

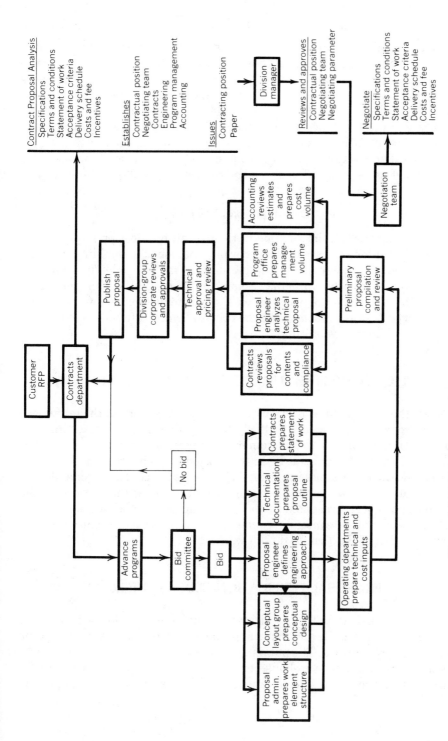

Figure 9.2. Proposal flow chart showing completion of proposal cycle.

through final copyediting. Word processing conversion to final printed copy, however, must be tested thoroughly beforehand to be sure that the vendor's computer equipment and software are compatible with that of the company and that the digital information can be transferred with great speed and with no difficulty. It is a good idea to go through a dry run of this final computerized typesetting process with the typesetter using sample proposal information to assure that there will be no bugs in this final phase of proposal production. Even after computer typesetting is accomplished, a final proofing is required to check the consistency and quality of output.

Distribution and Delivery

Assuming that sufficient time in the overall publication schedule has been allowed to take care of the sheer physical job of assembling, packaging, wrapping, and shipping the giant proposal to its destination, this phase should pose no difficulty. Some companies feel at this point that duplicate shipments are justified, with separate messengers and separate transport routings to *assure* that the proposal will get to the customer and that it will get there on time.

THE CUSTOMER SHOULD "EXPERIENCE" THE PROPOSAL

Whether the proposal is one of just a few pages, or one of the mammoth proportions just described, a skillful job of organizing, writing, editing, and publication will allow the customer to "experience" the proposal rather than to just read it or scan it. In writing and publishing a high quality proposal, the evaluator's attention is not just attracted but demanded by the careful, meticulous, and accurate presentation of the facts—and the proposal has been presented in an interesting and compelling way that is designed to stimulate interest, evoke a decision, and to culminate in action: the selection of the firm to do the work.

PROPOSAL PUBLICATION CLOSES THE LOOP

As shown in Figure 9.2, publication of the proposal "closes the loop" in the proposal flow cycle and triggers prenegotiation activities that precede actual contract award. The published proposal is sent to the customer and is distributed to those in-house organizations that have to prepare for action when the firm is selected and the contract is awarded to do the work.

10

HOW IS THE PROPOSAL EVALUATED?

. . . but glory, honor, and peace to every one that worketh good.
Rom. 2:10

Now that the proposal has been prepared, it will be useful to have the knowledge of how it will most likely be evaluated. This knowledge will be a basis for a proposer to exercise wisdom in the preparation of the proposal and will provide an understanding of the entire acquisition process. If the proposal, bid, quote, or presentation to management is more than merely a "bottom-line" cost or price (and the majority of proposals are), chances are that there is going to be some structured evaluation process. The same basic factors are considered both in structured and unstructured evaluations. The knowledge of the evaluation factors, how they are treated and scored, what adjustments will be made to the proposal, and what comparisons are likely to be made between one proposal and those of competitors will be invaluable.

SOURCE EVALUATION VERSUS SOURCE SELECTION

Before describing the details of the source evaluation process, it is necessary to define the difference between source *evaluation* criteria and source *selection* criteria. The source evaluation board, committee, or team chairperson has the responsibility for *evaluation* of the proposal and for presenting the results of this evaluation to a source selection official. In order to be selected as the chosen contractor or firm to perform a given job, the proposal must rate high in the evaluation process. *But* a high rating in the source evaluation process does not necessarily guarantee a contract award. The reason for this is that the source selection official may not elect to follow the source evaluation board chairperson's recommendations. The source selection official may elect to give a higher weight to unscored criteria or criteria not contained in the request for proposal in making a decision. In any event, the source selection official has final authority and is authorized to select whichever firm he or she chooses. It should be kept in mind that the official is unlikely to choose a firm that develops and presents a poor proposal. The purpose of the following discussion is to provide the reader with the maximum amount of information that, if followed, will result in the greatest likelihood of being chosen to do the work.

SOURCE EVALUATION BOARDS: HOW THEY WORK

The most structured and organized proposal evaluation procedure comes from the establishment and operation of a formal source evaluation board. Formal source evaluation boards are most frequently formed to make recommendations to source selection officials for government procurements, but the same formalized process can be used in commercial selections such as selection of a geographical location for a new production plant, expansion of a product line, or introduction of a new product or service into the marketplace. The evaluation process itself, if not properly organized, adequately staffed, and efficiently carried out, can take an inordinately long time and can result in inconclusive results. A good rule of thumb is to provide at least as much time for proposal evaluation as was expended in proposal preparation. Often, excessive proposal information is requested that cannot feasibly be digested in a reasonable time period or with a reasonable amount of manpower or resources. The procuring organization, however, will learn a lot about the work or product that it can expect to receive from a supplier if a thorough evaluation is accomplished using a structured evaluation process and evaluation organization, whether it is called a source evaluation board, committee, or team. The principal function of a source evaluation board is to collect the knowledge necessary to allow or permit a wise and objective selection recommendation to be made.

To obtain the wisdom required to evaluate a proposal and to recommend selection and contract award, it is necessary for the source evaluation board, committee, or team to obtain knowledge about the potential ability of a firm to perform the work in a manner that will be more advantageous to the procuring organization than that of any competitors. The source evaluation organization collects this knowledge from several sources, described in the following sections.

The Proposal

As mentioned in previous chapters, the proposal is the principal and sometimes the only source of knowledge provided to the proposal evaluation and selection individual or organization. As a supplement to the information in the proposal, however, evaluators often obtain additional information and knowledge from the other sources listed below.

Plant or On-Site Visits

Proposal or source evaluators frequently make on-location visits and inspections to the site or sites where the work will be performed. Hence, it is necessary to be accurate in matching the claims in a proposal to the actual on-site situation. Credibility can be seriously damaged if the on-site visit reveals a situation that is not accurately depicted in the written proposal.

References and Experience Verification

Proposal and source evaluators will usually call, write, or visit previous customers to determine the quality, timeliness, accuracy, and overall responsiveness of previous work. This type of investigation will sometimes lead to a different evaluation than that which results from a written submission. The best policy is to pursue markets where a reputation for outstanding or at least acceptable performance has already been established; this will assure good recommendations from these references.

Oral Presentations

Occasionally, evaluation organizations will request that a proposer provide an oral briefing to accompany or supplement the proposal. This oral briefing gives the evaluator or evaluators an opportunity to personally observe the confidence, demeanor, technical expertise, and credibility of the proposing organization's proposed management team. Since a selection to perform the work will result in a close working relationship between supplier and customer, these oral presentations can become key elements in imparting and maintaining a personal, living credibility to what is otherwise merely a written document.

Written Questions and Answers

After proposal evaluators have had an opportunity to initially review a proposal, questions may arise in their minds relative to the proposed technical approach, the organization proposed to accomplish the job, or the proposer's understanding of the resources required. Frequently these questions (and their answers) are of such importance to the evaluation and selection process that the procuring company or organization will submit one or more questions in writing to one or more of the proposers. Each proposer will be allowed sufficient time to prepare a clarifying response and will submit the answers as a supplement to the proposal.

Best and Final Offers

In negotiated procurements it is a common practice to allow the pro-posers to submit "best and final offers." These are final price quotes based on updated information developed by the proposer prior to completion of the evaluation process. Best and final offers must be made based on a company-developed cost estimate and should not be overly influenced by the knowledge of competitor's prices.

ORGANIZATION OF A SOURCE EVALUATION ACTIVITY

To collect and digest the knowledge needed to make a knowledgeable recommendation, the source evaluation activity usually contains the fol-lowing elements:

Source evaluation ground rules (a plan)

Source evaluation personnel (a team)

Source evaluation board functions

Physical location for the evaluation

Source evaluation schedule

Source Evaluation Ground Rules

Source evaluation ground rules usually take the form of a source evalu-ation plan which spells out the activities of the source evaluation board, committee, or team. In many instances this plan calls for the evaluation board, committee, or team to prepare requests for proposal or requests for quotation that are issued to call for the proposals. Structuring the request for proposal or request for quotation in a knowledgeable way prior to release can save considerable effort in the evaluation process by eliminat-ing unnecessary requirements and assuring that certain vital information and data needed for a wise and objective evaluation is provided in the proposals. These ground rules will contain the scoring factors, criteria, and the importance of each criterion in advance of the evaluation process. Numerical scoring of factors and subfactors is often used to reduce the subjectivity of recommendations that might be made by the source evalua-tion board or team.

Source Evaluation Personnel

Qualified personnel are chosen by the procuring or acquiring organiza-tion to evaluate the technical, organizational, and business aspects of the proposal. These individuals are usually among the best available in a given discipline and are given considerable latitude and authority to draw on the resources of the entire evaluating organization to thoroughly evaluate a proposal. Although procuring organizations seldom have the personnel or expertise to match the proposal preparation team on a one-for-one basis, they do have technical experts and business managers with considerable expertise, and their access to multiple proposals for the same or similar jobs allows them to gain a rapid familiarity with a specialized subject. They can cross-check and compare a proposal with others submitted by other companies and/or organizations. A source evaluation board, team, or committee usually contains sufficient expertise to locate weaknesses and/or strengths in a proposal and to identify "discriminators" between two competitors. A typical proposal evaluation organization is shown on Figure 10.1.

Functions of the Source Evaluation Board

Many of the functions of the Source Evaluation Board are administrative in nature and are similar to the functions that have been performed in the proposal evaluation process. In general, the three basic volumes or sections of a proposal will be evaluated by the three committees, respectively, shown on Figure 10.1. There are some important interactions between these committees, however, that may affect the style or approach to proposal development.

First, the cost committee does more than just check the mathematics in a cost proposal. The cost committee is usually charged with the important and usually controversial task of making cost adjustments to a proposal to develop the "Most Probable Cost of Doing Business" with a company. Some of the cost committee's inputs to make these adjustments will come from the correction of mathematical or pricing errors or from labor rate or factor adjustments; but the major adjustments will come from resource adjustments (labor-hours and materials) derived by the organization and management committee and technical committee.

The organization and management committee will make adjustments, if appropriate, to management labor hours based on major or minor weaknesses they find in staffing level, skills, or percentage of management attention to the project. They will be asked by the cost committee to estimate the impact of correcting these weaknesses in terms of labor-hours, materials, and/or subcontracts and will be required to submit time-phased estimates of the recommended changes, *along with detailed rationale for the changes*, to the cost committee. The organization and management committee will also identify any needed *reductions* in estimated effort due to any perceived overestimates on the part of the proposer. These adjustments are then priced by the cost committee and used to develop the "most probable cost" estimate of the proposal. Any adjustments, upward or downward, are reviewed and approved by the source evaluation board chairperson as well as the cost committee chairperson, prior to incorporation in adjusted costs.

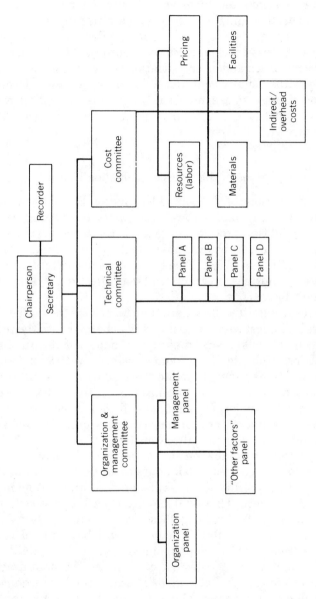

Figure 10.1. Proposal evaluation organization.

Likewise, the technical committee, in identifying major or minor strengths and weaknesses in a technical proposal, will be asked to estimate the labor-hours, materials, or subcontract costs required to correct weaknesses or to reduce overestimates. Technical committee adjustments are also approved by the source evaluation board chairperson prior to incorporation in the adjusted cost estimate.

Physical Location for the Evaluation Process

Since proposal evaluations are usually conducted in a highly competitive atmosphere, a secure and isolated office space is chosen for the evaluation board, committee, or team. When a large amount of money is at stake in a given competition, industrial espionage is not uncommon, and protection of sensitive information is a necessity. Planned or inadvertent release or disclosure of sensitive information could result in a company having an unfair advantage and the filing of a legal protest.

Source Evaluation Schedule

Figure 10.2 is an overall schedule showing how proposal-related activities are phased into the activities leading to a new contract. The schedule shown covers a nine month period from the time the project advocate within an organization requests management approval to proceed until a contract is awarded to the selected company. This time period will vary significantly and depends upon the size, complexity, and importance of the work output or work activity being evaluated. In general, the sequence of events will be in the order shown on this figure:

Request management approval of project

Management approval to proceed

Prepare request for proposal (if not unsolicited)

Proposal preparation

Proposal submittal

Source evaluation

Source selection

Contract negotiation

Contract award

The source evaluation board is sometimes organized during the time that the request for proposal is being prepared so that key members of the evaluation team can participate in and/or approve the format, content, and requirements in the proposal request. Figure 10.3 is a typical sequence of proposal evaluation for an eight week source evaluation activity.

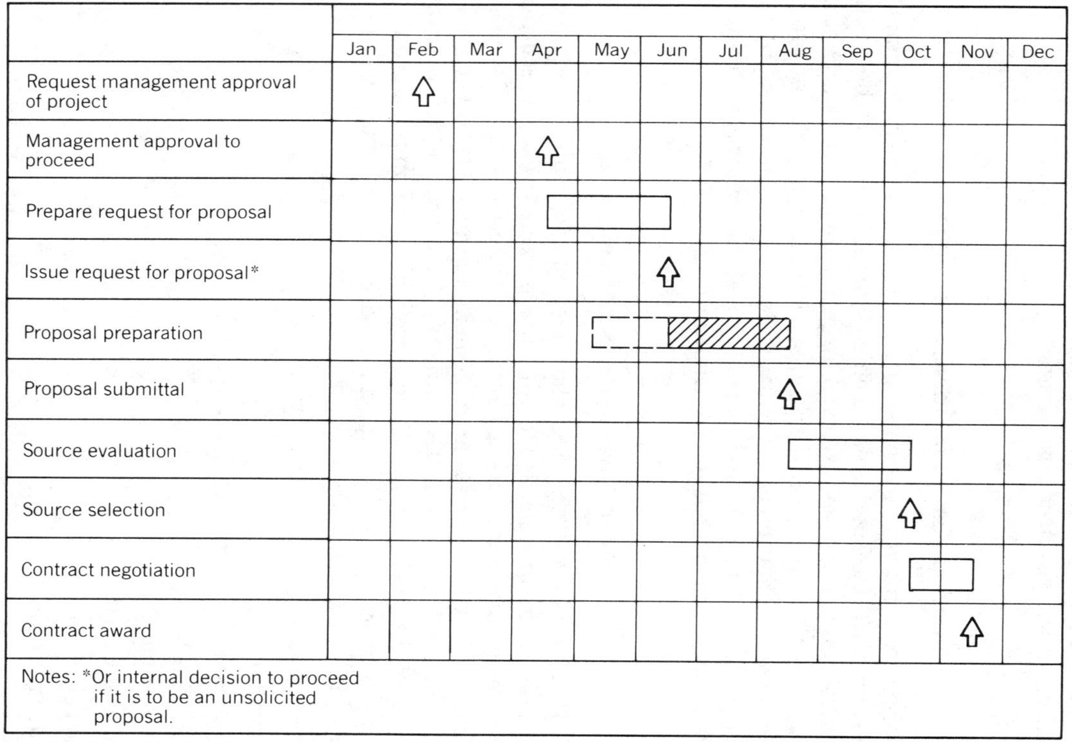

Figure 10.2. Overall schedule showing proposal related activities.

222

Preliminary review of proposals	1ST week
Questions submitted to proposers	2ND week
Identification of major strengths and weaknesses	3RD week
Preliminary cost adjustments identified	3RD week
Preliminary oral team reports to board	3RD week
Preliminary board report to selection official	3RD week
Answers received from proposers	4TH week
Oral discussions with proposers	4TH week
Best and final offers received	4TH week
Identification of major and minor strengths and weaknesses	5TH week
Resource assessment of strengths and weaknesses	6TH week
Final pricing of adjustments—reports to board chairperson	7TH week
Final board report to selection official	8TH week

Figure 10.3.   Sequence of Proposal Evaluation Activity.

EVALUATION FACTORS AND CRITERIA

Most proposal and source evaluation organizations establish evaluation factors and criteria before they solicit proposals and then continue to use these preestablished evaluation factors and criteria throughout the evaluation process. The purpose of establishing these factors and criteria is to designate what areas of schedule, cost, or performance are considered important in the planned work output or work activity, and to provide a structure for the assignment of weights and scores to be applied to each factor and criterion. A scoring scheme or plan is developed for the purpose of reducing or at least "leveling" the effects of subjectivity in the evaluation process. By employing a numerical scoring process, each evaluation team member is required to mentally rank the expected work accomplishment against a given standard. Although this method does not completely eliminate personal bias, opinions, and preferences, it has a tendency to produce a more equitable rating, particularly if a number of persons are doing the rating in adjacent or overlapping areas of performance.

There are three major categories of evaluation factors: (1) performance suitability factors, (2) cost factors, and (3) other factors. In general, the only factors that are weighted and scored are the performance suitability factors, although this policy has been found to vary between organizations. Performance suitability factors consist of those factors that reflect the capability of an organization to perform to a specified set of requirements and include both technical and management factors. Cost factors, usually not weighted and scored, include a detailed cost evaluation using an independent cost estimate as a baseline and a "most probable cost of doing business" which is an adjusted cost estimate developed by the cost evaluators.

"Other factors" include a company's experience and past performance; the financial condition of the company; labor relations, small business, and minority business record; and the geographical location and distribution of the work. Socioeconomic and geopolitical objectives are given particularly important emphasis if the proposed work is to be performed for federal, state, or local governments. Each of these factors and the criteria under which they are evaluated are discussed individually below.

Performance Suitability Factors

Performance suitability factors, sometimes called mission suitability factors, are selected and weighted to provide an indication of how well the offeror or proposer understands the requirements for the work output or work activity. The evaluation of performance suitability factors and criteria requires the evaluators to technically penetrate the proposal and to discern if and how much the proposer understands the intent, purpose, and method of successful completion of the work. Using these factors and criteria, the evaluator can and should determine if the proposer is merely repeating the request for proposal requirements or if they are truly understood in a way that will permit successful performance of the project's objectives. The criteria set forth by the evaluation team is applied to determine the offeror's comparative rating in performance suitability potential, including its understanding of the requirements, approach to the work, and the competence of the personnel to be directly involved.

There may be a great many varied and complex areas that bear on how well an organization can be expected to produce a work output or perform a work activity. The evaluation organization must be able to identify, analyze, and score those discrete criteria that determine how well the product or service can be expected to meet their performance demands. If individual criteria and weights have been prudently determined, the summation or integration of all of the scores of the various criteria will give a representative picture of the relative merit of each offeror from the standpoint of performance suitability.

In developing performance suitability criteria, emphasis has been on the identification of significant discriminators rather than a multitude of criteria which tend to average out when integrated (too *many* criteria have proven as detrimental to the effective evaluation of a proposal as too *few*). The evaluation organization evaluates *significant discriminators* among proposals, rather than many relatively unimportant differences which could result in overly numerous criteria. To the proposer, this means that the *significant discriminators* must be identified. Some performance suitability factors that have been found by experience to be relevant to virtually all procurements and that are generally included in the evaluation process by most evaluation teams are described below:

Understanding the Requirement. A proposer's understanding of the requirement depends on the comprehension of what the work is; how it should be most effectively performed; and what data should be generated, controlled, or submitted in the performance of the work. A proposal will be closely scrutinized to determine if the proposer truly comprehends both the content and magnitude of the task. Although costs are usually analyzed separately by the evaluation board, committee, or team, they are of significant value to the evaluator in indicating understanding of the resources, both human and material, required for performance of the work. The assessment and estimate of the resources required is also indication of an understanding of the work itself. Too high an estimate or too low an estimate will give an indication to the evaluators that a proposer may not have the proper conception of the magnitude, complexity, or content of one or more segments of the work. Because of this, proposal and source evaluation organizations usually make full utilization of the cost proposal to help them determine the understanding of the requirements spelled out in the request for proposal, drawings, or specifications for the job. Hence the importance of cross-referencing and compatibility of the technical and cost volumes as emphasized in Chapters 7 and 9.

Management Plan. The management plan in a proposal is also a frequently scored performance suitability factor. The evaluators will score the *proposed organization*, the recognition of *essential management functions*, and the *effective overall integration* of these functions. Evaluators will be assessing the arrangement of internal operations and lines of authority, as well as external interfaces with the customer and other organizations. Clearly defined lines of authority, a closely knit and autonomous organization, and identification of all essential management functions will be important in providing a high score in this area. Particularly important will be the relationships with subcontractors and associate contractors. The authority of the project manager and this person's position in the company hierarchy, the project manager's relationship with the next higher echelon of management, and the project manager's command of company resources generally will be also the subject of key criteria in the evaluation. Since the management plan usually also includes various schedules for the logical and timely pursuit of the work, accompanied with a description of the offeror's work plan, the organization, logic, sequence, and flow of this plan is also likely to be the subject of a scored evaluation.

Excellence of Proposed Design. If the project or product is hardware oriented, the excellence as well as the detail presented in the design and specification portions of the technical proposal volume is generally a major aspect of the competition. In order to arrive at an informed judgment, the source selection official requests the evaluators' views on the merits of competing designs—both against the stated requirement and against each other. Generally, the best design will be the one that promises to provide the required performance at a reasonable cost. Evaluation of proposed designs varies from a top level evaluation to a detailed evaluation of each subsystem and component, depending on the expertise of the evaluation team, the time provided for evaluation, and the expected unknowns in product/project design.

A large and important indicator of the excellence of a proposed design will be the amount of laboratory or prototype testing that has been done to demonstrate that the design concept is feasible and workable. A high score in this area means that the source evaluation activity is convinced not only that a proposer has a unique and innovative approach but that sufficient work has been done to demonstrate to a reasonable extent that the design will perform its function in an operational environment. A primary indicator of the maturity of the design is the degree of actual testing in scale model, mockup, or prototype form; and the maturity of the subsystem, parts, or components of the design. If the design includes mature, commercially available, well proven components, evidence to this effect will be a persuasive influence on the technical committee of the source evaluation activity.

Key Personnel.   The qualifications, education, experience, and past performance of the proposed key personnel usually represent a large percentage of the scored points in a major competition. Evaluators look for a proven record of high quality performance by the top six or eight managers, engineers, scientists, technicians, writers, or specialists who will manage and perform the work. Written résumés play their part in the evaluation of the quality of key personnel, but they are usually only considered as baselines from which the real evaluation of these individuals begins. Personal reference checks are made with people who are knowledgeable of a given individual's training, experience, and performance. These checks are made at levels commensurate with the proposed status or proposed role of the individual being checked. First-hand observations of the personality, performance, knowledge, and competence of key personnel can be, and usually is, derived from oral discussions with the proposer's team.

Corporate or Company Resources.   An evaluation board, committee, or team comparatively assesses the resources proposed by each offeror in the general areas of manpower and facilities. For example: Are the proper numbers and types of skills available in the company, and will they be assigned in a timely fashion to perform the work? Are the general type and capacity of facilities and (where required) special test equipment being offered suitable and adequate to assure timely performance of the work? If the proposer does not possess adequate resources, has the ability to acquire them been demonstrated through subcontracts or otherwise? These are all questions that are asked by the evaluation organization in the realm of corporate or company resources.

Cost Factors

Cost factors indicate what the offeror's proposal will *most probably cost* the customer or procurement organization. Unless a proposal is a fixed price bid and a company has a known reputation for being able to perform and deliver acceptable performance under fixed price bidding conditions, the evaluating organization will want to analyze the cost proposal in depth to: (1) determine the credibility of the cost estimates, (2) determine if necessary cost elements have been left out or added, and (3) establish a "most probable cost of doing business" for the given work activity. *Most probable cost* is determined by an in-depth analysis and evaluation of the proposal to identify strengths and weaknesses and by adding additional expected costs, if necessary, to bid price to correct the weaknesses and take care of obvious omissions. In some "fixed price" bid situations, procuring companies or government agencies have found it necessary to do an independent cost analysis of the work to determine if a company is underbidding or overbidding. (Aquisition of a fixed price contract at low cost does no good to the customer if the job is not completed due to lack of funds or if the supplier goes out of business.) More will be said about the evaluation of cost factors later. Even though cost factors themselves are not scored, they can have a significant impact on a company's standing in the competition.

Experience and Past Performance

Many proposers overlook the impact of the "experience and past performance" portion of their proposal. As mentioned in Chapter 4, a company should not even bid unless its experience and past performance indicate that it can accomplish the job. Hence, it is necessary not only to possess this experience and record of outstanding performance but to convey this information to the evaluator in a way that it can be analyzed, scored, and verified. Since this section of a proposal is similar to the résumés of key personnel in that it is a résumé of a company, the evaluation team will amend and supplement their knowledge of the capabilities through their own investigations and outside contacts. If the purchasing organization has had experience with a company on other projections, the evaluators will collect and organize information related to quality of production, timeliness of completion, and responsiveness to direction. If there is no experience record between the proposing and evaluating organization, the evaluator(s) will be polling previous and current customers to determine the quality, timeliness, and efficiency of performance.

Other Factors

Other factors that are evaluated but not scored are in the so-called socioeconomic, geographical, and geopolitical realms. They include factors such as labor relations, geographical location and distribution of the work, financial condition of the company, and small business or minority performance—the latter being most important in government procurements.

WEIGHTING AND SCORING PROCEDURES

When a formalized proposal evaluation or source evaluation procedure is used, the evaluation board, committee, or team usually assigns a weight to each factor, then grades the proposal based on observed strengths and weaknesses to determine how much of that weight is to be added to obtain the total score. In a typical example, shown on Figure 10.4, the evaluation team has established a maximum of 1,000 points and has assigned these 1,000 points among five performance suitability factors. Other point totals and factors can be used depending on the type, complexity, and importance of the activity being evaluated. In the example shown on Figure 10.4, however, the evaluation team considered Excellence of the Proposed Design as a predominantly important factor, with Key Personnel, Understanding of the Requirement, Management Plan, and Corporate or Company Resources of lesser importance in descending order. The proposal of Company A was then graded on a scale of one to ten under each factor, and points were computed from ten to one hundred percent respectively for the proposer for each performance suitability factor. The grades received for each factor are a result of analysis of major and minor strengths and weaknesses found through an in-depth study of the proposal and a comparison of the proposed work activity with stated work requirements. Some evaluation boards employ even more complex and sophisticated weighting and scoring techniques with subfactors and sub criteria, assignment of points to major and minor strengths and weaknesses, and nonlinear averaging of grade points to achieve an overall score. These high degrees of sophistication of weighting, grading, and scoring are of doubtful value since the process is itself based on subjective judgements at the lower level. Some form of structured weighting, grading, and scoring process is helpful, however, to reduce personal biases of evaluators and to provide a convenient numerical method of determining the approximate relative standing of several proposals.

Figure 10.5 is a comparison of the grading and scoring of four hypothetical companies for an imaginary project. Although the example is fictitious, it is not uncommon to see wide variations in grading and scoring of companies bidding for the same task. Also shown on this figure are bid price ranking and most probable costs as a percentage of an adjusted independent estimate.

Performance Suitability Factors	No. of Points Assigned	PROPOSAL SCORING		
		Grade	Grade Percent	Grade Points
Understanding of the Requirement	125	10	100%	125
Management Plan	100	5	50%	50
Excellence of Proposed Design	500	9	90%	450
Key Personnel	200	9	90%	180
Corporate or Company Resources	75	6	60%	45
Total Score	1000	—	—	850
(Minimum acceptable grade)	(600)			

Major strengths: Well developed, detailed design completed, with prototype hardware demonstrated.

Company is well versed in the product line, having already produced other similar items

Minor strengths: Project manager is experienced in one other identical program.

Major weaknesses: None

Minor weaknesses: Management team lacks complete cohesiveness: must be corrected prior to negotiations.

Company is small with fewer assets than competitors. Present growth rate makes this a minor weakness.

Figure 10.4. Example of proposal scoring process.

	Company A	Company B	Company C	Company D
Understanding of the requirement	125	115	50	75
Management plan	50	75	100	75
Excellence of proposed design	450	500	250	400
Key personnel	180	160	160	140
Corporate or company resources	45	75	55	65
Total score	850	925	615	755
Average score	85%	92.5%	61.5%	75.5%
Bid price ranking (percent of independent estimate)	110%	150%	85%	105%
Most probable cost ranking (percent of adjusted independent estimate)	95%	130%	105%	100%

Figure 10.5. Example Comparison of Scoring and Ratings (Four Proposals).

COST PROPOSAL ADJUSTMENT AND "MOST PROBABLE COST"

One of the functions of the technical evaluation panels on a proposal or source evaluation board, committee, or team is to identify resource adjustments that must be made to correct any weaknesses found in the proposed plan of action. Another function is to recommend adjustments that must be made in the independent cost estimate based on strengths, weaknesses, and comparisons found in the proposals. These adjustments are used to develop a "most probable cost of doing business" for each proposer and to update an independent estimate (if an independent estimate was made) after receipt of proposals. Experience has shown that bids will be lower than an independent estimate made by the procuring organization primarily because the bidders are acutely aware of price competition. The procuring organization does not encounter these competitive pressures to reduce resource projections from an estimated cost to a competitive bid price.

Adjustments to proposal cost estimates to arrive at most probable costs can be large enough to change the relative cost ranking of bidders because proposers sometimes omit vital cost elements (or add unnecessary items) in their cost structure. On several occasions firms that bid on a price negotiable contract found that the lowest bidder did not get the job because the most probable cost of doing business with that bidder was actually more than that for a proposer with the higher bid price. It is obviously very important for the evaluation team to document the rationale and support for any adjustments to bid price because selection of other than a low bidder could cause a protest and ensuing investigation of the evaluation procedures. Evaluation teams are very aware of this precaution and do not make adjustments to proposers' cost estimates unless these adjustments can be fully substantiated and backed up by factual information and the best expert opinion and advice available.

The two lines at the bottom of Figure 10.5 labeled "Bid Price Ranking" and "Most Probable Cost Ranking" illustrate how the ranking can change after adjustments are made. There have been frequent instances where cost adjustments by evaluators have caused a change in cost ranking, and, in many of these instances, this change in ranking has resulted in a different contractor selection than would occur if the selection decision were made on bid price alone. In the example shown, Company C's bid was the lowest, being eighty-five percent of the government estimate. After the evaluation process had been completed, however, and cost adjustments made, the most probable cost of Company A was the lowest when compared to the adjusted independent estimate. Use of the adjustment process and the development of a most probable cost are prudent actions and can be important factors in avoiding underestimates and overruns. The knowledge that this practice may be used will provide an incentive to a proposal team to leave no stone unturned in identifying all work elements, schedule elements, and cost elements. As mentioned in Chapter 1, the acquisition of new work must be based on providing cost-effective work rather than on oversight or excessive competitive optimism. Since cost is an important nonscored factor in many procurements, it is important to supply as much credible and substantiated backup data and rationale for the cost estimate as possible within the confines of the proposal page limitations. If a company is bidding for a fixed price contract, it is still important to record the rationale and backup data for all cost estimates for use by the company management, for use as a takeoff point for estimates in future proposals, and for use in tracking actual occurrences against the estimate.

In source evaluation activities the cost is a highly important but not always an overriding criterion. For example, a proposal rated last technically, or one with an unacceptable score on the management volume, or even one found unacceptable and nonresponsive, will seldom win just because the dollar bid or the adjusted "most probable cost" is the lowest. For most procurements complex enough to require a proposal, that proposal must first be technically acceptable and then deemed satisfactory regarding management aspects. Only those proposals which have survived the technical and management hurdles will be evaluated from a cost or "most probable cost" point of view. Among those proposals that are still in contention after the technical and management hurdles are successfully passed, the "most probable cost to the customer" becomes the all-important criterion.

The amount of cost-sharing proposed by the bidder can also be an important but not necessarily overriding factor in the cost evaluation. For example, say Company A and Company B are both acceptable technically and from a management point of view. The cost evaluation comparison is as follows:

	Company A's Proposal	Company B's Proposal
Total proposed price	$20m	$16m
Cost share dollar amount	6m	4m
Price to customer	14m	12m
Estimated customer in-house costs	1m	1m
"Most probable cost" to customer	$15m	$13m

Company A has proposed the greatest cost-sharing dollar amount both in absolute dollars ($6m over $4m) and percentage wise (30% over 25%). But Company B still has the least "most probable cost" to the customer.

DETAILED EVALUATION PROCEDURES

A general knowledge of some of the detailed evaluation procedures that are likely to be used on a proposal will be helpful in structuring the proposal. A proposer will want to avoid being downgraded because of the omission of vital information or placement of improper emphasis on certain areas. For this reason, some detailed procedures that probably will be used on a proposal are described below:

Management Plan

Most procuring companies and government organizations want to know that their process, project, product, or service is going to have the attention of the supplier's top management. Thus, the organizational level of placement of the project or activity in a company will have a large bearing on the grading of some of the more subjective aspects of the management plan. If the procurement is a large project, one would expect the project manager to report directly to the vice president, general manager, or another corporate officer. For important projects that are multidisciplinary in nature, clear and distinct lines of authority across the company organization are necessary.

For long term projects it is often appropriate to establish a new department or other organizational entity to manage the project. Usually, a combination of line and matrix-type organization is the most practical: the line type organization being one where all full time direct personnel on a project report directly to the project organization, and a matrix type organization being one where full time direct personnel are located in existing company departments but are responsive to a project manager. A combined line and matrix-type organization uses direct line control for those work phases and activities that involve meeting critical cost, schedule, and performance goals and uses matrix-type features for functions requiring checks and balances and part-time participation of special functions such as quality control monitoring, reliability, and safety.

Evaluators will be looking for distinct lines of authority that will provide the maximum assurance of on-schedule and within-cost work performance. The request for proposal will often request specific information in the management plan on how the proposed performer will track or monitor the work; make needed corrections; report deficiencies and corrections; report progress to the customer; control and report costs; and perform safety, logistics, and reliability management functions.

Excellence of Proposed Design

There are several ways in which a proposed design and/or plan of action will be evaluated. The design may be compared with an existing design of an earlier model produced by the proposing company or another company. It may be compared with an independent in-house design developed by the purchasing company or agency, or it may simply be compared with that of other proposers. In all instances it is highly desirable not only to possess, but to display in the proposal sufficient working drawings, assembly drawings, manufacturing plans, installation drawings, interface drawings, and product specifications to demonstrate in-depth knowledge of the work output.

Key Personnel

The principal place where qualifications, experience, and quality of key personnel will be displayed and evaluated is in the résumés that accompany the management plan. There are many good publications on the effective preparation of résumés, some of which are referenced in the bibliography. Most résumé writers emphasize the importance of adapting the résumé to the proposal to properly emphasize the individual's applicable experience. In most cases this means more than just a change in writing style or content. It usually means a direct face-to-face interview with the proposed performer to draw out verifiable applicable information from past experiences and activities. Many individuals have had applicable experience in a wide variety of areas that they do not even remember unless some memory-jogging is done by an inquisitive and positive discussion. The evaluators of résumés can determine rapidly if background and experience is falsely expanded or "stretched" to cover a job. But factual information is easily verified and always appreciated by the evaluator.

Corporate or Company Resources

A proposal will be evaluated to determine if the company has convincingly demonstrated that the appropriate skill categories are available to the project and will be assigned to the project. Skill categories will also be scrutinized to determine if a reasonable mix of skill levels within that category are available and will be used in performance of the work. Utilization and application of advanced technology equipment in the project will also be highly regarded by evaluators.

Experience and Past Performance

Admittedly, the assessments to be made regarding experience and particularly past performance may be and usually are very difficult for those evaluating the proposal. In the more straightforward or simple cases this assessment may be based on well documented evidence of varying degrees of either favorable or unfavorable experience and past performance. More often, though, these assessments will have to be made from data which is much less clear because of the difficulty of measuring and recording performance and recognizing that other customer and individual appraisals may be subjectively motivated. Therefore, evaluators are usually extremely careful and judicious in making the decisions required of this category of evaluation.

Experience is the accomplishment of work by an organization submitting a proposal which is comparable or related to the work or effort required under the proposed work. Activities of a comparable magnitude which include technical, cost, schedule, and management elements or constraints similar to those expected to be encountered in the proposed work are clearly relevant. Other experience or past performance (favorable or unfavorable) is indicative of the proposer's overall motivations, capabilities, and abilities. The evaluation of experience and past performance is usually not limited to the experience (or inexperience) of the design, management, or production team specifically committed in the proposal to performance of the resulting contract. This evaluation is of the overall corporate or company experience.

Past performance is especially pertinent: how well a company has performed previously on similar jobs is considered to be a strong indication of how well it can perform the task at hand. It is perceived by most evaluators of proposals that many organizations exhibit characteristics that persist over time: for example, resiliency in the face of trouble, resourcefulness, determination to live up to certain commitments or standards, skill in the development of key people, and acquisition of new high technology equipment and machines are indicative of desirable traits in a performing organization. The evaluation team will be collecting and developing information to establish and verify performance in these areas.

Other Factors

The evaluation team and the selection official will consider factors other than performance suitability factors, cost factors, and experience and past performance when evaluating proposals. These other factors and their treatment by evaluators are each described briefly below:

Financial Condition and Capability. Although evaluators can usually obtain a financial background of a company from a number of financial institutions and/or publications (Dunn and Bradstreet, Standard and Poors, *The Wall Street Journal*), the insertion of the latest financial statement or report to stockholders in a proposal usually satisfies this requirement. This information is all the more important to an evaluation team if a company is not well known.

Importance of the Work to the Company. The priority or importance that the corporate level of the proposing company places on the work being proposed is an important "other factor." Indications of this priority, if not clearly stated in the proposal or its transmittal letter, can be gleaned from various parts of the proposal. The evaluators must often read between the lines to gain a knowledge of the emphasis and importance the parent company, home office, or corporate management attaches to the proposed work. This can be seen in the quality of personnel assigned, the level of the proposed project organization in the company, the corporate resources dedicated to the job, and the overall quality and content of the proposal itself. Evaluation of this other factor is highly subjective and, therefore, great care is taken to avoid giving it too great a place in the overall evaluation—but it is a factor that is evaluated.

Stability of Labor-Management Relations.   This factor usually pertains to the historical and present quality of relations between labor and management in a company, particularly as it relates to the potential for labor unrest; poor worker morale; or an extended, prolonged, and costly strike. If there is a recent history of poor performance in this area, special assurance from management and labor alike that performance will proceed on a highly efficient, uninterrupted basis will probably be necessary to retain a high likelihood of selection to do the work.

Extent of Minority and Small Business Participation.   Minority and small business participation is particularly important for government prime and subcontracts, but this factor is often considered in commercial activities as well. The effectiveness of the Equal Employment Opportunity (EEO) and affirmative action programs are usually considered as an "other factor" in the evaluation.

Geographic Location and Distribution of Subcontracts.   Geographic location of a plant or office and that of subcontractors can often have a bearing on the capability of a company to carry out a task due to the possibility of labor shortages, natural disasters, and transportation disruptions. Also certain geopolitical influences in government contracts address the importance of providing more employment in areas of high unemployment. Although this factor is usually not a "swinger" in the decision, two equally qualified proposers may find that this factor will come into play in the evaluation and selection process.

LEARNING FROM PAST MISTAKES

Organizations which prepare and submit proposals may become overly discouraged if and when their firm is not selected for the job. It is in this "nonselection" area that the structured evaluation process can provide a greater service to the proposer's organization than is usually realized. Most evaluation proceedings provide for a debriefing if requested. It is through a debriefing that the proposer can determine a great deal of what went wrong and how to make improvements in the next proposal. In the instance that a company does not win the contract, the entire process can be looked upon as a learning experience. The "we play until we win" approach will pay off as a company continues to learn from its experiences.

This does not negate the advice given in Chapter 1 that a company go into the proposal as if it is going to win the contract. Further, the debriefing will not only point out the negative aspects of the proposal but also the positive aspects—strong points—which can be maintained and further strengthen a firm as it competes for new work. Assuming that a good work output or activity design was presented, factors should be thoroughly reviewed such as: (1) the original decision to bid—what were the influences and motivations; (2) what skill mix and skill level matrix were presented; (3) were there any overriding geographical or political influences on the selection decision; and (4) did the organization and its individuals have the appropriate kind and depth of knowledge and experience about the work output or activity? A close introspection will sharpen a company's proposal preparation skills and increase its assurance of winning the next time.

THE PURCHASING AGENT'S MOTIVES

Many purchases by government or industry are too small to warrant the issuance of a request for proposal or request for quotation, and many which are not too small for an RFP or RFQ do not use formal evaluation techniques. These purchases of goods and services are usually handled by purchasing agents or buyers who may or may not require some form of proposal along with a price quote. With the advent of higher technology work activities and outputs, these procurements are more frequently requiring supplemental information with the bid quote to fully describe and define the work. This supplemental information essentially constitutes a proposal and must be presented in a way that adheres to many of the principles presented in this book in order to enhance the proposer's potential for success.

It should be kept in mind, in selling to any organization, that the main objective of the buyer is profitability for *the purchaser's* organization. A proposal or supporting information for a price quote should emphasize how it is profitable *to the buyer* to purchase the item from a particular firm. Although the lowest price quote is usually what the purchasing agent or buyer is looking for, it is often more important that a work activity or work output be offered that *exactly* meets the specifications and that is delivered *exactly* on time to meet requirements. A buyer's profitability may depend on timely delivery more than a low cost, as delays in production may be more costly than a higher price. Therefore, *timing* of the work performance can be of vital importance to a customer as well as quality and suitability of the work. These factors need to be evaluated, as mentioned earlier, in the original decision to bid. If a company perceives that it has and can supply exactly the right service or product at exactly the right time or place, and that competitors are not in an equally good position, it does not have to compromise by offering a price that is significantly lower than costs plus a reasonable fee or profit. Thus, being in the right place at the right time has a value in itself.

McGraw-Hill's *Purchasing Handbook,* Third Edition, compiled by George W. Aljian points out and describes many of the techniques used by purchasing agents and buyers to assure that their company gets most for their money. This means buying the right *quality,* the right *quantity,* and at the right *time,* at the right *price,* and from the right *source.* Notice the order of these criteria. Quality, quantity, and timing precede *price* in the list. And the *source* is listed last. The source will be determined by the other criteria. If all other criteria are met, the *source* (experience and qualifications) could be a determining factor in the selection. Notice that the pricing criteria is the *"right"* price and not necessarily the *"lowest"* price.

Purchasing agents will look for much the same information that a source evaluation board will, except usually in less detail. In making a purchase they will consider the following technical or product characteristics:

Industry standard specifications

Manufacturer's specifications

Brand name

Part drawing

Part specification

Tolerances

Finishes

Material specifications

Manufacturing process specifications

Quality control system requirements

Acceptance tests

Packaging specifications

Performance specifications

Warranty provisions

Distributor provisions

Field service requirements

Resale requirements

In addition to technical or product characteristics, purchasing agents and buyers will look for and evaluate various *availability*-related features such as:

Quantity

Usage rates

Lead time

Long-term requirements

Transportability

Chronic short supply problems

In evaluating the bidders themselves, purchasing agents and buyers will evaluate the supplier's management capability, technical capability, manufacturing capability, labor-management relations, past performance, financial strength, and company ethics. To obtain this information, purchasing agents and buyers will use supplier proposals, quarterly or annual financial reports, trade and industry information, field surveys, and quality surveys as inputs to their decisions.

CONTINUING EVOLUTION IN SOURCE EVALUATION

As the sophistication of work outputs and work activities increase, so also the methods of evaluating proposals increase in sophistication. The methods, techniques, and skills used in source evaluation are continually improving and expanding to include the consideration of even more factors in the selection process. Customers are becoming more aware of the techniques of profitability analysis, life-cycle-costing, and detailed industrial engineering type man-hour and material based cost estimating. Some private firms and government agencies have developed computer programs that not only mathematically check resource estimates down to the lowest level in the work element structure but are able to compare an estimate on a line-for-line basis with the estimates of other bidders or of independently prepared estimates. These computer programs will provide labor-hour, material, dollar, and percentage differences between proposal line items of competitive or independent estimates. Having been provided with this information, evaluators can then dig deeper into the reasons for the larger deviations and selectively analyze a proposal in detail for completeness and credibility.

Commercial, industrial, and business customers are beginning to exercise greater care and to employ more advanced analysis techniques to determine if the work will result in a higher or lower profitability to the customer than the work of competitors. It should be remembered that the customer will be doing a profitability analysis on a proposal from *the customer's* viewpoint just as the proposer has carefully employed profitability optimization techniques in the proposal marketing and market analysis phase of new business acquisition. Knowing that evaluations are beginning to include these subtleties of business acumen, analysis of *customer* profitability during the marketing phase as well as a proposer's own profitability becomes even more important.

11

A FEW KEY ELEMENTS REQUIRED FOR SUCCESS

Let it be carried out with all diligence.
Ezra 6:12

Some basic principles are covered in the earlier chapters that bear restatement, emphasis, and expansion. These principles are vital to winning in today's business environments. They are the keys to success; therefore, they should be reviewed carefully in light of any specific proposal. Appendix 1 is a sample proposal preparation manual or handbook that can be adapted to a specific company. If a critique committee or "red team" is used, a checklist similar to that shown in Appendix 2 should be utilized to determine if the proposal is complete, accurate, credible, and persuasive.

TECHNICAL EXCELLENCE: A MUST

Being a winner in today's business environment requires *technical excellence*—in the company, in the work activity or work output offered, and in the means of accomplishing the work. It grows out of the desire to be the best in the field from two seemingly conflicting objectives in business: specialization and diversification. Specialization tends to narrow the scope of one's activities to those on which one can concentrate skills and abilities. Specialization of a company can result in that company carving out a "niche" in the industrial or commercial sector of the economy where a need exists and where techniques of fulfilling that need have been identified and can be profitably marketed. If the proposing organization has specialized in the work activity being proposed, this specialization should be described and supported by documented historical evidence or recorded actual experience. On the other hand, diversification can also be an asset to a proposer if the work being proposed can benefit through input from other disciplines or other aspects of the company's activities. Technical excellence means having the best personnel, equipment, and facilities available to do the job and having a management structure that will motivate personnel to use these resources to achieve superior results. A proposal must convey enough information to the customer to provide the assurance that technical excellence will be maintained in all of these areas. Technical excellence falls into three general categories: (1) meeting the specification, (2) providing on-schedule performance, and (3) controlling costs to meet budgets.

Meeting the Specifications

The function of the technical portion of the proposal is to convince the buyer or evaluator that the specified performance for the activity or product will be met. In areas where specifications cannot be met, sufficient description, discussion, and evidence should be presented to demonstrate that a deviation from specified performance will not affect the overall desirability and quality of work except, perhaps, to improve it. If a stated requirement is unrealistic or unattainable, an alternative should be proposed that points out *why* the original requirement is unrealistic. Recognizing an unrealistic or unachievable performance, quality, or operation goal and proposing an alternative requirement is often an indication of knowledgeability and confidence rather than limitations and is often graded as a plus rather than a minus in evaluations.

Providing On-Schedule Performance

The overall technical, organization and management, and cost proposal volumes must emphasize and demonstrate confidence and ability to perform the work as proposed and to complete the work on schedule. Timeliness of performance can mean the difference between the customer's success or failure and can make a difference in long-term profitability. Often, the completion of *the supplier's* work will be keyed to *the customer's* overall objectives and goals. An assurance of a proposer's timely completion of intermediate as well as final milestones can be a determining factor in the choice of a particular company to do the work.

Providing Consistency in Quality

Both the technical and management volumes of the proposal should provide convincing evidence that the company intends to provide a high quality service or product. The organization and management volume should provide evidence of independent checks and balances of quality of work. The technical volume should detail the methods, procedures, personnel, and equipment that are planned for inspecting, testing, checking, and correcting deficiencies during and after performance of the work. The experience and past performance portion of the organization and management volume should emphasize a record of continuous improvement in quality—through detailed evaluation of past mistakes and implementation of corrective measures.

INNOVATION AND CREATIVITY

Two qualities that are easily recognized and highly regarded by proposal evaluators are *innovation* and *creativity* in designing a work activity or work output that will fulfill a need. A willingness to use modern, advanced techniques and equipment for management, design, and production will improve credibility and demonstrate management and technical competence. Innovation and creativity will be evident in a company's acquisition of new skills, techniques, and equipment as they become available. Both the awareness and use of emerging methods of improving efficiency, economy, and effectiveness will be a clear indication of a proposer's desire to provide the customer with the most for the money.

Use of High Technology Methods and Materials

High technology is affecting virtually every type of work activity and work output in our nation. Businessmen are discovering that in order to remain competitive, they must be ready and willing to take advantage of the speed, accuracy, and efficiency offered by high technology skills, methods, and equipment. Decreasing costs, size, and improving quality of sensors, microprocessors, computers, automated office business systems, computer-aided design techniques, and automated factory manufacturing, assembly, handling, and testing equipment have caused a new industrial revolution in many fields. More businesses are adopting high technology methods each year. A recognition that there is no such thing as *status quo* is an important attitude to maintain while submitting a proposal. Each new job acquired is an opportunity to update work activities and outputs to take advantage of these evolving high technology methods.

Efficient Design and Manufacturing Techniques

Companies that are involved in design, manufacturing, and production are finding that highly organized and controlled scheduling techniques are not only useful but necessary to reduce or eliminate wasted time, effort, and materials. Any new product or service activity that has not included systems or methods for assuring precision in sequencing of hand

and automated operations should analyze these systems and include them where appropriate to be competitive. The "just-in-time" system originated by the Japanese but now spreading through United States industry is one which requires each operation to be performed and each part to be delivered "just-in-time" to be mated with its related operations and parts: not too soon or too late. Too early delivery of a part or performance of an operation can cause wasted storage or maintenance time for parts and too late delivery can result in wasted human and machine time in waiting.

In the field of design, computer-aided design techniques can save a significant number of man-hours by reducing or eliminating a draftsman's time-consuming manual production of drawings and by reducing the designer's time to essentially creative rather than mechanical work. Drawings and designs can be stored on magnetic tape or disk, rapidly updated, and reproduced by printer or plotter on demand in almost any size or shape desired. The use of three-dimensional and color graphics is also reducing or eliminating the many hours of technical artwork required to convert a drawing into an isometric, perspective, cutaway, or exploded view of a part, subsystem, or product. This time-conserving technology can be of considerable value to the preparer of proposals because designs do not usually have a high degree of maturity at the time a proposal is submitted. Computer-aided design allows preliminary concepts to be converted to realistic drawings and isometrics in a very short time.

Production, logistics, and materials handling are also now using advanced electromechanical and computer technology to increase the speed and accuracy of these functions. Computer-aided manufacturing, robotics, and automated storage and retrieval systems are being used with increasing frequency in industries of all sizes to reduce labor hours required to accomplish industrial functions and to enhance production quality and speed. A dedication to investigate, analyze, and adopt these systems in marketing new products or services will enhance one's competitive stature when proposing and performing new work.

The "People-Oriented" Approach

The use of innovation and creativity in motivating and rewarding employees is becoming a recognized and effective way to build timeliness and excellence into a work activity or work output. The "people-oriented approach" to solving problems, when coupled with the high technology approach, has proven to be an unbeatable combination for competing in today's business environment. Employee stock ownership, profit sharing, employee pension trusts, quality circles, and other motivational programs are demonstrating their immeasurable value in motivating employees to become interested and contributing members of the management of a company. These programs have increased team spirit, quality consciousness, and profitability in virtually every instance where they have been properly applied. An organization and management proposal should demonstrate the people-oriented approach to improving efficiency, economy, and effectiveness of operations, and the proposal should outline the ways in which the company plans to continue to use these programs to assure a continuation of high morale and high productivity. In-company proposals should also show how these programs will increase overall company and resulting customer profitability. Evidence of successful programs in other organizations, advice from consultants and motivational program experts, and reviews of the latest literature will assist a proposing company in building a convincing argument for including these programs in plans for future work acquisitions.

STABILITY OR FLEXIBILITY OF LABOR BASE?

When structuring the labor base for a new work activity or work output, it is necessary to review and analyze all available options pertaining to the use of the existing company's work force and the hiring or employment of new personnel, consultants, or subcontractors. The company's management should be involved in this part of pre-proposal planning because it bears not only on winning the present job but on the company's posture for the acquisition of future work. Company growth and expansion plans must be correlated with the work acquisition under consideration to determine how the skill categories, skill levels, and salary structure will be affected by performance of the new work. To be a winner in today's business environment, the work force itself must be continually updated, trained, motivated, and periodically supplemented to assure a competitive posture and a high capture potential for new contracts. Several interacting factors are important elements of this analysis: (1) stable base of skilled personnel, (2) hiring at the low end, (3) use of consultants and subcontractors, (4) part-time and temporary employees, and (5) cross-training of the work force.

Stable Base of Skilled Personnel

The solid foundation on which most companies build their future is a stable base of loyal, long-term, skilled, and experienced personnel. A company that has built its capabilities and reputation by continually improving and rewarding its employees is in an excellent position to assure the customer that this stable base will continue to be available to perform work in a satisfactory if not outstanding manner. Because long-term employees continue to receive merit, longevity, and quality salary increases, however, this stable work force will tend to escalate in cost as time progresses, making older companies less competitive than newer companies unless the older companies continually supplement and add to their labor base at the lower end of the salary scale.

Hiring at the Low End

To replace personnel losses caused by retirements and attrition, a company should bring in and train personnel at the lower end of the salary scale, and proposals should reflect the use of these newer employees as soon as possible in the work cycle. Presuming that the basic skills required to perform a proposed mission have been built up over a period of years through training, development, motivation, and advancement of personnel, new skills should be acquired and developed from the ground up rather than hired in from other companies at high salary levels. Maintaining this long-term approach requires considerable discipline because the temptation will exist to hire highly paid experts as an expediency to perform a short-term job when this job might just as well have been performed by a consultant or subcontractor. Hiring at lower levels and promotion from within are still the best practices if the appropriate skill categories and skill levels can be acquired for new work in this manner. Then the phasing-in of these skills in each new job on an appropriate time-based scale will make each proposal more competitive.

The Use of Consultants and Subcontractors

When it is anticipated that specalized skills not readily available within the company will be needed to perform work on a potential contract, consultants and/or subcontractors can be highly effective in supplementing and complementing the skills and experience of the work force. These performers bring in skills that could not be developed or obtained from within the company, and they can be employed contingent upon receipt of the contract. The skillful planning and use of consultants and subcontractors, therefore, is an integral part of preproposal planning both by the proposal team and the company's management and should be a part of the overall labor base analysis that precedes the acquisition of new work.

Part-Time and Temporary Employees

An increasing number of families have more than one individual who is or can be considered as part of the labor work force. Where there is a full-time breadwinner, there is often a spouse, child, or parent that can and does engage in part-time or temporary work to assist in earning "discretionary" income for the family. Because there is a full-time breadwinner, these family members do not object to (and often desire) part-time or temporary employment. There is a readily available market, therefore, of part-time or temporary skilled and unskilled employees who can be brought in during peak workloads but need not be considered part of the permanent work force.

Wives or husbands who are the "second breadwinners" in families may have just the skills needed for the project's duration. An expanding population of retirees exists, many of whom have retained their skills, vigor, and desire to do productive work. Companies, universities, and government organizations are finding that the experience, maturity, judgment, and seniority of many early and not-so-early retirees can be of remarkable benefit to an organization at a relatively low cost and commitment.

The increasing costs of education have caused many students to search for temporary or part-time employment to supplement their income as well as to provide them with experience in applying their newly found knowledge. Students are excellent temporary or part-time contributors to profitable business ventures. This labor market should not be overlooked when structuring a proposal for new work as it may enhance a proposal significantly from a price and skill mix standpoint.

Cross-Training of Work Force

Modern behavioral studies are showing that employee motivation increases as employees identify with a larger part of the job and as they realize and recognize the part that their work plays in the overall work activity or work output. A company policy of cross-training and broadly scoped jobs will reflect itself in a cost-effective proposal because some flexibility exists in work assignments.

If one person has the potential to perform several types of jobs, the hiring of two or three people may be avoided. Effective cross-training and judicious use of cross-trained employees can result in significant savings in labor-hours required to do a job and can avoid excessive buildup (above a company's stated growth objectives) of a workforce that must subsequently be fed with new, profitable work.

Specialization of *company* objectives and goals does not necessitate or require overspecialization of *personnel*, although every company must have a certain percentage of specialists in its work force in order to maintain technical excellence in its field. Today's business environment requires proposals based on a careful analysis of the degree of skill specialization and the degree of cross-training required for and provided to each task. A common fault in proposals is the use of highly qualified and highly paid personnel for work that starts out needing their services but which can eventually be delegated to lower skill levels. These highly qualified and highly paid individuals should be transferred to the *next* new job as soon as possible (1) to reduce the composite labor rate as soon in the project as practicable and (2) to make these highly qualified personnel available as early as possible for new projects that require high front-end skill levels.

Experience shows that, as a job progresses through time or quantity related experiences, the skill level required to do the job will decrease. The more highly paid employees that are needed to start new projects can train newly hired, lower paid personnel as the job becomes more well defined and more routine. Then these skilled workers can be moved on to establish new jobs and to train more new employees. This time-phasing of skill mix and skill category should be used to advantage in structuring the tasks and subtasks of the proposed work and in demonstrating to the customer that skill application and utilization has been optimized.

COMPETENCY IN SCHEDULING

The successful proposal must demonstrate to the customer not only that meticulous care has been taken in scheduling the work but that the tools, techniques, and methods of scheduling are both available to and understood by the proposer for use in rescheduling the work as required as the work progresses. Development and maintenance of a detailed multifaceted work activity usually requires the use of one or more of the generally accepted methods of network analysis or bar chart scheduling. Operations analysis tools designed specifically for large, long duration, multitask projects were brought to bear by the Special Projects Office of the U.S. Navy and published in 1958 as the PERT (Program Evaluation and Review Technique) system. Since that time, various versions of PERT, critical path bar charting, procedure diagrams, bubble methods, and method of potentials have been developed for both manual and computerized usage. These methods interrelate jobs in sequence or time and provide the assistance a manager needs that go beyond the limit of mental planning capacity in a multifaceted project. When a project is underway and the inevitable deviations from plans occur, the network or bar charting techniques help the manager to determine the importance of these deviations and to take effective corrective action. Two of the many good books on critical path analysis and bar charting are: (1) *The Critical Path Method* by Arnold Kaufmann and G. Desbazeille (see Bibliography), a book using complex mathematics adaptable to computer use; and (2) *Analysis Bar Charting*, by J. E. Mulvaney (see Bibliography), a book that can be used for manual bar chart analysis.

Even the simplest proposal should have some form of time-oriented display of the activities that must be carried out in parallel or in sequence in order to accomplish the work on time. Presentation of this type of display in the proposal will demonstrate to the customer that intermediate milestones have been established and that detailed planning has been carried out in anticipation of the contract award. Master schedules, backed up by detailed schedules of each phase of the work are required for more complex projects. In a complex project, the customer will want to know what type of scheduling technique will be used, how often it will be updated or adjusted, how corrective actions will be input to rescheduling exercises, and to what degree the scheduling methods will be integrated into overall project performance. An important precaution to take in the scheduling discussion is to avoid indicating a fascination with the scheduling technique itself: recognize that the scheduling and rescheduling methods are only there to help the project be completed on time.

PROPOSAL REVIEW BY MANAGEMENT AND OTHERS

Throughout the proposal preparation process, as shown in the flow diagrams accompanying appropriate chapters, critical reviews of the proposal are made by the proposal team, by middle management, and by disinterested experts. Some bidders use a technique known as "Story-Boarding" which involves the production of large hand-produced charts containing various proposal elements displayed on a conference room or office wall. These charts provide a real-time focal point for proposal team interaction and discussion. Some companies form steering committees or advisory boards consisting of middle or senior managers to review the proposal elements during various stages of preparation. Although there is no standard or recommended way of achieving this third-party or independent review, it is recommended that qualified individuals outside of the proposal preparation team itself be formed into what some companies call a "red team" or "murder board" to give the initial plans, outlines, and drafts, as well as the final published proposal, a critical review before it proceeds to the next step in the preparation process or is submitted to the customer. Third party reviews can often catch errors that are overlooked by those who are working with the proposal manuscript on a day-to-day basis and can identify inconsistencies that may be generated by last minute changes. After such interim and final reviews, the proposal is much more likely to be error-free and to represent the desires and policies of company management.

HONESTY AND INTEGRITY

Being a winner in today's business environment need not involve a compromise in a company's honesty and integrity. It should be recognized that there is a difference between honesty and optimism, but that the two are compatible. Optimism is a necessary element in proposal preparation. The entire proposal preparation activity must be carried out with a winning attitude in order to win. The *positives* that are in the proposing company's favor should be pointed out and not the negatives that are not in its favor. But a proposer must honestly believe that the job can and will be done in the manner, on the schedule, and with the resources and costs stated in the proposal.

FINAL GUIDANCE

There is some final guidance that the authors must provide in order to make this book complete. This final guidance is in the form of subjective but important factors that will spell success in a proposal preparation effort.

Be Complete!

A proposer should provide *all* required information in the proposal. A key piece of information left out could have disastrous effects on the capability of winning. Often the only thing the evaluator has to go on is the content of the proposal. Evaluators are sometimes not allowed to consider other information than that in the proposal even if this information is of general knowledge!

Be Organized!

An organized flow of information in the proposal that permits the evaluator to follow the thread of rationale will result in a positive reception of the proposal. Careful consideration of the interrelationship of the technical, organization and management, and cost or price proposal volumes is an absolute necessity. Organization in the proposal will be a clear indication of an ability to properly organize the proposed work!

Be Objective!

A proposer should avoid emotional comparisons, flowery words, and unfair judgments in the proposal. Frankness and objectivity are appreciated by the recipient.

Be Informed!

By *listening* to the customer's requirements and to the marketplace, a proposer can provide an up-to-date, timely proposal. The degree to which one is informed on the work content and the customer's requirements will "show through" in the proposal.

Be Innovative!

A proposer should not hesitate to present new approaches and ideas as long as they are backed up by planning and analysis. Most customers do not merely want "yes-men" to conform unquestioningly to their requirements.

Be Factual!

A proposer should not overstate or understate capabilities or costs. An accurate cost estimate should be presented and a reasonable fee requested.

Be Professional!

Proposal evaluators appreciate a professional, well-organized proposal!

Follow Up!

A proposer should not forget to follow up the proposal with responsive answers to requests for supplemental information. A contract is sometimes won based on this last minute information.

Finally, a proposer should remember that compatability with the request for proposal or "requirements" is a measure of *responsiveness*. Responsiveness is a key factor in the evaluation of any proposal. Internal compatability of the proposal within volumes and between volumes is a measure of *credibility*. Although credibility is not a scored factor, it is an important characteristic, the lack of which can cause rejection of the proposal in its entirety. The quantities and types of resources that are proposed to apply to each aspect of the job is a measure of an *understanding of the requirements*, which is a scored criterion, and which is a clear indicator to the evaluator of a proposing firm's technical competence in the work being proposed.

12

A CASE STUDY: PROPOSAL FOR "COSTREND™"

... it will turn out exactly as we have been told.
Acts 27:25

Because space is limited it is not possible to present in this book samples of all elements of the proposal preparation process for a large or even a medium sized hardware or software proposal. To provide an example of the principles covered, however, a small, unsolicited proposal for a software development project is included in this chapter. The sample proposal, prepared by a hypothetical company, Data Systems, Incorporated (DSI), and presented to a hypothetical professional society, the American Estimating Institute (AEI), is for the Costrend cost estimating system. The trademark Costrend™ is owned by Data Systems, Incorporated. The work is to be completed in a twelve-month period. AEI is to fund the development. Data Systems, Incorporated will forego the receipt of fee or profit on the development with the understanding that a licensing agreement with AEI will call for division of the income from software sales between AEI and DSI.

Data Systems, Incorporated, following principles outlined in Chapters 1 through 11 of this book, developed their proposal using the six basic steps of proposal preparation: marketing, analysis, planning, design, estimating, and publication.

MARKETING

Data Systems, Incorporated, using some of its independent research and development and proposal preparation funds, employed a traveling consultant to do a complete market survey of existing cost estimating systems

250

to determine if there was a need for a simplified, low-cost, "generic" cost estimating computer software system for preparing detailed, industrial engineering type, labor-hour and material-based cost estimates. The company had observed (1) that the cost of computer hardware was decreasing rapidly because of increased competition among computer companies, (2) more microcomputers, using a simplified form of computer language, were becoming available each year with greater capability for information handling and storage, and (3) competition in business was forcing all businesses, small and large, to do a better job of cost estimating. The marketing team was charged with the responsibility of interviewing potential customers of cost estimating computer systems and determining the desirable system features if a new, flexible, economical system were developed.

ANALYSIS

Analysis of the marketing data obtained by the traveling team over a six-month period proved that a need existed and that a basic system could be developed for use by all but the larger estimating organizations in industry and government for budgeting, estimating, planning and resource allocation. Further, the analysis showed that a "work element structure"-oriented system was needed to adapt to the increasing complexity of conventional and high technology work activities and work outputs. The market analysis showed that the system must be "user-friendly" and transportable between various computers.

PLANNING

Internal company planning meetings were held by Data Systems, Incorporated to develop ground rules, a system description, and a time schedule for development of the Costrend system. Priorities were assessed to determine what degree of manpower could be used for the new job and in what time sequence. At this point it was agreed within the company that it would be profitable over the long term to proceed with initial design and documentation of the system, and that further design, cost estimating, and publication of a proposal would be fruitful based on the anticipated market sales potential. The company decided to continue to invest funds in the next steps required to increase credibility of its proposed system, even though the exact method of sales and recovery of costs had not been identified. It was subsequently decided to approach the recovery of invested and continuing costs through the development and submittal of one or more unsolicited proposals.

DESIGN

Detailed preliminary design of input and output formats was completed during this phase to provide programmers with the required system constraints. A work element structure was developed for use as a basis for cost estimating, and detailed ground rules and assumptions were derived. Initial programming was completed on the input, edit, and error message portions of the program to provide a basis for testing the user-friendliness of the program. Based on preliminary trial input runs, suggestions were made by potential operators concerning input mode, input format, and input content.

ESTIMATING

Based on the preliminary design, assumptions, ground rules, time schedules, and skills used, a detailed cost estimate was developed using the basic methods included in the Costrend system itself. Program development was laid out on a yearly schedule and labor hours and material costs were estimated for each month for each element of work.

PUBLICATION

Once the preliminary estimate was complete, a more detailed technical description was prepared for the proposal technical section. Organization and management arrangements were developed for the organization and management section of the proposal, and the cost estimate and estimating rationale was updated and/or derived for the cost portion of the proposal. The resulting proposal is presented in its entirety as the balance of this chapter.

LETTER OF TRANSMITTAL

DATA SYSTEMS INCORPORATED
P.O. Box 3000
Knoxville, Tennessee 37919

October 16, 1984

Dr. David Dooley
Executive Director
American Estimating Institute
404 Kimberly Industrial Park
Cambridge, Massachusetts 02138

Dear Dr. Dooley:

Data Systems, Incorporated, is pleased to submit an unsolicited proposal for the development of Costrend™ which is a user-friendly, transportable computer software package for performing detailed industrial engineering type man-hour and material based cost estimates. As you will see in our cost proposal, DSI proposes that the American Estimating Institute fund the development of the Costrend computer program and market this program through your "Forecaster" magazine, technical meetings, newsletters, and displays. DSI proposes to forego fee on the development provided that your society will agree to a commission of ten percent of gross sales of the Costrend package, payable to DSI at the end of each calendar quarter.

Our market surveys show that there is an urgent and pressing need for the Costrend system among small and medium sized organizations that are just getting into the development of detailed cost estimates for governmental and industrial high technology programs. As a professional society, AEI is uniquely suited as a marketing agent for this software package. Your nonprofit status and overall goals for enhancement of the estimating profession put AEI in a position of impartiality which allows you to recommend the best system available without regard to political, company, or geographic pressures. Further, the introduction of Costrend puts AEI into a position of offering a standardized, uniform, cost estimating system that can be acquired and used by a large number of companies without the possibility of compromising corporate proprietary systems.

Data Systems, Incorporated has exhibited its confidence in Costrend by doing preliminary programming and demonstration of a prototype software package. This prototype package has shown us that a fully developed and documented commercially usable system can be developed within the time schedule and resources stated in this proposal.

We look forward to working toward the negotiation of a successful performance contract which will be mutually beneficial to AEI and Data Systems, Incorporated.

Very truly yours,

Encl   Ralph Roberts
a/s   President

TECHNICAL PROPOSAL

Introduction

Costrend is a user-friendly, transportable cost estimating system that is adaptable to a wide variety of cost estimating situations for small, medium-sized, and large work activities or work outputs. It is a software system designed for use on microcomputers as well as mini and main frame computers. Written in the BASIC computer language, Costrend can be easily adapted to the many versions of the BASIC language used on micro, mini, and large computers. Fundamental to Costrend's utility are the two features: (1) user-friendliness and (2) transportability.

User-Friendliness. User-friendliness means that Costrend's operational procedures and documentation are so simple that the system can be operated by the most inexperienced of cost estimators. The video display screen of the computer displays menus, questions, and responses from which the operator can select options in a conversational manner. Knowledge of computer languages and conventions are not required because all interactions with the computer are in plain English. A handy operator's manual clearly describes each step the operator must take to develop a cost estimate and describes what the computer is doing to develop the cost estimate.

Transportability.   Since Costrend is transportable among a large number of brands and types of computers, it has the potential of becoming a standardized, well-known and understood cost estimating system. It is easily adaptable to any computer through the use of BASIC computer language which is widely known and used by both professional and nonprofessional computer users. A company or organization that employs a number of different computer types and sizes will have little difficulty adapting the system to the several computer types and sizes. Figure 12.1 is a photograph of a Texas Instruments DS990 Model 1 microcomputer that is currently using prototype Costrend software for cost estimating seminars, software demonstrations, and development of cost estimates.

Basic System Description

Costrend is designed to develop an industrial engineering type labor-hour and material-based cost estimate from the ground up. It uses a work breakdown structure or work element structure to input, collect, compute, and print out cost estimate results. Costrend performs all mathematical and clerical functions on numbers entered by the operator and prints the results in letter quality for direct insertion in proposals, financial reports, cost summaries, or preliminary estimates. The operator needs the following six inputs to develop a cost estimate:

1.   The work element structure (the top level of the work element structure is the name of the project).
2.   Names of the labor skills or individuals.
3.   Labor rates for each labor skill or individual for each calendar period.
4.   Labor-hours for each labor skill or individual for each calendar period.
5.   Direct material (and subcontract) costs and other direct costs for each calendar period.
6.   Overhead, general and administrative, cost of money, and fee percentages.

Costrend™ multiplies labor rates by hours for each labor skill or individual to develop labor costs; computes overhead costs, adds material costs; and computes and adds general and administrative costs, cost of

Figure 12.1. Costrend computer system.

money, and fee or profit to develop a total cost estimate spreadsheet that is printed out on a calendar basis and summed vertically into calendar period totals. Inputs are provided at the lowest level of the work element structure. The computer sums all costs of lower work elements into their respective higher work elements and prints out all work element sheets for each cost estimate. Four printout formats are available, each representing a different calendar base for the estimate (monthly, quarterly, yearly, and free-form). A free-form calendar mode merely numbers each of twelve calendar periods which can represent days, weeks, months, quarters, or any other preselected calendar period (labor rates, hours, and materials costs are input based on the preselected calendar periods).

Because of its simplicity and flexibility, Costrend is ideal for use by the small or medium-sized business or organization that is contemplating or acquiring work that needs more detailed cost estimating methods than currently practiced. Programming assistance is available on a special subcontract basis to adapt Costrend to special requirements brought about by each company's unique situation. It is a system that can be easily adopted, learned, and used to provide immediate response to cost estimating requirements while forming a baseline for an expanded system if required.

Background and History

Because of the competitive nature of cost estimating, there has been very little, if any, sharing of cost estimating computer programs among various companies and organizations. This restriction of interchange of information on cost estimating computer programs is unfortunate because the basic *methods* of estimating are similar and often identical among competing organizations. The competitive element really should lie only in the *content* of the cost estimate and not in the mathematical computer program used to *compute* the estimate. The misconception that cost estimating computer programs cannot and should not be shared has resulted in the unique development of a computer program for *each* organization or company, resulting in the use of thousands of different computer programs to perform basically the same function. Costrend, however, can be used or adapted by any organization or company that is performing industrial engineering type labor-hour and material-based cost estimates. Since the development cost of Costrend can be spread among hundreds, even thousands of potential users, an economical system can be made available for use on small computers by those who are just entering the realm of detailed cost estimating. Standardization of operating procedures, terminology, and format will be welcomed by the many customers of organizations or companies using Costrend because there will be greater consistency in comparison, assimilation, and analysis of cost information. Costrend is a data base system where changes can be made without reinputting all inputs.

System Specifications

(a)   Written in BASIC and COBOL languages.

(b)   Operable on microcomputer (with minimum of 64K memory), mini-computers, or main frame computers.

(c)   OPERATIONAL PROCEDURE: Inputs

(1)   Operator puts in time and date of estimate.

(2)   Operator selects calendar baseline and starting year.

(3)   Operator inserts the number of skills or individuals.

(4)   Operator inserts a name for each skill or individuals.

(5)   Operator selects constant dollar or escalation mode.

(6)   Operator inserts labor rates for each skill (in the constant dollar mode only the first year is required).

(7)   Operator inserts overhead percentage, general and administrative percentage, cost of money percentage, and fee percentage.

(8)   Operator inserts labor hours, material dollars, and other direct dollars for each skill or individual, for each calendar period, for each work element.

(d)   OUTPUT FORMATS (Horizontal)

(1)   *Monthly*: The monthly format has a full calendar year across

the top. Twelve months are presented starting with a prespecified month. The year represented is printed in the heading. Cost elements are summed vertically for each month. A total yearly sum is provided for key labor and cost elements.

(2) *Quarterly*: Three years are presented with subtotals for each year. Quarters are numbered, and the total of all three years is provided.

(3) *Yearly*: Twelve years are presented with a grand total for all twelve years. Cost elements for each year are summed vertically.

(4) *Free-Form*: Twelve columns are presented and summed. Columns are merely numbered one to twelve and can represent days, weeks, months, quarters, years, or any other calendar period as long as labor rates, hours, and dollars are input in these same calendar period elements. In addition, each column can be used for a distinct company division, product, or product line when a time-based estimate is not required.

(e) FILE-DRIVEN SYSTEM: Inputs are stored, accessible, and can be changed if desired prior to printing out Costrend.

(f) PRINTERS: Output data can be printed either on letter quality printers or high speed dot matrix printers.

(g) WORK ELEMENT STRUCTURE LEVELS: Costrend^{TM} is capable of accepting inputs down to level five of the work element structure.

(h) WORK ELEMENT SUBDIVISIONS: Costrend^{TM} accepts up to nine subdivisions for each work element structure.

(i) COMPUTATION TIME: Computation time does not exceed twenty minutes. Search and retrieval time does not exceed thirty seconds for each search, retrieval, and replacement.

(j) ZERO ASSUMPTIONS: If an element or number is not inserted, it is assumed to be nonexistent or zero (by element we mean material, other direct costs, overhead, general and administrative costs, cost of money or fee).

(k) WORK ELEMENT STRUCTURE CONVENTION: [The work element structure convention is that shown in the author's book *Cost Estimating* (see Bibliography).]

Growth Potential

The software programming for Costrend^{TM} is done in such a way that it keeps in mind the following growth features:

1. The use of a constant or varying escalation percentage for labor rates, materials, or other direct charges.

2. Subdivision of materials and subcontract costs and other direct costs into further breakouts.

Development Schedule

Since all systems analysis and prototype system development work has been completed by Data Systems, Incorporated as part of this unsolicited proposal effort, detailed final software programming can start in January 1985. Minor changes in systems requirements can be mutually agreed to after contract go-ahead (December 1, 1984) but must be incorporated in the system requirements and finalized prior to the start of programming in January 1985. The contract will be accomplished in four major phases: programming, testing, documentation, and support. The timing of these four phases is shown on Figure 12.2. These four schedule elements coincide with the level two breakouts in the work element structure used for developing the Costrend cost estimate.

Programming (1.1).   Programming includes the development of all program coding for inputs, edit routines, error messages, and output reports. Also included in the programming effort are program additions and modifications to improve user-friendliness and ease of operation brought about by inputs from the "testing" phase (1.2). Additional user-oriented modifications required beyond the testing phase will require supplemental effort and additional contract coverage.

Testing (1.2).   Testing includes in-house testing by Data Systems, Incorporated testing on a real estimating situation selected from the open market by the American Estimating Institute, and testing of user feedback and program updates.

In-House Testing (1.2.1).   In-house testing will include a thorough "wringing out" of the system to verify that the system can and will successfully develop cost estimates with inputs from levels two, three, four, and five in the work element structure; and that estimates can be successfully run when up to nine skills are prespecified by name and labor rate structure versus time. Real year and constant year dollar estimates will be run using the monthly, quarterly, yearly, and free-form output modes. Off-optimum runs will be made based on requirements that may be specified in the future that do not coincide with currently envisioned system capabilities. For example, methods will be developed, in these test runs, to accomodate more than nine skills, more than twelve calendar periods, and more than five levels in the work element structure. It must be recognized that these "off-optimum" runs will require: (1) some reinputting of resource estimates, (2) modification (by typewriter) of output format headings, or (3) relabeling output formats after computer production.

Market Use Testing (1.2.2).   During the last month of the Costrend™ testing program, an estimate will be performed for a "real" customer

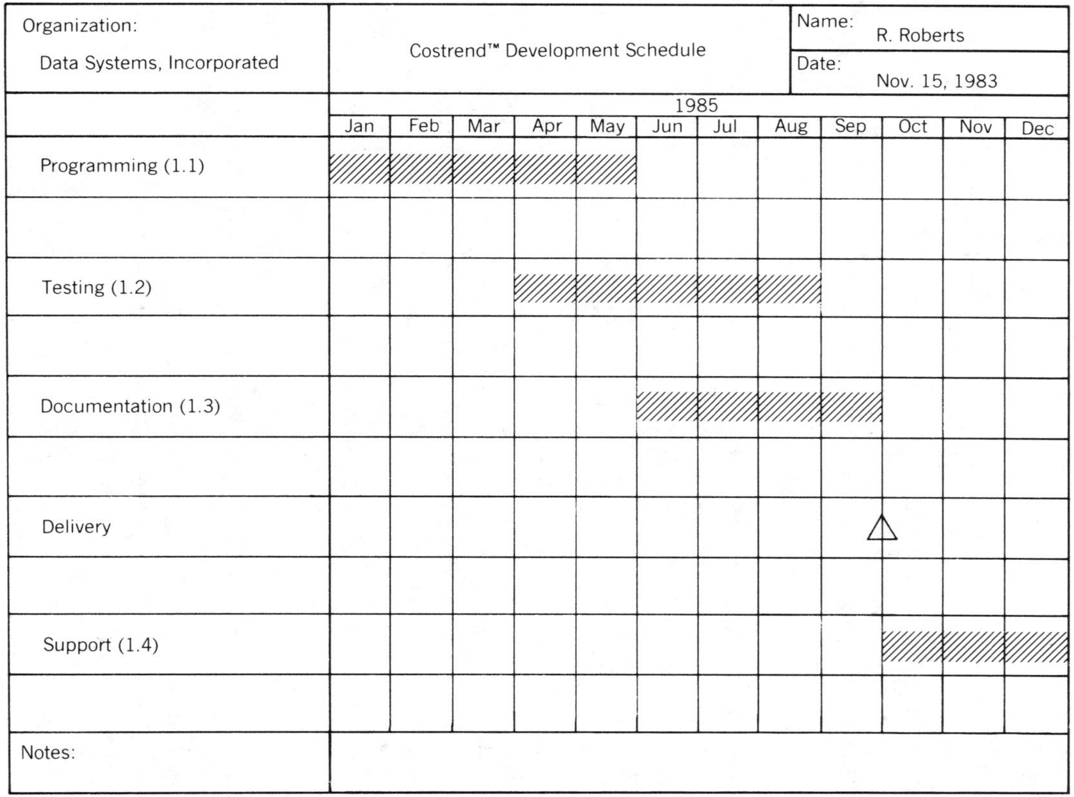

Figure 12.2. Schedule for Costrend development.

specified and designated by the American Estimating Institute. This real application must be selected prior to July 1, 1985. If AES fails to designate a real application within the capabilities of the Costrend system by that date, Data Systems, Incorporated reserves the right to select an application and to perform the market use test estimate on this selected application.

Testing of User Feedback and Updates (1.2.3). During in-house and market-use testing, Data Systems, Incorporated will recommend modifications and test these modifications for incorporation in the final product or in future modifications of the final product. Only modifications recommended or incorporated before August 1, 1985, will be incorporated in the test program.

Documentation (1.3). Documentation of Costrend includes: (1) expansion and updating of the basic system description included in this proposal throughout the development cycle; (2) the writing, editing, and publication of an operator's manual; (3) the development and publication of sample problems and solutions to estimating situations using Costrend; and (4) documentation of user feedback and updates. The basic description will occupy about ten single spaced pages, the operator's manual will encompass approximately thirty single spaced pages (including figures, input tables, and output examples), and the sample problems and solutions will be contained in a document of about twenty single spaced pages (including figures, input tables, and output examples). User feedback will be accumulated, organized, and reported to the American Estimating Institute to provide a baseline for future system modifications and growth.

Support (1.4). Support to Costrend includes installation, training, modifications and update, and field service for one user to be selected by the American Estimating Institute. "Modifications and Updates" are limited to those that can be accomplished by 160 labor-hours of effort by Data Systems, Incorporated. Modifications and/or updates that require more than this expenditure of labor-hours will be covered by a supplemental contractual agreement. During the installation phase, the on-site team will provide real-time assistance to the user in placing the program into operation. During the training phase, example problems will be worked and one or more operators will be able to observe the system in use, ask questions, and participate in "hands-on" use of the system. Field service includes an additional visit to the user after the initial installation and training period to answer questions, identify problem areas, and to propose suggested solutions.

ORGANIZATION AND MANAGEMENT PROPOSAL

Company Background and Experience

Data Systems, Incorporated has had ten years experience in the development of computer programs and systems for cost estimating, cost analysis, financial, and cost tracking applications. The following programs were developed on time and within their budget and cost constraints:

Name of System	Customer	Completed
General Ledger System	Data Services, Inc.	1975
Learning Curve Programs	Scientifics, Inc.	1978
Depreciation Programs	Dollard Business Services	1980
Inventory Program	Triad Research	1982
Cost Data Base System	Semco Corporation	1983
Budgeting Program	US Army: NPG	1984

In addition to its programming and computer system development capabilities, Data Systems, Incorporated carries a line of minicomputers, microcomputers, and software for business, financial, cost estimating, and cost analysis applications.

Project Organization

The project organization for the development of Costrend consists of a program manager, a programmer, a technical report writer, and a systems data analyst. The program manager reports directly to the president of Data Systems, Incorporated and will work closely with the American Estimating Institute to initiate, carry out, and complete the entire activity shown on Figure 12.2.

Company Financial Capability

As shown on the balance sheet and income statement on Figure 12.3, Data Systems, Incorporated has total assets in the amount of $2,410,000 and earned a net income of $236,000 in 1983. Using a measure of various solvency ratios, Data Systems, Incorporated is in good financial condition. The current ratio (current assets divided by current liabilities) is 2.6 to 1; the quick ratio (cash plus accounts receivable, divided by current liabilities) is 1.5 to 1; and the debt to equity ratio (all liabilities divided by stockholders equity) is .64 to 1. The year 1983 was a very successful year for Data Systems, Incorporated, because the return on total stockholders equity was sixteen percent (up from ten percent the previous year).

Balance Sheet
1983

Current Assets			Current Liabilities		
Cash	$ 482,000		Accounts Payable	$ 310,000	
Accts Receivable	616,000		Accrued Expenses	82,000	
Inventory	720,000		Income Tax Payable	47,000	
Prepaid Expenses	70,000		Notes Payable	300,000	
Total Current Assets	$1,888,000		Total Current Liabilities	$ 739,000	
Fixed Assets			Long-term Notes Payable at 10%	$ 200,000	
Machiner, Equip., Furniture & Fix	$ 952,000		Stockholders Equity		
Less Depreciation	430,000		Paid-in Capital	$1,271,000	
Book Value	522,000		Total	$1,471,000	
			Total Liabilities and		
Total Assets	$2,410,000		Shareholders Equity	$2,410,000	

Income Statement
1983

Sales Revenue		$4,576,000
Cost of Goods Sold		3,120,000
Gross Profit		$1,456,000
Operating Expenses	$728,000	
Depreciation Expense	206,000	934,000
Operating Profit		$ 522,000
Interest Expense		50,000
Profit Before Income Tax		$ 472,000
Income Tax Expense		236,000
Net Income		$ 236,000

Figure 12.3. Balance Sheet and Income Statement: Data Systems, Inc.

Key Project Personnel

The four key project personnel who will be engaged in the development of Costrend are listed below:

Program Manager: Mr. Joseph Goodloe

Programmer: Mr. Robert Eddins

Writer: Mr. Stuart Douglas

Systems Data Analyst: Ms. Maryann Lindsey

Résumés of each of the above personnel follow:

Mr. Joseph Goodloe

Education: M.S. Administrative Science
                    Mississippi Technical Institute

B.S. Electrical Engineering
Tennessee Polytechnic Institute

Experience: Mr. Goodloe was program manager for DSI for the development of computer hardware/software systems for the period of 1978 to 1982. In this capacity, he managed DSI's efforts for marketing, systems analysis, and development of three major programs dealing with financial and estimating functions. Prior to joining DSI, Mr. Goodloe was systems analyst for IBM for five years, with responsibility for developing financial, business, and word processing programs. He served in the United States Army as a communications and electronics officer responsible for tracking and data acquisition programs.

Awards: Mr. Goodloe received the George Pendray Award in 1981 for outstanding contributions to the data processing field by the development of SYNTAX machine language that speeds the compilation of conventional high order languages. He is a Fellow Member of the Computer Society of America and is listed in "Who's Who in Microprocessing."

Publications: Mr. Goodloe prepared the published operator's manuals for SYNTAX, DDBMS, and MICRO-WORD systems. He has authored two articles for the magazine, "DATAMASTER," and is currently working on a textbook for the teaching of simplified machine languages.

Mr. Robert Eddins

Education: B.S. Computer Science
University of Alabama in Huntsville
B.S. Mathematics, Troy State College

Experience: Mr. Eddins developed the program structure and did all of the programming for the cost data base system and budgeting programs completed by DSI in 1983 and 1984. He is an accomplished programmer in BASIC, COBOL, FORTRAN, PASCAL, PL-1, and several machine languages. Prior to joining DSI in 1982, Mr. Eddins was employed for three and one half years by Scientific Systems Software, Incorporated where he performed systems analysis and programming for energy-related data base systems.

Awards: Mr. Eddins received the "Outstanding Employee for 1983" award and has received numerous merit and achievement awards for his outstanding programming ability.

Publications: Mr. Eddins prepared all program documentation and operators manuals for TRACE, a total resource and cost estimating system developed by Scientific Systems Software, Incorporated.

Mr. Stuart Douglas

Education: B.A. Journalism, Cornell University
Associate Degree in Computer Science
Auburn University, Montgomery, AL

Experience: Mr. Douglas has been responsible for the development of simplified, user-oriented handbooks and instructions for computer programs developed by DSI since 1978. He has developed six such handbooks which include text, illustrations, and simple operator instructions. Prior to joining DSI, Mr. Douglas was associated for eight years with Olin Matheson Chemical Company where he prepared technical reports and manuals; and for five years with the United States Army Corps of Engineers where he prepared specifications for construction projects.

Awards: Mr. Douglas received the 1982 American Graphics Institute Award for his series of flowcharts and instructions for operating microcomputers. His work was published in the July 1981 Journal of the American Graphics Institute.

Publications: Mr. Douglas is the author of *Computing Aids to Small Business* published in 1978 by Worth-Hall Publishers.

Ms. Maryann Lindsey

Education: B.A. Computer Science
               Triton Technical Insitute
               Associate Degree in Engineering
               Brown Community College

Experience: Ms. Lindsey is an accomplished systems data analyst, having been responsible for customer interfaces for the majority of DSI projects since its inception. She has served as a consultant to several large corporations contemplating installation of data-based cost systems and has written proposals, pamphlets, and manuals on several of DSI's products. Prior to joining DSI she served as systems analyst for the United States Navy's Ship Development Works at Puget Sound, where she is credited with the development of computerized cost tracking and payroll systems.

Awards: Ms. Lindsey has received the Company President's Award for Outstanding Achievement, a $1,000 suggestion award for proposing a new cost control system, and several merit bonuses for superior performance.

COST PROPOSAL

Introduction

The cost estimate for Costrend development was prepared in accordance with the work element structure shown on Figure 12.4. The method of estimating used was labor-hour-loading based on the availability of the four skills: program manager, programmer, writer, and data analyst. The following labor rates were used as the calendar year 1985 labor rates for each skill:

1. Program Manager:	$35.00 per hour
2. Programmer:	30.00 per hour
3. Writer:	18.00 per hour
4. Systems Data Analyst	12.00 per hour

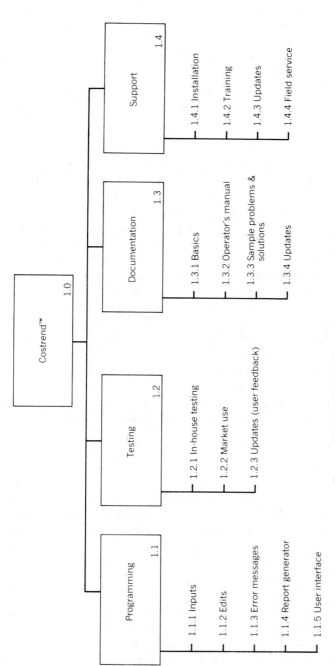

Figure 12.4. Work element structure for Costrend.

265

The estimate assumes an overhead rate of forty-three percent, a general and administrative expense rate of 2.5 percent, and a "cost-of-money" percentage of 0.5 percent. A fee of ten percent was calculated in the cost estimate but was later deducted in view of financial consideration offered to Data Systems, Incorporated in the form of a ten percent commission on the gross sales income from Costrend software packages.

Costing Rationale

Programming. The programming effort of 140 hours per month, which occupies eighty-eight percent of one programmer's time, is time-phased with the bulk of the programmer's work in the first month devoted to the input programming. Some programmer effort (approximately ten hours each) is required for each of the other four phases of programming activity: edits, error messages, report generation, and user interfaces. The Program Manager will be spending one hundred percent of his contracted work on the user interface during the first month of the contract. In subsequent months, the Program Manager's effort will reduce to eighty, sixty, and then forty hours per month as the user interface becomes more fully established. Programming effort is time-phased to permit a single programmer to take the lead in each phase of the programming activity. Hence, programmer man-hours peak in February, March, April, and May for each of the subsequent phases of edits, error messages, report generation, and user interfaces. The technical writer must spend about ten hours per month in research, study, and interaction with the other team members to gain and maintain familiarity with project content.

Testing. The testing effort for Costrend requires heavy participation of the systems data analyst. Systems testing starts in the first two months with in-house testing, proceeds through market testing for the next two months, and is completed during the last month of testing when modifications fed back from users will be evaluated and tested. Programming hours are required during the latter part of the testing effort to modify the coding to incorporate user feedback. The technical writer must stay "on board" by spending a few hours each month familiarizing himself with the activities and results of the test program.

Documentation. The activities of the technical writer come heavily into play during the documentation period, the bulk of the time being spent on writing the operator's manual. The systems data analyst will be spending full-time during this period in developing sample problems and examples for the operator's manual and in assisting in the preparation of other phases of program documentation. The program manager and programmer will continue to participate in the documentation phase in reviewing, editing, and providing inputs into the documents as they are developed.

Support.   The support phase of the project will occupy all team members on a part time basis during installation, training, updates, and field service. The programmer hours will be spent in working closely with the customer in adapting the BASIC language of Costrend to the specific form of BASIC language employed in the customer's computer. The program manager will continue to oversee the entire operation to ensure rapid response and satisfactory solution to problems and questions that may arise during the initial field use of the system. The writer will prepare and issue updates to the operator's manual, if required, during this period.

Material Costs

Two hundred dollars per month have been allocated for computer disks, direct mailing costs, special subcontracts, and handling costs.

Other Direct Charges

Two trips per month are planned during the programming and field support phases of the project. One trip per month is planned for the remaining months. Travel costs include airline fare, per diem, rental car, and miscellaneous expenses. Travel costs are estimated to be $1,000 per trip.

Overhead Costs

Of significant benefit to customers of Data Systems, Incorporated is the unprecedentedly low overhead and general and administrative expenses. This low overhead has been demonstrated over the past several years and is brought about by maximum and multiple-use of facilities and equipment, the use of part-time or temporary employees and subcontracts rather than hiring a large full-time work force, low energy costs, low interest costs, and a demonstrated low cost escalation history.

Detailed Cost Breakout

A detailed cost breakout is shown on Figure 12.5.

Cost Summary

The total estimated cost, including a fee of ten percent, for the development of Costrend as described in this proposal is:	$224,946.10
Fee amount to be foregone in lieu of licensing commission	$ 20,449.65
Total Contract Price	$204,496.45

Figure 12.5 Cost estimate for Costrend.

```
                              ****  COSTFORM ESTIMATE WORKSHEET   ****

Base Yr: 1985                                                        PAGE:   1
WES. #  : 1.1
                         PROJECT - COSTREND DEVELOPMENT
                         WES TITLE: PROGRAMMING   DATE: 10/16/84
```

COST ELEMENT	JAN	FEB	MAR	APR	MAY	JUN	JUL	AUG	SEP	OCT	NOV	DEC
PROGRAM MANAGER												
HRLY $$ 35.00	35.00	35.00	35.00	35.00	35.00	35.00	35.00	35.00	35.00	35.00	35.00	35.00
HOURS 100	80	60	40	40	0	0	0	0	0	0	0	0
total hours for this cost element = 320												
Senior PROGRAMMER												
HRLY $$ 30.00	30.00	30.00	30.00	30.00	30.00	30.00	30.00	30.00	30.00	30.00	30.00	30.00
HOURS 140	140	140	140	140	0	0	0	0	0	0	0	0
total hours for this cost element = 700												
TECHNICAL WRITER												
HRLY $$ 18.00	18.00	18.00	18.00	18.00	18.00	18.00	18.00	18.00	18.00	18.00	18.00	18.00
HOURS 50	50	50	50	50	0	0	0	0	0	0	0	0
total hours for this cost element = 250												
SYSTEMS DATA ANALYST												
HRLY $$ 12.00	12.00	12.00	12.00	12.00	12.00	12.00	12.00	12.00	12.00	12.00	12.00	12.00
HOURS 150	150	150	0	0	0	0	0	0	0	0	0	0
total hours for this cost element = 450												
SYSTEMS ANALYST 1												
HRLY $$ 0.00	0.00	0.00	0.00	0.00	0.00	0.00	0.00	0.00	0.00	0.00	0.00	0.00
HOURS 0	0	0	0	0	0	0	0	0	0	0	0	0
total hours for this cost element = 0												
SYSTEMS ANALYST 2												
HRLY $$ 0.00	0.00	0.00	0.00	0.00	0.00	0.00	0.00	0.00	0.00	0.00	0.00	0.00
HOURS 0	0	0	0	0	0	0	0	0	0	0	0	0
total hours for this cost element = 0												

Base Yr: 1985
WES. # : 1.1

****** C U M U L A T I V E   T O T A L S ********

Material Dollars Per Period :

200.00	200.00	200.00	0.00	0.00	0.00	0.00	0.00	0.00

Other Direct Cost Per Period :

2000.00	2000.00	2000.00	0.00	0.00	0.00	0.00	0.00	0.00

-- Cumulative Sub Totals Per Period ---   (NOTE: $$ = RATE X HOURS per period;   HR = TOTAL MANHRS per period)

$	10400.00	9700.00	9000.00	6500.00	0.00	0.00	0.00	0.00	0.00
HR	440	420	400	230	0	0	0	0	0

total manhours for all cost elements =   1,720

S U M M A R Y   A N A L Y S I S

```
TOTAL LABOR DOLLARS   =   $42,100.00
  + Labor Overhead    =   $18,103.00     (at 43 % rate)
                          ----------
        *** sub total ***   $60,203.00
  + Material Dollars   =    $1,000.00
  + Other Direct Cost  =   $10,000.00
                          ----------
        *** sub total ***   $71,203.00
  + G & A Factor       =    $1,780.08     (at 25 % rate)
  + Cost Of Money      =      $356.02     (at 05 % rate)
                          ----------
        *** sub total ***   $73,339.09
  + Fixed Fee          =    $7,333.91     (at 10 % rate)
                          ----------
******* GRAND TOTAL *******  $80,673.00
                          ==========
```

(Continued)

Figure 12.5. (Continued)

```
****  COSTFORM ESTIMATE WORKSHEET  ****

      PROJECT - COSTREND DEVELOPMENT

      WES TITLE:  SYSTEMS TESTING            DATE: 10/16/84
```

COST ELEMENT	JAN	FEB	MAR	APR	MAY	JUN	JUL	AUG	SEP	OCT	NOV	DEC
PROGRAM MANAGER												
HRLY $$	35.00	35.00	35.00	35.00	35.00	35.00	35.00	35.00	35.00	35.00	35.00	35.00
HOURS	0	0	0	20	20	40	40	40	0	0	0	0
total hours for this cost element = 160												
Senior PROGRAMMER												
HRLY $$	30.00	30.00	30.00	30.00	30.00	30.00	30.00	30.00	30.00	30.00	30.00	30.00
HOURS	0	0	0	10	10	40	50	60	0	0	0	0
total hours for this cost element = 170												
TECHNICAL WRITER												
HRLY $$	18.00	18.00	18.00	18.00	18.00	18.00	18.00	18.00	18.00	18.00	18.00	18.00
HOURS	0	0	0	15	15	15	15	15	0	0	0	0
total hours for this cost element = 75												
SYSTEMS DATA ANALYST												
HRLY $$	12.00	12.00	12.00	12.00	12.00	12.00	12.00	12.00	12.00	12.00	12.00	12.00
HOURS	0	0	0	150	150	150	150	150	0	0	0	0
total hours for this cost element = 750												
SYSTEMS ANALYST 1												
HRLY $$	0.00	0.00	0.00	0.00	0.00	0.00	0.00	0.00	0.00	0.00	0.00	0.00
HOURS	0	0	0	0	0	0	0	0	0	0	0	0
total hours for this cost element = 0												
SYSTEMS ANALYST 2												
HRLY $$	0.00	0.00	0.00	0.00	0.00	0.00	0.00	0.00	0.00	0.00	0.00	0.00
HOURS	0	0	0	0	0	0	0	0	0	0	0	0
total hours for this cost element = 0												

	*******	CUMULATIVE	TOTALS	*******	*******
Material Dollars Per Period :					
0.00 0.00	0.00	0.00	200.00	200.00	0.00	0.00
Other Direct Cost Per Period :					
0.00 0.00	0.00	1000.00	1000.00	0.00	0.00	0.00

-- Cumulative Sub Totals Per Period ---   (NOTE: $$ = RATE X HOURS per period;   HR = TOTAL MANHRS per period)

| $ | 0.00 | 0.00 | 3070.00 | 3070.00 | 4670.00 | 4970.00 | 5270.00 | 0.00 | 0.00 | 0.00 |
| HR | 0 | 0 | 195 | 195 | 245 | 255 | 265 | 0 | 0 | 0 |

total manhours for all cost elements =   1,155

S U M M A R Y   A N A L Y S I S

```
TOTAL LABOR DOLLARS     =    $21,050.00
  + Labor Overhead      =     $9,051.50    (at 43 % rate)

        *** sub total ***      $30,101.50
  + Material Dollars    =        $400.00
  + Other Direct Cost   =      $2,000.00
                              ------------
        *** sub total ***      $32,501.50
  + G & A Factor        =        $812.54    (at  25 % rate)
  + Cost Of Money       =        $162.51    (at  05 % rate)
                              ------------
        *** sub total ***      $33,476.55
  + Fixed Fee           =      $3,347.65    (at  10 % rate)
                              ------------
   ******* GRAND TOTAL *******  $36,824.20
                              ============
```

(Continued)

Figure 12.5. *(Continued)*

Base Yr: 1985   PAGE: 5

WES. # : 1.3

PROJECT - COSTREND DEVELOPMENT

WES TITLE: SYSTEM DOCUMENTATION   DATE: 10/16/84

COST ELEMENT	JAN	FEB	MAR	APR	MAY	JUN	JUL	AUG	SEP	OCT	NOV	DEC
PROGRAM MANAGER												
HRLY $$	35.00	35.00	35.00	35.00	35.00	35.00	35.00	35.00	35.00	35.00	35.00	35.00
HOURS	0	0	0	0	0	35	20	20	80			
total hours for this cost element =					155							
Senior PROGRAMMER												
HRLY $$	30.00	30.00	30.00	30.00	30.00	30.00	30.00	30.00	30.00	30.00	30.00	30.00
HOURS	0	0	0	0	0	60	60	60	60			
total hours for this cost element =					240							
TECHNICAL WRITER												
HRLY $$	18.00	18.00	18.00	18.00	18.00	18.00	18.00	18.00	18.00	18.00	18.00	18.00
HOURS	0	0	0	0	0	145	145	145	160			
total hours for this cost element =					595							
SYSTEMS DATA ANALYST												
HRLY $$	12.00	12.00	12.00	12.00	12.00	12.00	12.00	12.00	12.00	12.00	12.00	12.00
HOURS	0	0	0	0	0	160	160	160	160			
total hours for this cost element =					640							
SYSTEMS ANALYST 1												
HRLY $$	0.00	0.00	0.00	0.00	0.00	0.00	0.00	0.00	0.00	0.00	0.00	0.00
HOURS	0	0	0	0	0	0	0	0	0			
total hours for this cost element =					0							
SYSTEMS ANALYST 2												
HRLY $$	0.00	0.00	0.00	0.00	0.00	0.00	0.00	0.00	0.00	0.00	0.00	0.00
HOURS	0	0	0	0	0	0	0	0	0			
total hours for this cost element =					0							

Base Yr: 1985

WES. # : 1.3

```
                        * * * * * * *    C U M U L A T I V E   T O T A L S   * * * * * * *

Material Dollars Per Period :
  0.00      0.00      0.00      0.00      0.00    200.00    200.00      0.00      0.00      0.00

Other Direct Cost Per Period :
  0.00      0.00      0.00      0.00      0.00   1000.00   1000.00      0.00      0.00      0.00

-- Cumulative Sub Totals Per Period ---    (NOTE:    $$ = RATE X HOURS per period;     HR = TOTAL MANHRS per period)

$  0.00      0.00      0.00      0.00   7555.00   7030.00   7030.00   9400.00      0.00      0.00

HR    0         0         0       400       385       385       460         0         0        0

total manhours for all cost elements =   1,630
```

```
          S U M M A R Y   A N A L Y S I S

          TOTAL LABOR DOLLARS   =    $31,015.00
        + Labor Overhead        =    $13,336.45     (at  43 % rate)
          ------------------------------------
          *** sub total ***          $44,351.45
        + Material Dollars      =       $400.00
        + Other Direct Cost     =     $2,000.00
          ------------------------------------
          *** sub total ***          $46,751.45
        + G & A Factor          =     $1,168.79     (at  25 % rate)
        + Cost Of Money         =       $233.76     (at  0.5 % rate)
          ------------------------------------
          *** sub total ***          $48,153.99
        + Fixed Fee             =     $4,815.40     (at  10 % rate)
          ------------------------------------
          ******* GRAND TOTAL ********  $52,969.39
                                      ============
```

(Continued)

Figure 12.5. (Continued)

**** COSTFORM ESTIMATE WORKSHEET ****

PROJECT - COSTREND DEVELOPMENT

WES TITLE: SUPPORT   DATE: 10/16/84

COST ELEMENT	JAN	FEB	MAR	APR	MAY	JUN	JUL	AUG	SEP	OCT	NOV	DEC
PROGRAM MANAGER												
HRLY $$	35.00	35.00	35.00	35.00	35.00	35.00	35.00	35.00	35.00	35.00	35.00	35.00
HOURS	0	0	0	0	0	0	0	0	0	60	60	60
total hours for this cost element =					180							
Senior PROGRAMMER												
HRLY $$	30.00	30.00	30.00	30.00	30.00	30.00	30.00	30.00	30.00	30.00	30.00	30.00
HOURS	0	0	0	0	0	0	0	0	0	200	150	125
total hours for this cost element =					475							
TECHNICAL WRITER												
HRLY $$	18.00	18.00	18.00	18.00	18.00	18.00	18.00	18.00	18.00	18.00	18.00	18.00
HOURS	0	0	0	0	0	0	0	0	0	50	50	50
total hours for this cost element =					150							
SYSTEMS DATA ANALYST												
HRLY $$	12.00	12.00	12.00	12.00	12.00	12.00	12.00	12.00	12.00	12.00	12.00	12.00
HOURS	0	0	0	0	0	0	0	0	0	160	160	160
total hours for this cost element =					480							
SYSTEMS ANALYST 1												
HRLY $$	0.00	0.00	0.00	0.00	0.00	0.00	0.00	0.00	0.00	0.00	0.00	0.00
HOURS	0	0	0	0	0	0	0	0	0	0	0	0
total hours for this cost element =					0							
SYSTEMS ANALYST 2												
HRLY $$	0.00	0.00	0.00	0.00	0.00	0.00	0.00	0.00	0.00	0.00	0.00	0.00
HOURS	0	0	0	0	0	0	0	0	0	0	0	0
total hours for this cost element =					0							

Base Yr: 1985

WES. # : 1.4

PROJECT - COSTREND DEVELOPMENT

WES TITLE: SUPPORT   DATE: 10/16/84   PAGE: 8

```
*******  C U M U L A T I V E   T O T A L S  *******
```

Material Dollars Per Period :

0.00	0.00	0.00	0.00	0.00	200.00	200.00	200.00

Other Direct Cost Per Period :

0.00	0.00	0.00	0.00	0.00	2000.00	2000.00	2000.00

-- Cumulative Sub Totals Per Period ---   (NOTE: $$ = RATE X HOURS per period;   HR = TOTAL MANHRS per period)

$	0.00	0.00	0.00	0.00	0.00	10920.00	9420.00	8670.00
HR	0	0	0	0	0	470	420	395

total manhours for all cost elements =   1,285

S U M M A R Y   A N A L Y S I S

```
TOTAL LABOR DOLLARS    =    $29,010.00
    + Labor Overhead   =    $12,474.30        (at  43 % rate)

        *** sub total ***    $41,484.30
    + Material Dollars  =       $600.00
    + Other Direct Cost =     $6,000.00

        *** sub total ***    $48,084.30
    + G & A Factor      =     $1,202.11        (at  25 % rate)
    + Cost Of Money     =       $240.42        (at  05 % rate)

        *** sub total ***    $49,526.83
    + Fixed Fee         =     $4,952.68        (at  10 % rate)

    ******* GRAND TOTAL *******    $54,479.51
                                   ==========
```

(Continued)

Figure 12.5. (Continued)

Base Yr: 1985

WES. # : 1.0

PROJECT – COSTREND DEVELOPMENT

WES TITLE: Grand Total Recap

DATE: 10/16/84

COST ELEMENT	JAN	FEB	MAR	APR	MAY	JUN	JUL	AUG	SEP	OCT	NOV	DEC
PROGRAM MANAGER												
HRLY $$	35.00	35.00	35.00	35.00	35.00	35.00	35.00	35.00	35.00	35.00	35.00	35.00
HOURS	100	80	60	60	60	75	60	60	80	60	60	60
total hours for this cost element = 815												
Senior PROGRAMMER												
HRLY $$	30.00	30.00	30.00	30.00	30.00	30.00	30.00	30.00	30.00	30.00	30.00	30.00
HOURS	140	140	140	150	150	100	110	120	60	200	150	125
total hours for this cost element = 1,585												
TECHNICAL WRITER												
HRLY $$	18.00	18.00	18.00	18.00	18.00	18.00	18.00	18.00	18.00	18.00	18.00	18.00
HOURS	50	50	50	65	65	160	160	160	160	50	50	50
total hours for this cost element = 1,070												
SYSTEMS DATA ANALYST												
HRLY $$	12.00	12.00	12.00	12.00	12.00	12.00	12.00	12.00	12.00	12.00	12.00	12.00
HOURS	150	150	150	150	150	310	310	310	160	160	160	160
total hours for this cost element = 2,320												
SYSTEMS ANALYST 1												
HRLY $$	0.00	0.00	0.00	0.00	0.00	0.00	0.00	0.00	0.00	0.00	0.00	0.00
HOURS	0	0	0	0	0	0	0	0	0	0	0	0
total hours for this cost element = 0												
SYSTEMS ANALYST 2												
HRLY $$	0.00	0.00	0.00	0.00	0.00	0.00	0.00	0.00	0.00	0.00	0.00	0.00
HOURS	0	0	0	0	0	0	0	0	0	0	0	0
total hours for this cost element = 0												

Base Yr: 1985

WES. # : 1.0

PROJECT - COSTREND DEVELOPMENT

WES TITLE: Grand Total Recap

DATE: 10/16/84

PAGE: 10

```
* * * * * *          C U M U L A T I V E   T O T A L S          * * * * * * *
```

Material Dollars Per Period :
200.00   200.00   200.00   200.00   200.00   200.00   200.00

Other Direct Cost Per Period :
2000.00   2000.00   2000.00   1000.00   2000.00   2000.00   2000.00

-- Cumulative Sub Totals Per Period ---
(NOTE: $$ = RATE X HOURS per period;   HR = TOTAL MANHRS per period)

$ 10400.00   9700.00   9000.00   9570.00   12225.00   12000.00   12300.00   9400.00   9420.00   8670.00

HR   440   420   400   425   645   640   650   460   470   395

total manhours for all cost elements = 5,790

```
S U M M A R Y     A N A L Y S I S
```

TOTAL LABOR DOLLARS	=	$123,175.00	
+ Labor Overhead	=	$52,965.25	(at 43 % rate)
*** sub total ***		$176,140.25	
+ Material Dollars	=	$2,400.00	
+ Other Direct Cost	=	$20,000.00	
*** sub total ***		$198,540.25	
+ G & A Factor	=	$4,963.51	(at 25 % rate)
+ Cost Of Money	=	$992.70	(at 0.5 % rate)
*** sub total ***		$204,496.46	
+ Fixed Fee	=	$20,449.65	(at 10 % rate)
******* GRAND TOTAL *******		$224,946.10	

(end)

```
******************************************************************
* C O S T   F O R M    E S T I M A T E    S Y S T E M *
******************************************************************


        ******    HEADER EDIT PROGRAM    ******


        FOLLOWING DATA FOR HEADER RECORD
...................................................................

(01)  PROJECT TITLE = COSTREND DEVELOPMENT

(02)  CALENDAR BASE = M

      START MONTH   =   JANUARY

(03)  OVERHEAD RATE =  .43

(04)  COST OF MONEY =  .005

(05)  G & A FACTOR  =  .025

(06)  FIXED FEE     =  .10

(07) # LABOR SKILLS =   6

      SKILL 1 - PROGRAM MANAGER

      SKILL 2 - Senior PROGRAMMER

      SKILL 3 - TECHNICAL WRITER

      SKILL 4 - SYSTEMS DATA ANALYST

      SKILL 5 - SYSTEMS ANALYST 1

      SKILL 6 - SYSTEMS ANALYST 2
```

Figure 12.6. COSTFORM™ header record.

The cost estimate in this chapter was run on COSTFORM™, an estimate system developed by Diversified Data Systems, Incorporated, of Huntsville, Alabama.

Figure 12.6 is a header sheet for the COSTFORM Estimate System. This header sheet shows the factors and skills used in the estimate.

Appendix 1

PROPOSAL PREPARATION

Sample Proposal Preparation Manual

INTRODUCTION

This sample proposal preparation manual assumes a hypothetical company which is a division of a larger company. The division is headed by a general manager who reports to the corporate management along with general managers of other divisions. A director of advanced planning is responsible for the division's acquisition of new work. Other directors manage various portions of the division's activities.

Section 1

PURPOSE

This manual establishes uniform guidelines for the preparation and processing of proposals within the company. Its purpose is to provide a general guide for proposal preparation and is not intended to limit or constrain any procedures made necessary by unique requirements, or special circumstances not addressed in this manual. Proposals in all cases should be prepared to meet specific customer requirements.

Section 2

SCOPE

This manual is applicable to all proposals for which a proposal task authorization is issued, or engineering change proposals for which a task authorization has been issued, regardless of cost/price basis or cost magnitude, and regardless of whether we are responding to a formal request for proposal or request for quotation or are making an unsolicited offer.

Section 3

APPROVALS

PROPOSAL TASK AUTHORIZATION

Proposal task authorizations for expenditure of $ _____ or less require approval of the cognizant director. Those in excess of $_____ require general manager approval. Supplementary proposal task authorizations increasing the cumulative authorization for a proposal to more than $_____ also require general manager approval.

PROPOSAL

Policy No. _____ specifies proposal signature authority and dollar amounts for the various levels of management.

Section 4

PROPOSAL CYCLE

GENERAL

The proposal is a primary mechanism for the acquisition of new business. It is the company's committed offer to undertake certain work for a firm dollar amount and to complete that work within a specified time. It is essential, therefore, that the proposal be:

Technically sound

Accurately cost-estimated

Structured for proper program control

Responsive to the customer's requirements

There are three distinct but interrelated parts of all proposals: technical, organization and management, and cost. The form in which they appear in the final published proposal as separately bound volumes, separate sections in a single volume, or merely separate paragraphs, is incidental to the preparation process, which in all cases must be thorough, orderly, and complete.

Because of the short time normally available for the preparation of proposals, the technical, organization and management, and cost sections are prepared concurrently—many times by separate groups. Because of the interrelationship of each section to the others, continuous liaison between groups is an absolute necessity.

The controlling authority throughout the proposal preparation process is the proposal manager. The proposal manager is responsible for the total proposal. He or she is designated by the director to whom the proposal has been assigned. Proposal team members normally include an assigned engineering staff; a contract administrator; an administrator from program management; a marketing representative; a cost analyst; a technical documentation/data management representative; and support personnel from such groups as program management, product assurance, manufacturing, reliability, design and drafting, procurement, and test. Support participation is solicited by the proposal manager and varies with the nature and scope of each proposal. Participation is required by all groups that will be committed in the proposal to do work on the job. A general checklist of proposal responsibilities is shown later in this manual.

Classified proposals are handled in accordance with standard security practices (Policy No. _____) or special requirements of the RFP/RFQ. The proposal manager is responsible for the overall proposal security under the guidance of the company security officer. The manager of technical documentation supervises the marking, handling, reproduction, and storage of sensitive proposals and related materials processed through technical documentation.

(A typical proposal flow chart is shown in Figure A1.1.)

PROPOSAL MEETINGS

Bid and Proposal Meeting

The contracts department, upon receipt of any RFP or RFQ, or if organizing an unsolicited proposal, advises and forwards data to the director of

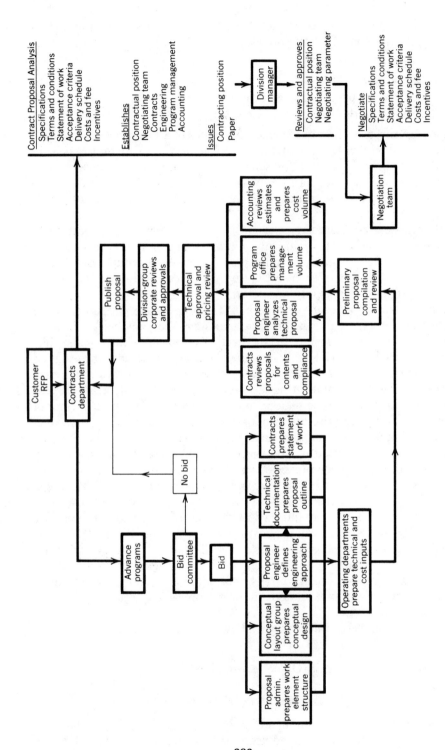

Figure A1.1. Typical proposal flow chart.

advanced planning for the division. The director of advanced planning reviews the RFP/RFQ or in-house propositon to determine its business potential and notifies the director of corporate advanced planning that a proposal cycle is being initiated.

If the RFP or RFQ is determined to be a joint division opportunity or to apply to another division, the director of division, advanced planning, forwards it and the data package to the director of corporate advanced planning.

When notification from the corporation offices to proceed is received, a "bid/no bid" decision meeting is scheduled in coordination with the appropriate director. At this meeting if a preliminary "bid" decision is made, a proposal manager is then selected.

If a decision is made *not* to respond to the RFP or RFQ, the director, advanced planning, informs the customer and corporate management. If it is to be accepted, the proposal manager in coordination with the director, advanced planning, prepares a preliminary proposal plan, which includes the following information:

1. Estimate of resources required to implement proposal.
2. Identity of the customer.
3. Proposal preparation time.
4. Preliminary proposal team.
5. Expected contract work scope (work statement).
6. Special requirements.
7. Funding available to the customer.
8. Type of contract anticipated.
9. Past relations with the customer and future prospects, including company's obligation to the customer.
10. Competitive chances to win the contract, including both the company's and the customer's competitive position.
11. Estimate of contract value and possible future business potential.
12. Preliminary proposal strategy.
13. Facilities required.
14. Equipment and/or property required.
15. Special terms and conditions.

The above information is summarized in a proposal task authorization (Figure A1.2). Also a cost estimate checklist (Figure A1.3) is attached to all proposal task authorizations in excess of $_____ .

The bid package, which includes a copy of the request for proposal, the proposal plan, and the proposal task authorization, is presented at the division bid committee meeting within *forty working hours* of RFP/RFQ receipt.

PROPOSAL TASK AUTHORIZATION

WORK ORDER	TASK	REV. NO.

TITLE	PRIME DIVISION

LOG NO.	CUSTOMER	BUSINESS AREA

REP.NO.OR CUST.MSG.NO.	SECURITY CLASSIFICATION	DEPARTMENT HAVING PRIME RESPONSIBILITY

PROPOSAL WORK STATEMENT

BUSINESS POTENTIAL, (ESTIMATED CONTRACT PRICE)- IS REQUIREMENT BUDGETED?   YES ☐   NO ☐   UNKNOWN ☐

MARKETING STRATEGY
 CONTRACT POSSIBILITY
 PAST RELATIONSHIP WITH CUSTOMER
 PRIME COMPETITORS
 CONVERSION DATE
 CONTRACT TYPE
  ☐CPFF ☐CPIF ☐FFP ☐T&M ☐FPI ☐OTHER

PROPOSAL TASK BUDGET
PREVIOUS AUTH. _____
THIS AUTH. _____
TOTAL AUTH. _____
(INCL. THIS PTA)

END ITEM USER	DOD	NASA	OTHER GOV'T	COMM'L	COMM'L PURCHASER SUPPLYING GOV'T

PROPOSAL BUDGET

DEPARTMENT		JAN	FEB	MAR	APR	MAY	JUN	JUL	AUG	SEP	OCT	NOV	DEC	TOTAL MM	$
	LAB $														
	N/L $													✕	
	LAB $														
	N/L $													✕	
	LAB $														
	N/L $													✕	
	LAB $														
	N/L $													✕	
	LAB $														
	N/L $													✕	
TOTAL LAB $															
TOTAL N/L $													✕	
*TOTALS $														THIS AUTH.	

DOES THIS CONTRACT REQUIRE SIGNIFICANT ADDITIONAL CAPITAL EQUIPMENT OR FACILITIES (DESCRIBE)	$ AMOUNT CAP.EQ.

IDENTIFY KEY CONTRIBUTORS REQUIRED FOR THIS PROPOSAL		PROPOSAL MANAGER		SUBMISSION DATE	
MARKETING (1)	DATE	DIR.ADV.PLAN (2)	DATE	DIR.ADV.PROG.(3)	DATE
DIRECTOR (1)	DATE	GEN. MGR. (2)	DATE	CONTROLLER (4)	DATE
DIV.CONTROLLER (1)	DATE	ASST.CONTROLLER (3)	DATE	SR.V. PRES. (4)	DATE

*IF IN EXCESS OF $1,000 REQUIRES BID COMM. APPROVALS-
TOTAL AUTHORIZATION DETERMINES APPROVAL LEVEL:
(1)$1,000 OR LESS ☐ (2)OVER $1,000 ☐ (3) OVER $10,000 ☐ (4) OVER $25,000 ☐

Figure A1.2. Proposal task authorization.

TYPE OF PROPOSAL

COST-TYPE	—	ENG STUDY	—
FIXED PRICE	—	BREADBOARD	—
ROM	—	PROTOTYPE	—

CONTRACT EFFORT

PRODUCTION	—	FIELD SUPPORT	—
SPARES	—		—
DATA	—		—

PROPOSAL VOLUMES

LETTER	—
TECHNICAL	—
MANAGEMENT	—
COST	—

REQUIRED EFFORT*	ELECT.	MECH.	TEST	SYS. INT.	REL.	DATA	INST.	ADV. PGMS.	Q-A	MFG.	TLNG.	P. MGT.	CMPTR.	TECH. STP.
BIDDERS CONFERENCE (INCL. TRAVEL)														
DETAILED PROPOSAL SCHEDULE														
KICK-OFF MEETING														
VENDOR/SUB SURVEY (INCL. TRAVEL)														
TEAMING ARRANGEMENTS (INCL. TRAVEL)														
DETAILED PROGRAM SCHEDULE														
PRELIMINARY DESIGN														
VALIDATE CUSTOMER SPECS.														
ENGINEERING COSTING														
HARDWARE COSTING														
DETAILED BILL OF MATERIALS														
SPECIAL TOOLING/TEST EQUIPMENT														
PROPOSAL PREPARATION (ROUGH, FINAL)														
CUSTOMER PRESENTATION (INCL. TRAVEL)														
NEGOTIATIONS (INCL. TRAVEL)														

*EXPLAIN ALL ITEMS CHECKED BUT NOT INCLUDED IN BUDGET REQUEST

Figure A1.3. Proposal cost estimate checklist.

285

The bid committee usually consists of the following management personnel:

General manager

Technical director

Cognizant activity director

Division controller

Director, administration and contracts

Director, advanced planning

Director, engineering

Director, advanced technology

Manager, contracts

In addition the following personnel may be members of the committee, as appropriate:

Director, corporate advanced programs

Director, corporate advanced planning

Director, manufacturing

Director, quality assurance

The division bid committee reviews the RFP/RFQ and:

1. If a decision is made *not* to bid, the data package is returned to the division director of advanced planning to inform customer/requestor accordingly.

2. If it is accepted, the committee approves the following, and forwards data package to the director of corporate advanced planning and the division controller:

    a. Proposal manager

    b. Proposal schedule

    c. Proposal task authorization

The division controller reviews the information in the proposal task authorization for compliance with bid and proposal guidelines, assigns a proposal charge number and returns the proposal task authorization to the proposal manager.

If an engineering change proposal is being processed, the contracts department will assign an appropriate "ECP" number. A task authorization is then issued by the program office, defining the ECP requirements. The task authorization goes through the same approval cycle as a proposal task authorization.

Proposal Kickoff Meeting

The proposal manager, within twenty-four working hours following proposal task authorization approval, convenes a proposal "kickoff" meeting. Attendees include representatives from all contributing, operating, and support departments as determined by the proposal manager. At this meeting, all pertinent information is distributed and discussed. As a minimum, the following is supplied to the attendees:

1. Proposal control form (see Figure A1.4).
2. Copies of the RFP/RFQ.
3. Proposal preparation schedule and budgets.
4. Marketing intelligence and proposal strategy.
5. Basic proposal theme and technical/costing guidelines.
6. Proposal preparation schedule of all proposal contributors.
7. Assignment of tasks, as appropriate.
8. Coverage of any other proposal effort items as applicable.

The proposal manager may appoint, if required, a technical team to evolve the technical aspects of the proposal and to determine conceptual feasibility and design, including risk areas and program scope.

RESPONSIBILITIES OF TEAM

Following the kickoff meeting, the customer's requirements are reviewed and the program manager and members of the proposal team prepare a work element structure (WES), a preliminary program schedule, and a program milestone chart.

The proposal manager and data management department prepare detailed proposal outlines (with writing assignments) for each proposal section:

Technical
Organization and management
Cost

The proposal team conducts a baseline concept review prior to initiation of final technical proposal preparation. The object of this review is to summarize the design concept, confirm proposal strategy, identify any further engineering/design to be done, and verify responsiveness to known customer requirements.

The team evaluates the adequacy of available drawings, sketches, and technical data for cost estimating purposes.

The proposal manager calls a management/cost meeting with representatives of management, accounting, and contracts, as appropriate. This meeting is the kickoff for the cost estimating activity required to support

PROPOSAL TITLE: _____

RFP TITLE AND NUMBER: _____

CUSTOMER NAME AND ADDRESS: _____

PROPOSAL CHARGE NUMBER: _____

PROPOSAL MANAGER: _____

PROPOSAL ADMINISTRATOR: _____

CONTRACT ADMINISTRATOR: _____

FINANCIAL REPRESENTATIVE: _____

TECHNICAL WRITER: _____

COURIER EXPEDITER: _____

CRITICAL DATES:

    TECHNICAL SECTION TO TECH WRITING: _____

    COST SECTION TO ACCOUNTING: _____

    SIGN-OFF MEETING: _____

    DELIVERY TO PUBLICATION ACTIVITY: _____

    MAILING DATE: _____

Figure A1.4.   Proposal control form.

proposal preparation. The meeting covers management and cost factors, such as:

    Organization and personnel availability
    Program management techniques
    Company capability and experience
    Facilities and equipment availability
    Program plan
    Task descriptions and task responsibility matrix
    Schedules

Work element structure

Cost estimating guidelines and instructions

Drawings/sketches/specifications

RFP/RFQ terms and conditions

At this point of the procedure, the three major proposal activities are underway concurrently:

Preparation of technical proposal drafts

Preparation of organization and management proposal drafts

Preparation of cost volume draft

As a guide in estimating the various tasks required, the definitions and procedures given in Sections 6, 7, and 8 should be utilized by assigned personnel.

Section 5

RATES

DIRECT LABOR

Direct labor rates (bid rates) are preestablished for the pricing of all proposals and are reviewed periodically to determine whether current conditions support their continued use. These rates are revised at least once a year, employing actual average rate data by skill category and skill level, and applying to these data an escalation factor which includes the effect of merit increase budgets, labor turnover, promotions, and reasonable anticipated changes in wage patterns.

Direct labor rates are applied in proposals by fiscal year to the estimated number of actual productive hours required to perform the required tasks.

OVERHEAD RATES

Overhead rates are calculated as follows for each overhead pool:

$$\frac{\text{Projected overhead expense dollars}}{\text{Projected direct labor dollars}} = \text{Overhead \%}$$

Overhead and direct dollar projections are based on the latest division workload and business projection and on related historical indices.

GENERAL AND ADMINISTRATIVE (G&A) RATES

G&A rates are calculated by adding the division expenses to corporate and independent research and development allocations that are based on cost input. The makeup of these expenses is as follows:

Local Division Expenses.   Based on the latest division cost projections for such functions as purchasing, contract administration, accounting, the general manager's office, and other support functions.

Independent Research and Development.   This amount, if applicable, is based on an annual advanced negotiated agreement and is allocated on projections of cost input by division.

Corporate Expenses.   Allocated to the division on a basis of cost input. Corporate expenses include bid and proposal costs which are fully burdened and covered by an advanced negotiated agreement.

Division cost input includes all direct labor, overhead, and nonlabor dollars in the month of expenditure.

It is the responsibility of the accounting department to insure that all cost exhibits, including computerized labor/cost estimates include the proper labor and burden rates.

Section 6

DIRECT LABOR

DEFINITION

Direct labor (ref. Policy No. _____)is the cost of productive time of personnel classified as direct labor employees based on the hourly rate paid. Productive time is not limited to labor input which is incorporated in the end product, but is limited to the effort which can be identified with a particular cost objective (e.g., that of engineers, designers, project administrators, mechanical assemblers). Personnel who are classified direct are those employees who can properly account for a majority of their direct productive effort and can properly charge a majority of their direct productive effort to cost objectives. Direct labor employees are outlined by job classifications on Table A1.1.

TABLE A1.1
DIRECT LABOR CATEGORIES

Job	Labor code
Senior Staff Engineer	1001
Senior Engineer	1002
Engineer	1003
Associate Engineer	1004
Junior Engineer	1005
Designer	1006
Mechanical Assembly Technician	1007
Electronic Technician	1008
Technical Writer	1009
Junior Production Engineer	1010
Field Service Representative	1011
Project Administrator	1012
Material Technician	1013
Production Engineer	1014
Metrology	1015
Machinist	1016
Tool Maker	1017
Product Electronics	1018
Calibration Technician	1019
Mechanical Shop Inspection	1020
Electrical Inspection	1021

ESTIMATING DIRECT LABOR

The estimating of direct labor embodies a variety of techniques and methods. In a specific instance, an estimate may represent a combination of many methods and techniques, and, of course, judgment. Figure A1.5 graphically depicts methods of estimating these labor requirements in addition to emphasizing specific aspects of each method. Whichever estimating technique is used, it must be for a specific task as defined by the work element structure or statement of work. It is the responsibility of the estimator to prepare a concise audit trail through the data and be able to demonstrate that prudent business judgment was used in making the decisions on the labor values selected.

After the basis for estimate has been determined, the estimator will complete the detailed estimating sheets using the number of actual productive hours estimated to be required to perform the task, or block of tasks, for which the particular estimator is responsible.

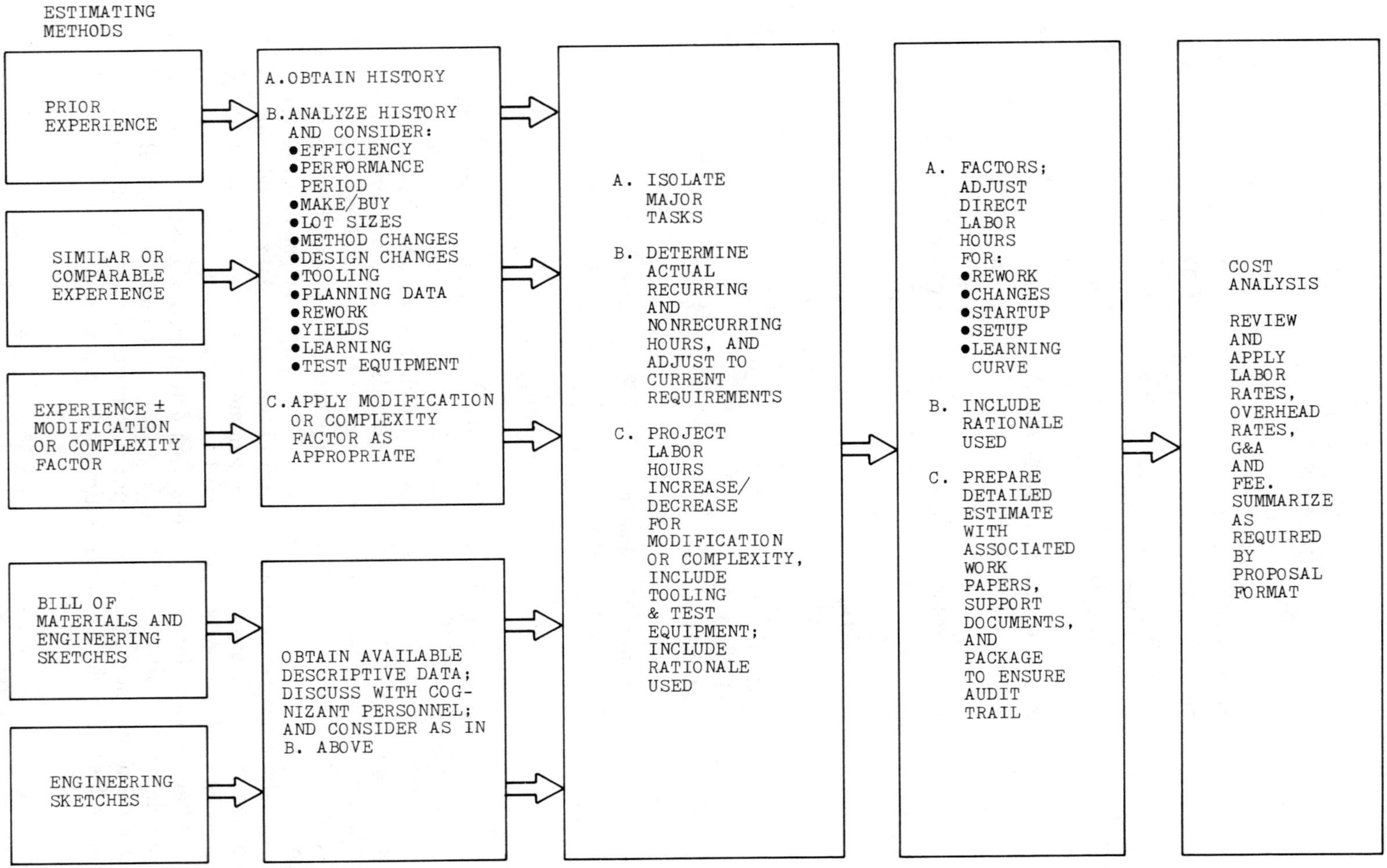

ESTIMATING METHODS

PRIOR EXPERIENCE

SIMILAR OR COMPARABLE EXPERIENCE

EXPERIENCE ± MODIFICATION OR COMPLEXITY FACTOR

BILL OF MATERIALS AND ENGINEERING SKETCHES

ENGINEERING SKETCHES

A. OBTAIN HISTORY

B. ANALYZE HISTORY AND CONSIDER:
● EFFICIENCY
● PERFORMANCE PERIOD
● MAKE/BUY
● LOT SIZES
● METHOD CHANGES
● DESIGN CHANGES
● TOOLING
● PLANNING DATA
● REWORK
● YIELDS
● LEARNING
● TEST EQUIPMENT

C. APPLY MODIFICATION OR COMPLEXITY FACTOR AS APPROPRIATE

OBTAIN AVAILABLE DESCRIPTIVE DATA; DISCUSS WITH COGNIZANT PERSONNEL; AND CONSIDER AS IN B. ABOVE

A. ISOLATE MAJOR TASKS

B. DETERMINE ACTUAL RECURRING AND NONRECURRING HOURS, AND ADJUST TO CURRENT REQUIREMENTS

C. PROJECT LABOR HOURS INCREASE/DECREASE FOR MODIFICATION OR COMPLEXITY, INCLUDE TOOLING & TEST EQUIPMENT; INCLUDE RATIONALE USED

A. FACTORS; ADJUST DIRECT LABOR HOURS FOR:
● REWORK
● CHANGES
● STARTUP
● SETUP
● LEARNING CURVE

B. INCLUDE RATIONALE USED

C. PREPARE DETAILED ESTIMATE WITH ASSOCIATED WORK PAPERS, SUPPORT DOCUMENTS, AND PACKAGE TO ENSURE AUDIT TRAIL

COST ANALYSIS

REVIEW AND APPLY LABOR RATES, OVERHEAD RATES, G&A AND FEE. SUMMARIZE AS REQUIRED BY PROPOSAL FORMAT

Figure A1.5 Estimating direct labor

Section 7

OTHER DIRECT COSTS

MATERIAL

Definition of Material

Material classified as direct is purchased and/or requisitioned from stores only for a sales order, work order, or divisional production order and will be incorporated into or become a part of a contract end item or will be consumed or expended in the performance of a contract. Further, material classified as direct should be easily and economically identifiable (and measurable) with a specific cost objective, which objective is necessary to meet the requirements of the contract. (Ref. Policy No. _____ , "Direct Versus Indirect Charging.")

Estimating Material Costs

The estimating of material requirements can encompass a variety and combination of methods. These are included in chart form in Figure A1.6. It is impossible to formulate an approach which will cover every condition, and prudent business judgment must always be exercised by the estimator. All purchased items identified as "buy" on the bill of materials will be substantiated by vendor quotations, a copy of the page indicating catalog reference, or a copy of a previous purchase order. If a previous purchase order price needs adjustment for quantity difference or anticipated increase due to inflationary factors, such adjustments must be accompanied by a reasonable explanation. Any "overages" for loss, shrinkage, breakage, waste, anticipated changes, or any other reason must be substantiated. Sources of all purchased item costs, if known, should be noted on a "Purchased Parts Justification Data Sheet." All procurements must conform to Policy No. _____ , "Make/Buy."

TRAVEL

Travel expenses are those expenses incurred by an employee which are necessary while the employee is engaged in duties away from the normal place of business. The classification of travel expenses should be consistent with the classification of the associated labor charges (i.e., if an employee charges labor direct while away from the normal place of business, the related travel expenses should be charged direct; if there is a proration to

ESTIMATING
METHODS

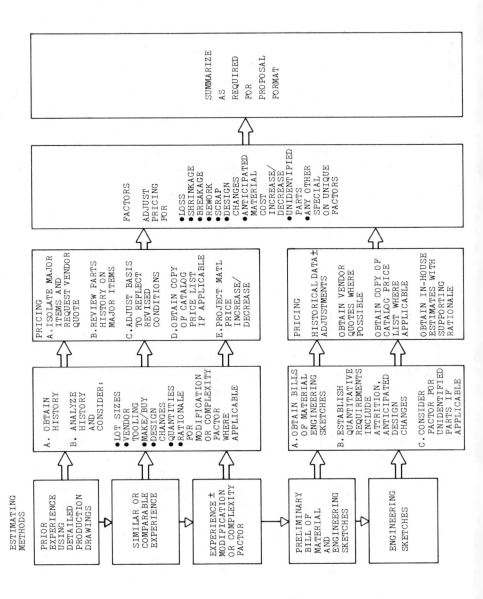

SUMMARIZE AS REQUIRED FOR PROPOSAL FORMAT

FACTORS

ADJUST PRICING FOR
•LOSS
•SHRINKAGE
•BREAKAGE
•REWORK
•SCRAP
•DESIGN CHANGES
•ANTICIPATED MATERIAL COST INCREASE/DECREASE
•UNIDENTIFIED PARTS
•ANY OTHER SPECIAL ON UNIQUE FACTORS

PRICING
A. ISOLATE MAJOR ITEMS AND REQUEST VENDOR QUOTE
B. REVIEW PARTS HISTORY ON MAJOR ITEMS
C. ADJUST BASIS TO REFLECT REVISED CONDITIONS
D. OBTAIN COPY OF CATALOG PRICE LIST IF APPLICABLE
E. PROJECT MATL PRICE INCREASE/DECREASE

A. OBTAIN HISTORY
B. ANALYZE HISTORY AND CONSIDER:
•LOT SIZES
•VENDOR TOOLING
•MAKE/BUY
•DESIGN CHANGES
•QUANTITIES
•RATIONALE FOR MODIFICATION OR COMPLEXITY FACTOR WHERE APPLICABLE

PRIOR EXPERIENCE USING DETAILED PRODUCTION DRAWINGS

SIMILAR OR COMPARABLE EXPERIENCE

EXPERIENCE ± MODIFICATION OR COMPLEXITY FACTOR

PRICING
HISTORICAL DATA ± ADJUSTMENTS
OBTAIN VENDOR QUOTES WHERE POSSIBLE
OBTAIN COPY OF CATALOG PRICE LIST WHERE APPLICABLE
OBTAIN IN-HOUSE ESTIMATES WITH SUPPORTING RATIONALE

A. OBTAIN BILLS OF MATERIAL ENGINEERING SKETCHES
B. ESTABLISH QUANTITATIVE REQUIREMENTS INCLUDE ATTRITION, ANTICIPATED DESIGN CHANGES
C. CONSIDER FACTOR FOR UNIDENTIFIED PARTS IF APPLICABLE

PRELIMINARY BILL OF MATERIAL AND ENGINEERING SKETCHES

ENGINEERING SKETCHES

direct and indirect of an employee's labor charges while away from the normal place of business, the related travel expenses should be prorated in the same manner.) (Ref. Policy No. ____ .)

Travel requirements will be specified by each participating functional department in terms of destination, duration, number of personnel, and the reason for each trip on a travel estimate form (shown in Section 9).

Travel and subsistence rates are supplied by accounting, utilizing the latest published airline fares and approved auto rental and daily subsistence rates.

COMPUTER COSTS

Computer costs are estimated for each task required to perform the contract.

In order to comply with company regulations and cost accounting standards concerning consistency in estimating, it is required to quote corporate computer facility costs in the manner in which they are accumulated.

Figures A1.7 and A1.8 are forms to be used for the backup of computer cost estimates. These forms *must* be submitted as backup for all proposals and "estimates to complete."

CONSULTANTS

In the event that the services of consultants are required, the proposal manager will inform the contracts department of the particular type of specialist required. A subcontracts administrator will be assigned to solicit quotations.

The support for a consultant cost should consist of an identification of the consultant by a brief biography of experience in his or her specialized field, the number of days the consultant is required, the fee rate per day, and travel expenses.

SUBCONTRACTS

Major Subcontracts

A "major" subcontract is distinguished from purchase orders and routine subcontracts by the following criteria:

1. A "major" subcontract is the procurement of a subsystem or major component, where the supplier has a systems management responsibility, or where the supplier performs to a work statement which includes development and/or performance specifications, or where the supplier performs engineering and design effort.

Proposal Number: _____

Project Name: _____

Task Number: _____

                                            Rate

Central Processing Unit
Computer Time (seconds)   _____ X   = $_____

Connect Time (hours)   _____ X   = $_____

Disk Storage (cylinder weeks) _____ X   = $_____

Miscellaneous*   = $_____

                                 TOTAL $_____

Estimate Prepared by_____ Date:_____

_____

*Miscellaneous charges result from
 the usage of dedicated terminals,
 tape drive, keypunching, plotting,
 etc. A separate form should be used
 to break down miscellaneous charges.

Figure A1.7. Estimate of computer charges.

2. A "major" subcontract excludes:
   a. Supplier catalog items.
   b. Supplier published specification items.
   c. Supplier items built to detail or assembly drawings.
3. It is not possible to define a "major" subcontract in terms of dollar value alone. However, experience indicates that all individual procurements in excess of $ _____ or which represent _____ % of the program's prime cost *normally* qualify as "major" under the definition outlined above.

4. In unusual circumstances, where a particular procurement does not meet the normal criteria established above, the potential procurement may be considered a "major" subcontract only after the circumstances are specifically documented in the procurement files and approved by the senior vice president.

5. All subcontracts that qualify as "major" within the definition outlined above will be reviewed and approved in writing by the controller prior to incorporation in a proposal or quotation which commits the corporation.

Routine Subcontracts

Subcontracts are designated as either "routine" or "major" for the purpose of determining whether the "major subcontract" handling rate should be applied or if "routine," the normal general and administrative rate is used.

Whether the subcontract qualifies as "major," as defined previously, or is considered "routine," the procurement and management of the subcontract becomes the responsibility of the subcontract administration section

```
Proposal Number: __ _____

Project Names: _____ _____

Task Number: _____
```

```
                                                        Rates
Dedicated Teletype Terminal      (months)_____ X         _____

Dedicated Computer Terminal      (months)_____ X      $_____

Magnetic Tape Drives             (hours)_____ X       $_____

Disk Drives                      (hours)_____ X       $_____

Keypunching or Verifying         (hours)_____ X       $_____

Temporary Diskspace     (cylinder hours)_____ X       $_____

Portable Terminals               (hours)_____ X       $_____

Plotters                         (hours)_____ X       $_____

                                 TOTAL                  $__
```

```
Estimate Prepared by _____ Date:_____
```

Figure A1.8.   Estimate of miscellaneous computer charges.

of the contracts department. Policy No. 5 defines specifically the process-ing responsibilities involved in this type of procurement.

Where it is necessary to subcontract "major" subsystems, subassemb-lies, critical components, or "black boxes," detailed information should be provided on subcontractors. When a subcontract is defined as "major," a special section of the proposal should be set aside to integrate the proposed subcontract work into the proposal. The subcontractor's proposal should be presented in the same format as that prescribed for the prime.

Request of Data from Subcontractor

In addition to complying with the description, work statements and specifications supplied to the bidders in conjunction with the RFP/RFQ requirements, the subcontractors proposal should include the following:

1. Type of contract.
2. Cost breakdowns for each task/item and a summary cost break-down for all tasks showing material, hours by labor classifications, wage rates, burden rates, and extended amounts in all areas.
3. Unit cost breakdown by element of cost for each type of equipment furnished.
4. Priced bills/list of major materials.
5. Exhibit of approved wage, burden, and other applicable rates. Spec-ify approving agency and approval period.
6. Furnish summary and separate manloading tabulation for each task and subtask specified in work statement.
7. Special tools and special test equipment should be priced in the same format as above but each as a separate item.
8. *Profit/fee.* If either weighted profit guidelines or profit incentives are applicable, the subcontractors should submit substantiating justification in support thereof.
9. If factors or contingencies are used, they must be explained and justified.
10. Any deviations from the terms, conditions, schedule, or technical requirements of the statement of work and specifications supplied by the buyer should be detailed.

INTERDIVISIONAL WORK

Request for interdivisional cost estimates will be initiated by the sub-contract administrator assigned to the proposal. If the request is for other than a price listed catalog item, the interdivisional proposal should be requested in the same format and detail as that prescribed for prime procurements.

Section 8

ESTIMATING

Engineering labor is estimated on the basis of the defined tasks in the work element structure and/or the statement of work. The engineering directorate is responsible for estimating tasks such as studies and analyses, design, reliability requirements and analyses, technical documentation, manufacturing liaison, subcontract, interdivisional work and vendor liaison, data/report manuscript preparation, customer reviews and liaison, and field support.

DESIGN AND DRAFTING

Design and drafting estimates are based on the drawing count and sizes established from the preliminary engineering design concepts, drawing tree, indentured parts list, customer drawing form requirements and estimated drawing complexities, and other available information. Standard drawing estimating factors are then applied against the drawing count.

TECHNICAL DOCUMENTATION (DATA MANAGEMENT)

Technical documentation estimates are based on customer data requirements and related internal requirements supplemented by page counts, illustration counts/complexities and overall scope of the writing, editing, and production effort as defined by the contract data requirements list, as well as the release and control of such documents (document control, data retrieval/retention/microfilming). Estimates also consider labor involved in managing subcontractor data requirements utilizing routine surveillance/audit techniques and communications.

RELIABILITY

Reliability estimates are based on the labor involved in preparing a reliability program plan that includes a detailed listing of specific tasks and procedures to implement and control the reliability function. The magnitude of the reliability plan is determined by the operational use of the end-item produced as well as the military and/or specific standards required by the request for proposal. Reliability labor estimates include but are not limited to the effort involved in the identification, assessment, and solution of problems that impact the specified contract requirements.

Estimates include liaison efforts to disseminate and implement reliability requirements by all cognizant engineering, manufacturing, quality control and test personnel, as well as vendors and subcontractors.

MANUFACTURING AND TEST

Manufacturing labor is incurred when the primary function is the production of end-item hardware. This labor effort encompasses production planning; design and fabrication of special and production tools; special test equipment and handling equipment; parts fabrication and assembly; and in-process, final, and environmental testing.

Manufacturing labor and material estimates will be based on the drawing tree and/or the bill of materials as drawn up from the drawings supplied as cost estimating input, i.e., drawings, sketches and specifications from design and drafting, engineering, and the customer. Assembly and major subassembly conceptual layouts with overall dimensions, general tolerances, materials, similarity identifications, process specifications, and major special equipment identifications are considered the minimum for adequate manufacturing estimating.

Functional, acceptance, and environmental tests, as well as plans and equipment for the tests are the responsibility of this area, as are any modifications to facilities.

PRODUCT ASSURANCE

Product assurance estimates are based on the hardware concept, specifications, drawings, and assembly/test activities previously defined by the request for proposal or developed during the estimating activity. These estimates include the following areas:

a. *Quality control.* Source and receiving inspection, fabrication and assembly in-process inspection, test witness, discrepancy resolution, special process control, and subassembly build support.

b. *Quality engineering.* Design review, quality planning, malfunction analysis, subcontractor control, system test witness, discrepancy resolution, and field technical support.

c. *Configuration management.* Drawing and change control, as-built vs. design comparisons, configuration management audits, subcontractor configuration management control.

Section 9

COST COLLECTION AND SUPPORTING DATA

The project administrator for each contributing department or section collects all the pertinent data from the estimators assigned the various tasks or subtasks defined by the statement of work and work element structure. These data will consist of timephased input sheets, which detail, by labor classification, the hours per task per month or year for the duration of the program and the estimated nonlabor dollars shown in the time period of commitment. Each input sheet must be accompanied by a task element substantiation sheet (Figure A1.9) properly describing the task and the estimator's breakdown of the hours assigned each portion of the task with rationale for the estimate. When material costs are included, they are to be described and listed on a purchased parts justification sheet (Figure A1.10) showing quantity, unit cost, total cost, and the source or rationale for the estimated costs. If travel is anticipated in the task, a travel and subsistence cost substantiation form (Figure A1.11) must be submitted showing destination, number of people, number of days, and the reason for the trip.

Computer cost backup will be furnished as described in Section 7. Interdivisional and/or subcontract estimates, if required, will be supported as described in Section 7. The responsible project administrator reviews the cost data for proper format and backup material, and if satisfied, submits it to the department manager or section supervisor for review and signature approval. The various cost packages are then submitted to the proposal program management administrator for review.

If the data meets the approval of the proposal administrator, it is then transferred to the cost analysis office. The cost analyst assigned to the proposal reviews the cost packages for errors, omissions, format, and the overall reasonableness of the material cost justification. Travel forms and computer estimates are checked for proper rates and all calculations verified. The input forms for engineering, manufacturing, and, if applicable, field support are reviewed and corrected, if necessary, for titling, hour-count, and period of performance. Interdivisional and subcontract costs are compared with the latest interdivisional and subcontract proposals for proper costs and period of expenditure. The information on the input data sheets is then entered into the computer and a timephased, dollar, and manpower computerized run is produced. The cost analyst checks the tab run for proper rates and keyboard input errors. If all is in order, the analyst prepares the cost volume or cost proposal (including any updates or changes) and the cost backup packages are placed in the cost analysis master proposal file.

SECTION_____ TITLE_____ DATE_____

The labor and non-labor elements of cost summarized below are
required for performance of the following functions:

Element and Amount	Description of Performance

SPO NO.	TASK NO.	TITLE	SHEET
			OF

Figure A1.9. Task element substantiation.

The cost proposal, together with the technical and management proposals (considered preliminary at this time), are then reviewed by the proposal management team for technical and pricing approval. If no revisions or updates are required, the proposal package is then submitted for division and corporate review and approval, as required by company policy.

The proposal cost analyst, with the cooperation of all departments that input estimates to the proposal, will inform the proposal manager and the

PARTS – TOOLS – TEST EQUIPMENT

REPORTING SECTION:

ATTACHMENT:

| PART NO. | VENDOR | ESTIMATE SOURCE | | | QTY. | PRICE | | LOT CHARGE | TOTAL PRICE | NOTES: |
		PO	QUOTE	DATE		UNIT	TOTAL			

PROPOSAL NO.:

TITLE:

SPO:

TASK:

Figure A1.10. Purchased parts justification sheet.

DESTINATION	1 NO. MEN	2 NO. DAYS	3 TOTAL MAN DAYS (COL.1 X COL.2)	4 SUBSIST (COL.3 X $34)	5 AUTOMOBILE RENTAL (SEE TABLE A)	6 AIRFARE	7 TOTAL TRIP COSTS (COLS.4 + 5 + 6)	8 NO. OF TRIPS	9 TOTAL (COL.7 X COL.8)	REASON FOR TRIP

Figure A1.11. Travel and subsistence.

division controller of any revisions or additions to previously provided cost information that affect the proposal. Any significant changes are brought to the attention of the appropriate management team and the contracts department notifies the customer. In the event that the division succeeds in winning the contract, this updating process continues up to the time of contract negotiations.

Section 10

MANAGEMENT REVIEWS

The review cycle for proposals is as follows:

Department managers review technical and cost estimates for text, format, supporting data, and compliance with statement of work and work element structure requirements.

Proposal administrator performs preliminary proposal compilation and review.

Proposal manager reviews technical and cost estimates.

Contracts manager reviews the proposal for contents and compliance with the request for proposal.

Proposal engineer/manager reviews the technical proposal.

Program office reviews the organization and management volume.

Cost analysis reviews estimates and prepares the cost volume.

At this point in the review cycle, any revisions necessary are completed and the proposal package is again reviewed by the proposal team and approved for submission to management.

The proposal package is submitted for division management review and sign-off.

The proposal package is submitted for corporate review and sign-off (if required by corporate policy).

The final review will be conducted by the following personnel in addition to the division general managers:

Director of responsible directorate

Accounting—division controller

Contracts—manager of contract administration

Technical director

Marketing—director of advanced planning

Manager of applicable support groups if input is significant:
1. Purchasing
2. Product assurance
3. Reliability
4. Design and Drafting
5. Data management
6. Manufacturing and testing
7. Engineering

These personnel are notified after the responsible directorate has established a specific time and location for the general manager's review.

PROPOSAL RESPONSIBILITIES

A checklist of proposal responsibilities is as follows:

Directorate

PROPOSAL MANAGER

Overall proposal responsibility

Prepares proposal task authorization and identifies participants, services required, and special facilities/equipment

Establishes proposal schedule; calls key meetings

Furnishes copies of request for proposal to all participants as required

Establishes proposal budgets and assignments

Finalizes and disseminates proposal theme and approach

Supervises preparation and disseminates technical data, work element structure, and detailed program schedule for cost estimating

Supervises/reviews technical and management proposal

Keeps director informed of proposal progress/problems

Establishes program plan

Establishes program organization

Participates in preparation of, and approves, bill of material with incorporated make/buy decisions

Establishes technical, management, and pricing strategies

Approves technical proposal management proposal, and cost package

Writes statement of work

Approves program schedule

Serves as chairperson of proposal kickoff meeting, baseline concept review, all director reviews

Establishes proposal review cycle and resolves all reviewer comments

DIRECTOR

Assigns proposal manager

Approves proposal task authorization and general assignments

Approves technical, management, cost strategies

Approves proposal theme and approach

Approves technical, management, cost proposals

Recommends fee/profit structure

Approves statement of work

Recommends fact-finding, negotiation actions

Serves as chairperson of division review

Support Groups

TECHNICAL
DOCUMENTATION/DATA
MANAGEMENT

Writes assigned sections

Critically reviews, edits, and/or rewrites input material

Formats, illustrates, produces all volumes

Supervises security aspects, including marking, storage, and handling

Prepares estimates for documentation/data management support services

Recommends special artwork and presentation techniques

Prepares concept illustrations and engineering drawings

PRODUCT ASSURANCE

Prepares quality assurance program plans

Prepares quality assurance estimates

Prepares bill of materials addendum for special inspection equipment

Writes product assurance section of proposal

RELIABILITY

Conducts reliability analysis

Prepares reliability program plan

Prepares reliability estimates

Participates as an advisor in bill of materials preparation

Writes reliability section of proposal

MANUFACTURING, ASSEMBLY, AND TEST

Prepares preliminary and final bills of materials

Prepares manufacturing, assembly, test support estimates

Prepares bill of materials addendum for special test equipment

Writes manufacturing and test sections of proposal

CONTRACT ADMINISTRATION

Reviews request for proposal terms and conditions, identifies risks, recommends exceptions and/or qualifications

Establishes, via consultation with engineering and technical documentation, a position on "rights in data"

Establishes proposal restrictive legends and/or other proprietary-markings

Reviews statement of work

Prepares incentive/award fee plans

Obtains subcontract, interdivisional, and consultant quotations

Makes recommendations regarding contractual aspects

Furnishes and executes required certifications

Prepares transmittal letter in concert with proposal manager and advanced planning

Recommends fact-finding, negotiation plans

PROCUREMENT

Provides purchased parts quotations and delivery schedules

Identifies, with engineering, long-lead items (for both proposal quotations and program delivery)

Participates as an advisor in bill of materials preparation and make/buy decisions

Prepares procurement/manager plans

SECURITY

Provides overall guidance on security aspects

Handles all special security requirements

COST ANALYSIS

Provides any special cost estimating forms to all estimating groups

Prepares special cost volume writeups as required

Verifies final cost elements with contributors

Prepares all required cost exhibits, including computerized manpower/-cost spreads if required

Provides all labor/burden rates

Prepares computer use forms

Maintains proposal cost backup files

ADVANCED PLANNING

Furnishes marketing intelligence, including recommended technical, management, and pricing strategies

Recommends proposal theme and approach

Updates intelligence throughout proposal preparation with emphasis at proposal meeting, baseline concept review, cost/management kickoff meeting, and division review

Recommends proposal support tactics

Prepares proposal follow-up plan

Drafts corporate management interest letter and proposal submittal letter

Establishes proposal delivery method and date

Responsible for coordinating and controlling all contacts with customer during proposal preparation

Appendix 2

PROPOSAL PREPARATION

Checklist for Proposal Review

Technical Approach

Are the technical requirements as seen by the customer clearly interpreted and not simply parroted from the request for proposal?

Does the proposal reply to the basic minimum requirements as given by the customer?

In the event of deviations or alternatives, is detailed logic for these recommendations given, especially in terms of desirable results which the customer will receive? (These results might include such items as improved performance, lower costs, greater producibility, earlier delivery, and simpler maintenance.)

In the event that certain program objectives are incompatible with other program goals (e.g., range versus speed, payload versus speed, etc.) does the proposal show that the *optimum* solution, all factors considered, has been obtained?

Does the approach consider such matters as logistics, maintenance, retrofitting, and problems of the using organization?

If originality has been identified as a requirement, does the proposal present a unique, imaginative approach?

Does the approach avoid overengineering and oversophistication?

Technical Competence

Does the proposal provide convincing assurance of specific technical competence for this project?

Does the proposal give specific examples of similar projects successfully completed by the company?

Do the résumés of key personnel which have been designated to perform the program relate their experience to the specific needs of this project? Has extraneous biographic information been eliminated?

Is the availability of qualified manpower clearly detailed in terms of man-hours for both full- and part-time people?

Does the proposal clearly indicate that the company has adequate space and facilities, both general and special, to perform the work efficiently and on schedule?

Are special facilities (such as dust-free laboratories, data processing equipment, construction tools, special laboratory equipment, etc.) to be provided for the project clearly spelled out?

It is clearly indicated that all required facilities will be available when needed for this project?

Where arrangements with subcontractors are proposed, is specific evidence given of the subcontractor's commitment to make people and facilities available when required?

Schedule

Does the proposal provide convincing assurance that the customer's delivery and due dates will be met?

Is sufficient detail regarding master scheduling, programming, follow-up, and other like functions given to reinforce this assurance?

When subcontractors and major suppliers are involved, are sufficient safeguards built into the proposed scheduling system to ensure that their schedules will comply with the master program schedule?

Reliability and Quality Control

Does the proposal spell out reliability and quality assurance provisions in such a manner that the customer can have no doubt that quality standards will be met or surpassed?

Is a clear understanding of reliability and quality control requirements reflected in the proposal? Are deviations, if any, satisfactorily explained? Are testing procedures outlined in sufficient detail?

Is evidence given that the system of inspection guarantees the same high level of quality and reliability from subcontractors as in-house production?

Program Direction and Management

Does the proposal clearly demonstrate an understanding of the customer's concern with the management of this project?

Is evidence given that top level management effectively communicates with and inspires its personnel?

Does the proposal specify the required number of the right types of management people?

Is evidence given that supports the selection of subcontractors, not only from the standpoint of their technical and manufacturing capabilities but also their management philosophy and talent?

When subcontractors are involved, has it been clearly stated how their management will participate in the program?

Manufacturing Competence

Does the proposal clearly indicate that the company has adequate manufacturing space and facilities, both general and special, to perform the work efficiently and on schedule?

Are specialized equipment and processes required for the project given sufficient prominence in the proposal through photographs and descriptive information?

Does the proposal call attention to the high standards of production and test procedures?

Does the proposal specifically state that all required facilities are available for the project at the times required in the project?

Field Support

Does the proposal provide documented assurance that field service and support activity, as required by this project, is of a high caliber at reasonable cost?

Does the proposal highlight the magnitude and scope of field service and support area?

Does the proposal provide specific examples of accomplishment in the field services and support area?

Price

Is this the lowest price considering (a) long range versus immediate return and (b) probable competitive price range?

Is there adequate evidence that subcontractors and suppliers have submitted their lowest realistic cost estimates?

Have man-hour, space, facility, and other cost factors been estimated properly?

Are overhead, burden rates, and proposed profit or fee reasonable for this type of project?

Is the extent of pricing detail given consistent with the importance of these details?

Does the proposal provide convincing evidence that the company is properly oriented and organizationally structured to meet the specific management demands of this project, especially in terms of providing the necessary communication functions, both internal and external; of traceability of decision making; and of integration of all project bits and pieces?

Is evidence give of management's understanding of how the specific project fits into the customer's overall requirements? Does the proposal show how this project relates to long range business objectives of the company?

BIBLIOGRAPHY

Aljian, George W. *Purchasing Handbook*. New York: McGraw-Hill, 1973.

Ammon-Wexler, Jill. *How to Create a Winning Proposal*. Englewood Cliffs, N.J.: Prentice-Hall, 1978.

Crawford, Jack and Kielsmeier, Cathy. *Proposal Writing*. Portland, Oregon: Continuing Education Publications, 1970.

Heinritz, S. and Farrell, F. *Purchasing Principles and Applications*. Englewood Cliffs, N.J.: Prentice-Hall, 1981.

Holtz, H. and Schmidt, T. *The Winning Proposal: How to Write It*. New York: McGraw-Hill, 1981.

Kaufmann, A. and Desbazeille, G. *The Critical Path Method*. New York: Gordon and Breach Science Publications, 1969.

Larson, Virginia. *How to Write a Winning Proposal*. Carmel, California: Creative Books, 1976.

Lauffer, Armand. *Grantsmanship*. Beverly Hills, California: Sage, 1977.

Lefferts, Robert. *Getting a Grant*. Englewood Cliffs, N.J.: Prentice-Hall, 1982.

McCready, Gerald B. *Marketing Tactics Master Guide*. Englewood Cliffs, N.J.: Prentice-Hall, 1982.

Mulvaney, J.E. *Analysis Bar Charting*. London: ILIFFE Books, Ltd., 1969.

Society for Technical Communications. *Proposals and Their Preparation*. Anthology No. 1. Washington, D.C.: Society for Technical Communications, 1973.

Stewart, R. *Cost Estimating*. New York: Wiley, 1982.

Tracey, John A. *How to Read a Financial Report*. New York: Wiley, 1980.

United Nations. *Research Proposal Guide for Developing Countries*. New York: United Nations, 1973.

Zallen, Harold. *Ideas Plus Dollars*. Greenville, N.C.: Academic World, 1976.

INDEX

Acceptance time, 15
Administrator, proposal, 63
Affirmative action, 78
"AIDA" approach, 13
Allowances:
  cost growth, 175
  labor, 174
Analysis, financial, 24
Analyzing, 7, 251
Appendices to the proposal, 206
Assembly, 112
  skills required, 55

Basic truths about proposals, 9
Best and final offer, 41, 72, 218
Bidders conference, 35
Bid/no-bid committee decision, 21, 24
Bill of material, 168
Blackout period, 35
Brassboard, 32
Breadboard, 32
Bureau of Labor Statistics, 11
Business proposal, 65, 82, 125
Business skills required, 54
Buy-American, 78

Capabilities, company, 17
Changes, contract, 20
Checklists for proposal preparation, 212, 319
Commerce Business Daily, 12
Company:
  capabilities, 17
  experience, 147
  objectives, 16
  organization, 134
  resources, evaluation of, 226, 233
Competitive advantage, 25
Composing methods, 195
Computer demonstrations, 48

Computer software, 48
Conferences:
  preproposal, 34
  proposal preparation, 36
Configuration management, 119
Construction estimating, 112, 172
Contamination control plan, 115
Contingent fee certificate, 78
Contract:
  changes, 90
  negotiations, 42, 72
  options, 85
  planning, 74
  price, 42
  schedule, 84
Contracts:
  fixed price, 3
  negotiated, 4
Cost:
  accounting standards, 79
  adjustments, 230
  control, 140
  elements, 162
  estimating, 8
  evaluation, 229
  factors, evaluation of, 227
  growth allowances, 175
  management, indirect and overhead, 136
  proposal, 83, 155, 264
    content, 159
  volume, 83, 155
  volume manager, 65
Credibility, importance of, 155
"Cuspetitor," 17
Customer:
  action, 15
  attention, 14
  decision, 16
  desire, 14
  interest, 14

Customer (*continued*)
  involvement, 121
  knowledge of, 12
Customer-provided facilities, 79

Decision to bid, 24
Defining the proposal effort, 45
Delivery, 114
Delivery of proposal, 214
Demonstrations, 34
Design, 8, 112, 225
Design excellence (as an evaluation
    factor), 225, 232
Designs:
  conceptual, 8
  preliminary, 8
Detailed outline, 208
Development plan, 106
Direct management, estimation of, 176
Disadvantaged businesses, 79
Distribution of proposal, 214
Documentation costing, 169
Drawings as used in the proposal, 100
Drawing takeoff, 166
Drawing trees, 105

Education, key personnel, 144
Electrical analysis, 117
Employee training, 151
Engineer, sales, 63
Engineering skills required, 54
Equal opportunity, 78
Equipment:
  general purpose, 146
  special, 146
Estimating, 8, 75, 252
  factors, 143
  process, 159
Evaluation:
  boards, 216
  criteria, 223
  facilities, 221
  factors, 223
  functions, 219
  ground rules, 218
  methods, 80
  organization, 218
  personnel, 218
  procedures, 80
  of proposals, 215
  scoring procedures, 228
Executive summary, 204

Experience:
  evaluation of, 227, 233
  key personnel, 144
External proposals, 6

Fabrication, 112
Facilities, 90
  acquisition, 4
  general purpose, 146
  for proposal teams, 40
  special, 146
Factor, profitability, 20
Failure mode and effect analysis, 115
Fee, 135
  negotiation, 43
  payment, 88
  structure, 88
Figure positioning, 206
Finance skills required, 54
Financial analysis, 24
Flow diagrams as used in the proposal, 102
Flow of proposal, 51
Format of the proposal, 202
Front matter, 203
Functional elements, 128
Functional manager, 54

G&A rates, 135
General provisions, 92
Geographical advantage, 27
Giant proposals, 207
Government facilities, 79
Ground rules:
  review of, 44
  treatment of, in cost proposal, 165
Growth rate, 21

Illustrations, 200, 210
Independent research and development, 4
Index tabs, 206
Indirect cost control, 152
Indirect rates, 135
Industrial engineering skills required, 55
Information management, 141
In-process inspection, 172
Inspection, 113
Instructions, proposal, 75
Instructions to bidders, 73
Instrumentation lists, 118
Interdivisional relationships, 134
Internal proposals, 6
Inventory considerations, 167

Key personnel, 144
  evaluation of, 226, 233
"Kickoff" meeting, 43, 46
Knowledge of the customer, 12

Labor:
  allowances, 174
  base, flexibility, 243
  base, stability, 243
  burden, 152
  costs, 162
  rates, 142
Letter of transmittal, 203, 252
Logistics:
  management, 141
  proposal, 210
Long lead time items, 111

Maintainability, 116
Maintenance manuals, 165
Major system acquisition, 3
Make or buy decision, 111
Make or buy plan, 143
Management plan, 225
  evaluation of, 232
  review of proposal, 247
  reviews, 44
  visibility, 133
Management skills required, 55
Manager:
  business volume, 65
  cost volume, 65
  proposal, 58
  publications, 66
  technical volume, 65
Manual, proposal preparation, 279
Manufacturability, 116
Manufacturing costing, 170
  skills required, 55
Marketing, 7, 250
Market survey, 11
Mass properties analysis, 118
Material:
  burden, 152
  control plans, 118
  costs, 166
  handbooks, 167
  lists, 105
Materials control plans, 118
Mathematical skills required, 55
Matrix, skill, 129
Meeting, kickoff, 43

Mockups, 33, 48
Models, scale, 33
Most probable cost development, 229
Motion pictures, 48

Negotiation:
  fee, 43
  price, 42
  work statement, 42
Negotiations, contract, 42, 72
No-bid decision, 28
Nonconformance reporting, 115
Nonrecurring activities, 128
Nonsegregated facilities, 79

Objectives, company, 16
On-site visits, 217
Operability, 116
Operation, 114
Optimization, profitability, 18
Options, contract, 85
Oral briefings, 217
Organization and management proposal,
    125, 261
Other direct costs, estimation of, 176
Other factors, evaluation of, 227, 234
Outline, detailed, 208
Overhead costs, 154

Parts control, 115
Past performance, evaluation of, 227, 233
Performance suitability factors, 224
Period of performance, 88
Photographs as used in the proposal, 101
Physical elements, 128
Planning, 7, 251
  contract, 74
  proposal, 31
Plant:
  equipment, 146
  facilities, 146
  visits, 217
Political advantage, 28
Prebid meeting, 71
Preproposal conference, 34, 35, 71
Preproposal functions, 45
Price advantage, 28
Pricing, 75
Problem areas, discussion of, 122
Process control plans, 118
Processing the proposal, 211
Process planning, 170
Procurement management, 141

Procurements:
  fixed price, 3
  negotiated, 4
Producibility, 116
Product assurance, 114
Production planning skills required, 55
Profit goals, 22
Profitability, 7
  factor, 20
  goals, 23
  optimization, 18
Program control, 140
Project:
  control, 140
  direction, 139
  organization, 138
  plan, 106, 131
Property, 90
Proposal:
  administrator, 63
  binders, 201
  covers, 201
  drafts, 46
  evaluation, 215
  flow, 51
  format requirements, 82
  instructions, 75
  logistics, 210
  manager, 58
  planning, 31
  processing, 211
  production (printing), 212
  publication, 190
  resources, 40
  style manual, 211
  team, 40, 56
  writing, 191
Proposals:
  external, 4, 6
  government, 2
  in-company, 4
  Internal, 4, 6
  preliminary, 34
  skills need for, 54
  unsolicited, 34
Prototypes, 8, 32
Provisions, general, 92
Publication, 252
  department, role in proposal preparation,
    194
Publications manager, 66
Publishing skills required, 56

Publishing the proposal, 9
Purchasing agent, viewpoint in evaluation,
  236

Quality assurance, 114
Quality control, 114
Quantity buy considerations, 167

Recurring activities, 128
Reliability, 114
Repair manuals, 165
Representations and certifications, 78
Reproduction methods, 197
Request for proposal, government, 95
Request for proposal (RFP), 45, 69, 92
Request for proposal preparation, 40
Resources review, 44
Resumes, 144
Review of ground rules, 44

Safety management, 142
Sales engineer, 63
Scale models, 33, 48
Schedule for proposal preparation, 43, 45
Schedule of elements, 111
Schedule planning, 107
Schedule/skill interactions, 110
Scheduling, 8, 107
  a project, 246
  of the proposal process, 37
Schematics as used in the proposal, 102
Scrap allowances, 168
Sketches as used in the proposal, 100
Skill:
  level, adjustment, 151
  matrix, 129
  mix, key personnel, 145
Skills for proposal preparation, 54
Small business, 78
Socioeconomic objectives, 2
Software estimating, 174
Source evaluation, 2, 215, 216
Spare parts, 165
Spares, 165
Special tooling, estimation of, 173
Specification types, 104
Staffing, 145
Statement of work, 42, 84, 100
Statistical skills required, 55
Study and analysis, 111
Subcontractor relationships, 135
Subcontracts, 169

Subsystems analysis, 117
Supervision, estimating of, 76
Supplier catalogs, 167
Support services, 93
Survey, market, 11
Synergism, 17
Systems analysis, 117
Systems engineering, 116

Tables, 200
Team, proposal, 40
Technical:
  direction, 89
  proposal, 83, 98, 253
  skills required, 54
  specifications, 102
  volume, 82, 98
  volume manager, 64
Technological advantage, 26
Test equipment, estimation of, 173
Testing, 113
  estimating of, 173
Test planning, 119

Thermal analysis, 117
Training, employee, 151
Types of proposals, 6
Types of specifications, 104

Understanding the requirements, 120, 224
Unsolicited proposals, 34
Urgency in proposals, 9

Verification, 119
Video tapes, 48

Waste allowances, 168
Word processing, 194
Work breakdown structure, 126
Work elements, treatment of, 130
Work element structure, 126
  interrelationships, 129
Work statement, 42
Writing skills required, 56
Writing the proposal, 191
Written questions, 217
  to proposers, 36